THE ENIGMA OF ED GEIN

Ed Gein was a strange, eccentric little man with pale, icy eyes and a reserved manner, not given to idle chit-chat with his neighbors. People in rural Plainfield, Wisconsin would have admitted that, in retrospect, he always had been a bit of a weirdo. But no one could possibly have imagined just how weird Gein was until the day in November 1957 when the police arrived at Gein's farmhouse to check out the disappearance of Bernice Worden, the mother of a local store owner . . . and made discoveries so unspeakable that some of the officers felt their stomachs heave. . . .

CANNIBAL KILLERS

The History of Impossible Murderers

Moira Martingale

St. Martin's Paperbacks

First published in Great Britain by Robert Hale Limited, London.

Published by arrangement with Carroll & Graf Publishers, Inc.

CANNIBAL KILLERS

Library of Congress Catalog Card Number: 94-6405

ISBN: 0-312-95604-5

Printed in the United States of America

Carroll & Graf trade paperback edition/ August 1994
St. Martin's Paperbacks edition/ August 1995

St. Martin's Paperbacks are published by St. Martin's Press, 175 Fifth Avenue, New York, NY 10010.

10 9 8 7 6 5 4 3

Contents

Acknowledgments

During my research for this book, a number of people put themselves out on my behalf.

I should like to thank the FBI Public Affairs department, Lt. Ray Biondi of the Sacramento police department, Professor Herschel Prins of Loughborough University, Graham Nown, Poppy Martin, Professor David Dolphin—and especially my good friend Alan Bott, who went to a great deal of trouble for me and asked nothing more in return but a bottle of whiskey and a good lunch. Also my thanks to Chris, for sharing both the proof-reading and the nightmares.

"This Be The Verse" from *High Windows* by Philip Larkin, reproduced by permission of Faber & Faber Ltd.

Prologue

They brought the severed heads in first. On golden platters. Frozen in death, the faces of the young slave girls were still fresh and beautiful, the almond eyes lifeless. The men's mouths watered to think how sweet and tender their flesh would be when, in just a few minutes, it was served to them, the honoured guests.

And, week after week, hundreds, probably thousands, of guests banqueting at the court of Shih Hu, who ruled the Huns of northern China between 334 and 349 AD, savoured the delicacy of a young harem girl, killed and cooked to excite their palates. Part of the preprandial ritual was this passing-round of the platter similar, perhaps, to the manner in which we might now go to a fish restaurant and choose a live lobster to be cooked for us.

There is no record of any guest recoiling from this human feast. And until the early nineteenth century restaurants serving human flesh were common in China. But why? How could an ever-changing succession of families in China—a place that was, in many ways, a civilized and orderly society—sit down to dine upon another human being? How could the guests at Shih Hu's banquet enjoy the flesh of those wretched girls whose misfortune was that they looked good enough to eat?

It was, of course, an awesome demonstration of power . . . slaves were the stock of noble families, no more than their cattle. But more importantly, and more simply, they liked the taste. When all specious moral arguments are swept aside, these are the reasons we now eat animals: we have the unchallenged power to do so, and we enjoy the taste.

The fourth-century Chinese nobles were not alone.

Cannibalism runs like a blood-red thread through the tapestry of mankind's history. Man has always eaten meat and ancient man was not too worried about whether the prey he dragged back to his cave to devour had four legs or two.

Our fascination with cannibals—so brilliantly tapped by the Oscar-winning film *The Silence of the Lambs*, from the book written by Thomas Harris—suggests that old desires still lie buried within us. In a few people, the taboos of civilization are not enough to keep such savagery in check. They kill and consume their victims. They drink their blood.

This book looks at the present day cannibals of the Western world for whom one morsel of human flesh, one bitter taste of a victim's blood on the tongue, is never enough. What is it that drives them to act out our darkest thoughts? To begin to understand their psychology, we first have to see them against the maelstrom of history.

Fantasy abandoned by reason
produces impossible monsters;
united with her, she is the mother
of the arts and the origin of their
marvels

Francisco Goya: Epigraph
to *Los Caprichos*, 1970

3rd Fisherman: I marvel how the fishes live in the sea.
1st Fisherman: Why, as men do a-land;
            the great ones eat up the little ones.

William Shakespeare: *Pericles*, Act II, Sc. i

1

Overpowering Instinct

The mere memory of Man as I knew him had been swept out of existence. Instead were these frail creatures who had forgotten their high ancestry, and the white Things of which I went in terror. Then I thought of the Great Fear that was between the two species and, for the first time, with a sudden shiver, came the clear knowledge of what the meat I had seen might be. Yet it was too horrible! . . . Clearly at some time in the Long-Ago of human decay the Morlocks' food had run short . . . Even now man is far less discriminating in his food than he was—far less than any monkey. His prejudice against human flesh is no deep-seated instinct. And so these inhuman sons of men—! I tried to look at the thing in a scientific spirit. After all, they were less human and more remote than our cannibal ancestors of three or four thousand years ago . . . Why should I trouble myself? These Eloi were mere fatted cattle, which the ant-like Morlocks preserved and preyed upon.

H.G. Wells: *The Time Machine*

They call it "anthropophagy": literally, to consume humans. Cannibalism is the crime which probably shocks and disgusts more than any other. Yet, at the same time, along with the antipathy and horror, cannibalism and vampirism also exude a fascination. Why is that? Could it be something in our psychological make-up which harks back to the past? Have we the capacity, as H.G. Wells' Morlocks had, to slip back into that bestial nature of a primitive past which we all share? For although we consider that as civilized human beings it is not ethically agreeable for us to eat other human beings, this was not always the case. Archaeologists and anthropologists have turned up masses of evidence to show that as soon as man was able to walk upright he indulged freely in carnivorous activity and cannibalism was widespread.

The reasons were various: there was cannibalism resorted to in times of famine, or as the preferred form of protein. It was practised for magical, mystical or religious reasons. It was a form of revenge against enemies. And finally, then, as now, inevitably there would likely be a scattering of deviant individuals who obtained sexual gratification from acts of sadism and cannibalism. To try and comprehend the reasoning of this last small group, it is perhaps necessary to investigate the strength of the compelling subconscious power exerted by the reasoning of the former groups, set within the customs of their time and culture.

Nowhere was free of cannibalism. In Britain, one of the most recent archaeological discoveries which appeared to indicate that Britain's Stone Age population was cannibalistic was in 1987 during a Cheddar cave dig in Somerset [1]—and there are reports of it being practised in England and Ireland during the famine of the seventh century and in Scotland three hundred years later for the same reason. In fact it seems clear that there are few places untouched by cannibalism. It went on all over the world, except in Europe, until comparatively recently. In-

[1] Paul Barber, in his book, *Vampires, Burial and Death*, suggests that cut-marks on these bones might have been caused not by cannibalism but by a tribal burial practice called excarnation, in which the flesh was routinely separated from the bones of corpses both to facilitate disposal and to ensure the destruction of the body, which hastened the soul on its journey into an afterlife.

deed, if we investigate recorded history, we learn that our ancestors have throughout the centuries invented all manner of ways in which to attack and inflict the most cruel hurts upon their fellow humans, seemingly without conscience—and that includes eating them.

Mention has already been made of the fourth-century Chinese predilection for eating their slave girls, but proof that cannibalism still flourished in the Far East came from Marco Polo a thousand years later when he returned to Italy with horror stories from China and Tibet. Nineteenth- and twentieth-century missionaries and explorers—the fortunate ones—furnished us with much of our information about tribal cannibalism in places like Africa. Man's inhumanity to all other animals including man knew no bounds and there is a clear inability to empathize with others' suffering. In parts of Africa, slaves were paraded for sale in the market-place and, just as H.G. Wells' Eloi were used as cattle by the Morlocks, were fattened for food. Enemies slain in battle were also eaten, as were family members who died of natural causes. Adulterous women faced the same fate. Tribes which raised cattle, such as the Zulus, were not cannibals, but people-eating tribes could often be recognized by their teeth, which they would file to sharp points. There is even a dark suspicion that the practice may still go in far flung reaches of the world, or in the Congo, Uganda and Kenya. Over recent decades tyrannical African leaders Idi Amin and Emperor Bokassa have both been found guilty of eating their human captives.

In Papua New Guinea cannibalism was widely practised until fifty years ago—Japanese soldiers were said to have been captured and eaten during the Second World War. In one South American tribe, slave-women were impregnated in order that their captors could eat their babies. On other occasions, conscious victims had limbs removed and were made to watch while they were cooked and eaten. Sometimes, to underline the contempt

felt for them, they were offered some, and in Fiji human
flesh was craved in preference to animal flesh. It was
prized so highly that it even had a name—"puaka
balaca," meaning "long pig." Here a man exercised such
dominion over his wife that if he so wished, he could kill
and eat her without fear of reprisals.

The most infamous British cannibal in history was
Sawney Bean who with his wife—"a woman as viciously
inclined as himself," according to chronicler John Nich-
olson—and his numerous offspring, dwelt in a cave in
Galloway, Scotland, during the sixteenth century. He
abandoned his trade as a hedger and ditcher and opted
instead to prey upon other people. The family cave was
close to the sea and they lived by highway robbery: am-
bushing, killing and then eating passers-by. Any parts of
the body which they were not able to eat at once were
pickled in brine or hung in their cave. There were no
obvious sexual or mystical motives for their actions; they
robbed the people of their bodies and ate them in the
same way that they robbed them of their possessions
which they then, presumably, sold in the Edinburgh region.

Over a period of twenty-five years it was estimated that
Bean and his family, which had by now grown to forty-six
individuals—men and women who knew no other diet or
way of life, thereby offering living proof that "culture is
king"—were estimated to have killed and eaten more
than a thousand people. Because nobody survived their
attacks, there was no way for the local people to have
known of their existence. It was only when Bean and his
family became careless and began tossing surplus body
parts into the sea that they came to the authorities' attention and their actions began to strike fear into residents.
Even then, the perpetrators of such vile deeds could not
be traced. It was only when, during an attack on a man
and his wife (whom they killed), another group of travellers arrived to fight them off, that realization dawned on

the authorities. With a pack of armed men and blood-hounds, the Bean family cave was discovered and entered. The soldiers were horrified to see parts of human bodies hanging up to cure or being cooked over a fire. The family were taken to Leith where, without trial, they were executed in about 1700, using the obscene methods of the time—by having limbs cut off and being burned to death.

There are those—like writer Ronald Holmes—who believe that Sawney Bean did not really exist, but that he was merely the stuff of myth, a demonic bogey-man figure like the vampire or the werewolf—"a primeval presence from the dark past of the human mind," he says. But in addition to countering that the tale has been very well documented in its claim to be factual, it must be noted that unlike these mythological night monsters, there are no elements of magical or even devilish dimensions to Sawney Bean. There is a danger, too, in falsely believing that because a person's crimes are so unspeakably shocking as to defy the laws of humanity, they could not possibly have taken place in reality. One has only to look at historical figures like Vlad the Impaler (1431-1476), who cruelly relished the murder of thousands in the most bloody of ways, and is also said to have provided Bram Stoker with his inspiration for *Dracula*, or the sixteenth-century Hungarian Countess Elizabeth Bathory, a distant relative of Vlad's who bathed in and drank the blood of hundreds of virgin girls because she believed it would keep her youthful, to find actual perpetrators of evil far beyond the bounds of human compassion. It makes one realise that there is no reason at all why a one-off monster like Sawney Bean should not belong in history's chamber of real-life horrors.

Half a century later, and, curiously enough, in exactly the same part of Scotland, Nichol Brown was executed for killing and eating his wife. During his trial it became evident that flesh eating was not an unusual event for

him. It was revealed that one night, in his local inn in
Leith, he declared to his drinking companions that he
would go to the gibbet whereon hung the body of Norman Ross, a criminal who had been hanged a week earlier, and would bring back a piece of his body and
consume it in front of them. He went away and returned
with a lump of flesh from the dead man's thigh, cooked it
on the fire and ate it, fulfilling his promise as they
watched.

In desperate circumstances, man has always shown a
readiness to eat whatever protein was available in order
to save his own life. In the nineteenth century, a few
prominent cases of this sort of cannibalism arose in the
Western world, although during the court cases which
followed the American incidents there were doubts
raised about the manner in which victims died. Lewis
Keseberg, a German by birth, was, with his wife and two
children, among the Donner Party, a group of California-
bound settlers led by George Donner through the Sierra
Nevada Mountains in 1846. Appalling weather conditions forced them to slaughter their animals and then
fighting broke out between the members of the party.
Some people died of cold and starvation and the dead
bodies were eaten by others. It was then that the alleged
murders began, including one incident when Keseberg
took a small boy to bed with him one night and presented
his body to the others in the morning for butchering. The
others were convinced Keseberg had murdered the child.

Some of the travellers, including the Donners, had split
off from the main wagon train and it was these few, including Keseberg, who were left behind after repeated
rescue attempts had saved the forty-five remaining living
people out of the eighty-nine strong party. But when the
final rescue party arrived to take the Donners to safety,
only Keseberg remained in the carnage-littered camp,
looking fat and healthy, lying beside a simmering pot
containing the liver and lungs of a human being. The liver

belonged to Mrs. Donner, he told the horrified rescuers, adding, "She was the best I have ever tasted." They were suspicious because only weeks before Mrs. Donner had appeared healthy and nowhere near death, but Keseberg said she, the last survivor apart from himself, had died naturally. Keseberg was regarded as a murdering cannibal by his fellow-men, but at his trial he claimed that like the other members of the party, he had only resorted to cannibalism as an act of despair. He was freed by the court and within a few years he found a new career . . . running a steak house.

Thirty-odd years later, Alfred Packer was not quite so lucky. In 1873, Packer was a gold prospector who, despite warnings from Indians at an outpost that the weather conditions were appalling, persisted in guiding a party of men from Salt Lake into the San Juan Mountains . . . and ended up eating them. He had been paid well by the party, but weeks later he arrived back alone, saying the others had abandoned him. Suspicion was aroused because he looked very fat for someone who claimed to have been struggling in the snow in adverse conditions. In addition, he was laden with money, guns and knives which had belonged to the other members of the party. When the bodies of the five missing men were eventually found, four had had their skulls crushed, apparently while they slept, and the fifth had been shot. Four had been totally stripped of flesh and the other partially so. When he eventually came to trial ten years later, Packer was judged to be guilty of murder and sentenced to forty years' hard labour, but he was to be released after seventeen. During the sentencing of Packer, Judge Melville Gerry made an infamous remark which has since entered the annals of American history: "There were only seven Democrats in Hinsdale County, and you ate five of them, you depraved Republican son of a bitch!" It is doubtful whether the relatives of Packer's unfortunate victims were able to appreciate the unintentional humour of this remark.

At around the same time last century, England had its own tale of cannibalism to occupy the horrified masses. In 1884, Captain Thomas Dudley and Edwin Stephens were shipwrecked with the rest of their four-man crew hundreds of miles to the west of Africa and took to a dinghy with only two tins of turnips to sustain them. When seventeen-year-old cabin boy Richard Parker became ill after having drunk sea-water, Dudley killed him and the surviving men stayed alive by eating the boy. When they were rescued, Dudley freely admitted this. They were sentenced to death, but this was later commuted to six months' imprisonment.

A more recent incident took place in 1972 when an aeroplane travelling from Argentina to Chile crashed at an altitude of 23,000 feet in the Andes mountains, the most hostile of territories where, with sub-zero temperatures, there is no edible vegetation. Several of the passengers perished in the crash or soon afterwards; of the forty-five passengers, thirty-two found themselves stranded in an alien terrain, with no radio, food or hope of immediate rescue. That hope faded even more as the weeks passed, and as the pangs of hunger became unbearable, the survivors were left with only one option if they wished to remain alive: to overcome their revulsion and eat the flesh of their deceased fellow passengers. Some of them could not bring themselves to do it and refused. They died. Others kept alive for seventy days by eating the flesh raw, to preserve its nutritive value. When they were finally rescued, only sixteen survivors remained. The story was told dramatically in the 1993 film *Alive*.

But the "reasons" for using humans as convenience-food were not always strictly nutritional. Odd instances of cannibalism for revenge are sprinkled throughout history even until comparatively recent times. For instance, John

Johnson was a trapper who lived in the mountains of Montana in the United States in the 1880s and maintained a private war with the Crow Indians who had murdered his Indian wife and child. Whenever he came upon a Crow camp, he would attack it single-handedly, kill the Indians, butcher their corpses and, for some inexplicable reason, eat only their livers. He was known, unsurprisingly, as Liver-Eating Johnson and far from being ostracized for this horrid practice, later became a sheriff in Coulson, Montana, maintaining law and order for several years before vanishing into the mountains again.

But blood-drinking and flesh-eating customs in history are multi-dimensional. There was more than just sating the appetite or gaining the ultimate revenge involved in the activities of tribal cultures, such as those in Africa or Australia. There the belief was that by eating humans or drinking their blood one transferred their finer qualities to oneself. To eat a slain enemy was not only an act of revenge, it also enabled one to absorb his strength and courage. Slaughter was not always necessary: to eat dead relatives was to honour them and to devour a dead elder enabled one to absorb the aged one's greater wisdom. Australian aborigines believed that if a child ate his dead father he would inherit the father's hunting skills.

Blood has always been thought to contain mystical energies—strength, spiritual essence; indeed, life itself. The superstitions attached to blood were evidenced by the initiation ceremonies undergone by young aboriginal men who had to drink human blood for the sacred powers it bestowed upon them. In eastern Prussia, the blood of an executed person was considered lucky and, in other parts of Europe, to drink such fresh blood was thought to protect one against illness. The belief in several cultures was that to drink the blood of a dead person whom one suspects might return to haunt the living—perhaps as a vampire—protects against such an event. This belief is still said to exist among some Canadian Indians. Blood remains of symbolic importance in the "civilized" world: only last century bleeding with leeches was considered to be a medical cure for many ills, including lunacy. And in the present day in England, those individuals who take pleasure in the blood-letting rituals of hunting foxes and deer might pause to consider the symbolic significance of blooding a small child—that is, smearing the blood of the eviscerated deer upon his head—during his first hunt.

As *homo sapiens* evolved and his imagination developed, mystical beliefs came to dominate his life. Arrogantly, he awarded himself "god-given" spiritual qualities and advantages which he arbitrarily deemed were not present in other animals. The gods which he created were, of course, sympathetic to his aggressive interests and offered him clear, just "reasons" why he should continue to do as he had always done, including torturing, killing, inflicting unbearable pain upon other human beings, drinking their blood and eating their flesh. With this divine rubber stamp, humans continued to indulge their brutal, cannibalistic desires. Cruelty and slaughter therefore found their place as part of the blood-drinking and flesh-eating rituals and human sacrifice, all of which became central to many tribes' belief systems. In order to assure the fertility of their land and their people, many cultures appeased their gods with the blood of their weakest members. In Crete, the people were said to fertilize Mother Earth with the blood of their victims, and similar blood rituals could be found all over the world. The Aztecs of Mexico, for instance, worshipped so many blood-thirsting deities that barely a week went by without some helpless infant, young man or woman or captured prisoner being sacrificed by the priests. For the sun- or moon-god to bring fertility to the Aztec crops necessitated the removal of a live victim's heart, whereupon it was held aloft, still beating. The corpse was then distributed to the crowd and, with heavy symbolism and seriousness rather than greed it was cut up and eaten. Such customs were hard to break, even when European civilization reached the Aztecs and other related peoples. There were still reports of such ceremonies as recently as 1838. The North American Indians' belief in a host of gods and spirits also involved cannibalism. Known for the richness of their legends, the Indians understood that a cannibalistic spirit was able to take over a person's body, enabling him to eat human flesh, either from slain or captured enemies or from dead relatives. As the influence of civilization was felt, the literal interpretations of their beliefs were dispensed with, although they continued to be acted out symbolically during ritual dances. In Lapland, symbolic ceremonies surrounding death included naming a reindeer after the dead person (choosing an animal of a similar age and sex to the deceased), then ceremonially killing and eating it.

Before we "civilized" Westerners begin to feel superior about such atavistic impulses, perhaps we should glance at the major religions which prevail in the world today and their bases in either fact or myth. The Judaic tradition is based on the Old Testament wherein God gave man dominion over all the animals, to devour as we pleased. Blood-sacrifice and ritual played a major part in the religious lives of people during Biblical times and pages of the Old Testament are devoted to God's instructions to followers on the exact and bloody methods to be used on differing animals when making these sacrifices in honour of Him. Indeed, in Genesis 22 Abraham was called upon by God to sacrifice his only and dearly-loved son Isaac in a similar manner. Isaac was only saved by an eleventh-hour reprieve from the Lord, who then told Abraham that he had only asked him to do this as an act of faith. The assumed spiritual and mystical essence of blood were of great importance then and the vestiges of such belief remain today within the Jewish faith—and indeed, within other faiths—where, although meaning and requirements may have changed over the ages, blood is still believed to contain specific qualities. Notably, Jehovah's Witnesses refuse blood transfusions because of their literal interpretation of Biblical passages such as "Only flesh with its soul—its blood—you must not eat" (Genesis 9: 3-4). They do not, however, denounce meat-eating. Orthodox Jews and members of other religions eat only kosher meat; that is, animals which have been slaughtered in a certain way which drains them of blood.

By the time the New Testament was written, the emphasis on literal sacrifice—human or otherwise—was redundant. But as in many major religions, at the heart is the principle of the sacrifice of its central figure. Although Jesus Christ may have embraced the finer human values of compassion, kindness and non-violence, nevertheless he was bloodily sacrificed in primitive tradition. And it was this ancient primal custom of human sacrifice that he underlined symbolically when he dined with his disciples at the Last Supper. Offering them bread, he urged: "Take, eat; this is my body which is given for you," and with the wine, he said: "This is the new testament in my blood, which is shed for you" (Luke 22). This ceremony with all its mystical allusions of blood being a symbol of life still prevails today in the Christian church's service of Holy Communion. In fact, the Roman Catholic teaching since 1215 when Pope Innocent III ordered a new Catholic dogma, is that transubstantiation takes place—that is, that the bread and wine actually *turns into* Christ's body and blood, rather than being a mere symbolic substitute. What better illustration of our unconscious preoccupation with "magical thinking"— something which we may like to think belongs in our primitive ancestry, but is, in fact, very much a part of us still.

The black arts remain an area where blood sacrifice still persists, both of animals and, if we are to believe the claims, also of humans. Satanists glorify their unholy Master by offering blood. Drinking of blood or its symbolic substitutes forms a large part of cult activities in a hardly more sophisticated way than the tribal rituals indulged in by pagan cultures, despite our presumed civilized exterior. Incidentally, equally important during black magic ceremonies is sexual activity, and a similar inextricable linking of blood and sex in the imagination forms a combination which is crucial to the thinking of most of the murderers to be discussed in this book. The blood-sex link is also powerful for countless other serial killers and violent rapists who may be, but usually are not, Satanists. While we view their criminal activities as perverted and obscene, believing them to be far removed from normal sexuality, one can, perhaps, begin to perceive the unconscious depths wherein the roots of their perversions lie. But it is perhaps unsurprising that the Devil was blamed for such criminal outrages during the ignorant years of the Middle Ages, although as the witch hunts of the sixteenth and seventeenth century showed, the truly guilty were few in comparison to the number of innocent victims of the Church's persecution. It is well known that the early purveyors of Christianity achieved their remarkable success by, in addition to publicizing their beliefs, also superimposing Christian festivals and feast days upon existing pagan celebrations. Therefore, Christmas was determined as 25 December, not because Christ was born on that actual day but because this was the traditional Winter Solstice.

Despite the monopoly which Christianity had upon people's thinking, fear of paganism and devilish dabblings was rife. It lasted long after the appalling chapter in European history when such panic resulted in thousands of wretched individuals—mainly elderly women—being tortured, burned or murdered most cruelly by the authorities on the grounds that they were witches. It was not necessary to commit any offence to be denounced, tortured and slaughtered as a witch, and the scale of the murder was horrifying. In Germany at least 100,000 people were executed as witches, simply on the say-so of someone else—who might equally have been tortured to extract names. Death, after fiendish torture, was by burning alive. Indeed, the German authorities at Neisse in Silesia anticipated the Nazis by three hundred years by constructing an oven, in which were roasted more than a thousand people in the space of nine years, including children of between two and four years. So in an age when Satan invaded everyone's terrified sensibilities, it seems logical that when an individual really did behave in such an abominable and sickening way as to be beyond human comprehension, people fell back upon the Devil and his works to provide a comforting explanation.

Even accounting for the advances in global communication, it seems to be beyond doubt that the incidence of serial and sadistic killers, including those who cannibalize their victims, has increased over the centuries to the all-time high of today, for reasons which will be discussed later. But that is not to say that such disturbed people are solely a modern phenomenon. In 1573 at Dole, France, Gilles Garnier, a recluse who confessed to killing numerous children—their bodies were found mutilated and half-eaten—may have been one of the earliest recorded serial killers. An explanation for his deeds was demanded and, predictably, the Devil's sorcery came to the fore. Garnier admitted that he was a *loup-garou*, a werewolf, a condition he said he had acquired through witchcraft after meeting a phantom who taught him how to change at will into a wolf by rubbing an ointment over his body (a common method according to legend). After killing a child of twelve—by tearing her to pieces with his teeth and his wolf's paw, he said in his confession—he ate parts of her body, then cut a joint to take home for his wife, Apolline. He killed and ate three other children in a similar way and admitted that he had the same unnatural

inclinations even when he was in his normal, human state
rather than in werewolf mode.

He was, of course, burned alive. One cannot be sure
whether or not he was guilty of the crimes, since he was
doubtless tortured cruelly to produce a confession, or if
he really believed he was a werewolf, for the incident
occurred during a time when werewolf hysteria was at its
peak in Europe. Fifteen years later, in Bedburg, Germany, Peter Stump (also called Stubbe in writings) was
tortured and executed in the most vicious manner after
admitting a twenty-five-year spree of cannibal killings,
the barbarity of which turned him into a fearsome folk-
legend. Again, he said that the Devil had taught him the
art of metamorphosis and had given him a wolf's skin
(another common way of changing form) which he wore
when he pursued young women and children. But when
he caught his victims, he said he changed back into his
human shape while he raped and murdered them with
terrible cruelty. During the first five years after he had
made his pact with the Devil, Stump said he had murdered thirteen people, including two pregnant women.
With these, he admitted tearing the unborn babies from
their mothers' bodies and devouring their hearts "pant-
ing hot and raw." He also killed countless animals, he
said, but what caused the greatest shock was his admission that he had killed and eaten his small son, whose
mother, Beell, was Stump's own daughter with whom he
had an incestuous relationship. He told with relish how
he had found the boy's brains to be "most savoury and
delicious." The people of Bedburg and neighbouring vil-
lages were afraid to go out alone during this twenty-five-
year period and they regularly discovered bloody limbs of
men, women and children littering the fields. When
Stump was eventually executed, so were his daughter and
his mistress, who were judged to have been accessories to
murder.

As with Garnier, the torture methods used at this period in history were such that one cannot be certain whether Stump was really under the delusion that he was a wolf when he slaughtered and devoured. Werewolfery was second to witchcraft in the Middle Ages, seriously regarded as a canker in society which had to be rooted out, and confessions were extracted from "werewolves" —both male and female—in the same abominable way that they were wrenched from those accused of witchcraft. Stump's death was no less horrid than the pains he had inflicted upon his victims: he was tied to a wheel, had lumps of flesh torn out of him with red-hot pincers and his limbs were broken with a wooden hatchet before he was beheaded and his decapitated body burned.

Such barbarity on the part of the authorities always casts doubt upon the true guilt of the accused, but what cannot be disputed is that *someone* committed the crimes; the mutilated bodies bore testimony to the fact that there were sadistic cannibal killers then, as now. The Garnier and Stump cases, together with other similar ones, added a touch of authenticity to the werewolf legend, but over a period of a hundred years a staggering 30,000 cases of "werewolfery" were recorded in France alone—and it is obvious that there could not have been so many unhinged individuals, considering how few later centuries threw up, notwithstanding a larger world population. The twentieth century Western world has, indeed, surpassed itself not only in the number of cannibal and serial killers it has produced but also in the quantity of each killer's victims.

Interestingly, vampires and werewolves complement each other in that they are both mythical blood- and flesh-eating creatures which were called upon in past centuries to provide colourful descriptions in cases where these particular predatory crimes were committed, providing a mystical "explanation" to murders so horrible that they could not be countenanced. The myth of the werewolf—a human who changes shape on the night of the full moon [2]—continued to be called on for many centuries to explain the deviant behaviour of individuals. In 1849, Parisians were relieved to hear of the capture of the beast who had been breaking into graves of women and small girls in cemeteries and tearing the bodies asunder, then rolling in the bloody fragments. The culprit was a junior infantry officer called Sergeant Bertrand and his explanations about the compulsion which took hold of him prior to committing these outrages bears similarity to those of "werewolves" of earlier times. Someone with cannibalistic homicidal urges may hallucinate enough to convince himself he is a vicious animal, then venture into the night to satisfy his primeval blood-lust, transferring the blame on to his *alter ego*, the wolf. In the perpetrator's eyes, this makes it the crime of the wolf and transforms the shameful dimension of man-eat-man cannibalism into the more acceptable wolf-eat-man killing. Among the Canadian Indian tribes, the spirit of the werewolf—or Wendigo—was a persistent legend. It was believed that the Wendigo could possess a person and induce him to perform unspeakable acts, and in 1879 a Cree Indian named Katist Chen, who was also known as Swift Runner, claimed to have been visited by the Wendigo when he murdered and ate his mother, wife, brother and six children during a hunting expedition the previous year. His earlier claims that the family had starved to death were dismissed and he was found guilty of murder. Later he confessed to a priest about the Wendigo and said that the spirit had visited him in his cell

[2] Interestingly, "moon-madness" might well exist. Scientists believe that the waxing and waning of the moon can substantially affect behaviour, noting that there is an increase in all crime—including murder—on nights of the full moon. During the period of the lunar cycle when the moon is closest to the earth, homicides are more ruthless and bizarre. A New York study found a dramatic rise in the number of admissions to psychiatric hospitals on days of the full moon. This theory is called the "Transylvania Hypothesis."

and tortured him to make him confess. Only this way, Swift Runner said, could he banish the spirit. He was hanged, notably being the first man executed by the Royal Canadian Mounted Police.

Reports of lycanthropy continue even today, although in enlightened Western society it is now considered a clinical delusional disorder: sufferers—as with Gilles Garnier and Peter Stump, perhaps—believe themselves to be transformed into wolves and act accordingly, howling, unleashing bestial sexual attacks upon helpless victims and eating nothing but raw, bloody meat (other sufferers, who are among at least eighteen recorded cases in Britain and France over the past seventeen years, may believe themselves to be other animals like cats and dogs —and in one case, a thirty-five-year-old man thought he was a gerbil for three days). Robert Louis Stevenson's well-known *Dr. Jekyll and Mr. Hyde*, published in 1886, drew on this sort of delusional illness and also used it to illustrate man's innate desire for aggression.

Fearsome legends develop in all manner of ways: in 1985 Dr. David Dolphin, a Canadian chemist at the University of British Columbia in Vancouver, suggested there was a real physical condition which might have contributed to the werewolf and vampire legends during an age when scientific ignorance made people look for magical answers to inexplicable phenomena. Dr. Dolphin described to the American Association for the Advancement of Science the physical symptoms of porphyria. This is a genetic disease which strikes one in 200,000—which means there are 279 potential cases in Britian today— and results in a lack of heme, which is produced in the liver to make blood red and help carry haemoglobin. George III was a sufferer. Victims are so photosensitive that they can be disfigured by sunlight and can go intermittently mad. When exposed to light the upper lip recedes and the skin cracks, causing bleeding. Horrific skin lesions on the face cause loss of blood, and teeth become more prominent. The sufferer can crave blood and a major treatment for some porphyrias is an injection of heme. But in the Middle Ages, this could have been solved by drinking blood—and because of the aversion to sunlight, physicians would also keep sufferers secluded during the day. Porphyria is but one reason why the legends of werewolves and vampires might have prevailed; one also has to consider the powerful cultural determinants such as preoccupation with the magical quality of blood and ingrained beliefs about creation and prolongation of life. And there is also that other overwhelming biological instinct, sex.

The werewolf of legend had a fondness for tender flesh and warm, flowing blood, but he was quite prepared to devour the already-dead, unlike his fellow-monster of myth, the vampire, whose prey had to be living. But they both had an inclination to sexually attack victims. Interestingly, while in modern fiction—and by modern, I mean the last hundred years or so—the werewolf is still regarded as a fearsome brute with no redeeming qualities, the vampire has acquired a seductive, sensual magnetism which owes much to Bram Stoker's infamous creation who has been incarnated in more films than any other character—Dracula.

Before the nineteenth century mythical vampires were charmless creatures: red-faced, bloated and swollen like leeches with the blood they had consumed. In fact, such an appearance has a natural, rather than supernatural explanation, being consistent with that of a decomposing corpse which swells as the intestinal micro-organisms produce methane gas. The vampire's skin was said to be taut like the skin of a drum because of this bloating; the ancient Slavic view was that the vampire had no bones, but was merely a blood-filled sack—which would seem to render the monster immobile, but for the fact that he was facilitated in his ghastly endeavours by the Devil's powers. Compare this image with that of modern fiction: the

tall, dark, slender aristocrat in his black cloak, whose
pronounced canine teeth serve their primitive purpose
(the teeth of legendary vampires before this time were
unremarkable). A sexual dimension was certainly present
in vampires of folklore—they were said to be sexually
obsessive and those suspected vampires who were ex-
humed and found to have erections (again, a common
occurrence, caused by the bloating in corpses as they
begin the process of decomposition) fed this legend. But
until the nineteenth century the vampire did not use his
powers of seduction in order to achieve his ends; it was
during this period that the blood-lust of the fictional vampire became irrevocably entwined with primitive sexuality
through the rather obvious symbolism used, not necessarily consciously, by a sexually frustrated Stoker among
others.

Accepting that myth has always exerted a hold on past
and present beliefs, it is perhaps unsurprising that a sexu-
ally-obsessed Dracula tapped a rich vein of fascination in
human beings. Blood lust is presented as sexual hunger—
and this sexual metaphor, inspiring fear, sympathy and in
some cases arousal, says much about the primitive instincts which linger beneath the organized surface of our
lives. The maintenance of myth relies on that slight sub-
stratum of fact, which lies in our history and our subconscious. "Normal" sexuality does not involve ingesting
one's partner's blood; however, a minority of people do
regard blood-sucking as an erotic experience. Vampirism
is documented as deviant sexual behaviour by contempo-
rary researchers such as Krafft-Ebing and although usually found in association with other psychiatric disorders,
recent evidence suggests that as a clinical entity on its
own, it may be more common than we imagine, especially
when allied to criminal behaviour. Although, strictly
speaking, the term "vampirism" means the ingestion of
fresh blood, clinically it can also refer to—and occur
alongside—necrophilia (sex with a dead body) and nec-

rophagia (consumption of dead human flesh). Vampirism appears to occur in individuals functioning at a very primitive mental and emotional level and is seen "not infrequently" in association with serious sexual offending, where biting and the ingestion of blood are not uncommon phenomena.

As we approach the year 2000 we consider ourselves higher beings, putting a premium on finer emotions like love, compassion and protection of the weak. We call this "humanity" and are shocked and devastated when individuals break the ascribed rules of "civilization" and plummet to its lowest ebb. Last century it was people like Jack the Ripper, who in the late 1880s not only murdered five prostitutes in London, ritually disembowelling them, but also took the kidney of one victim, Annie Chapman and wrote to the police, saying it tasted "nise." It was German-born Adolph Luetgert, a Chicago butcher who, in 1897, murdered his wife and turned her into sausages, which he sold to his customers. And it was twenty-nine-year-old Joseph Vacher, "The French Ripper," who operated at about the same time and confessed to eleven murders—seven women, four youths—in the south-east of France. He killed by strangulation or stabbing, then raped, mutilated, disembowelled, castrated and inflicted terrible injuries with his teeth. He went to the guillotine in 1898.

One hundred years on, in Russia Andrei Chikatilo operated using exactly the same methods, but his terrible toll was fifty-five victims—the worst individual serial killer the modern world has known. In the twentieth century more, not fewer, cannibal killers have emerged. Men like Dean Baker, who in 1970 confessed to a Californian patrolman: "I have a problem: I'm a cannibal." Whereupon he pulled from his pocket a man's severed fingers and admitted killing someone and eating his heart raw. Men like Albert Fentress, a history teacher in New York, who invited an eighteen-year-old boy into his house then shot him, cut up his body and ate parts of it. He was committed to a mental institution indefinitely in 1979. Men like Marcelo Costa de Andrade, who was arrested in Rio in December 1991 and confessed to killing fourteen boys, aged from six to thirteen, and drinking their blood "to become young and pretty like them" during the previous eight months. Walter Krone, a German cannibal who went to jail for seven years in 1980 for eating parts of a girl who had died in a street accident. And men like Mark Heggie, aged twenty-three, who drank the blood of his victim after trying to kill her in North London in 1992. He told detectives he often drank animals' blood and obtained work in abattoirs to satisfy his craving. He was sent to a mental hospital. And, although rarer, there are women, too: twenty-six-year-old Anna Zimmermann from Mönchen-Gladbach, Germany, who in 1981 murdered her lover, cut him into manageable, pan-sized steaks and, after saving them together with a finger, an ear and his penis in the freezer, fed him to her two children aged six and four—something she had previously done with the family pets. And Tracey Wigginton, who murdered a man she met at a Brisbane dance in 1989 and, according to the friends who were with her, feasted on his blood in the belief that she was a vampire.

In the pages which follow, such perversions occur time and again, each preceded by the murder of the victim by a killer in the grip of a sexual compulsion. For, having looked at dietary need, desperation, magic, religion and cultural factors as reason for cannibalism and blood-drinking, here is the final reason, the only one truly in operation today: sexual desire—inspired, one might conclude, by the sort of primal instincts which I have described. Blood-lust is a motivating factor, but the incidents in the following chapters are not remotely like those in fiction like *Dracula*, in which a victim falls helplessly beneath the vampire's voluptuous spell and willingly surrenders to his desires, experiencing something approaching orgasm during the vampire's "love bite." These murders involve victims who are torn apart and brutally savaged in a way which would have had more in common with the mythical werewolf than the vampire. For we are looking here at the lowest point on an imaginary scale of sexual behaviour. And could it, perhaps, compare with man's evolution? Man emerged from the slime, passed through aeons of blood-filled ritual ruled by primal instincts like cannibalism and blood-drinking, and now we imagine we have reached the pinnacle of evolutionary sophistication and civilization. As this book illustrates, some of us clearly have not. And what of the rest of humanity? In the Middle Ages the powerful were delightedly slaughtering "witches," but as events in recent history prove, the human ability to abandon civilized principles and indulge in unspeakable cruelty—even genocide—still needs little prompting. For all the horror with which we regard the modern witch-hunt—the Nazi atrocities of the Second World War—similar events still persist: in Iraq, regiments of apparently normal people are easily induced by Saddam Hussein to wipe out thousands of Kurdish people; in Tibet, the Chinese commit similar outrages; in the former Yugoslavia ordinary humans show a shocking enthusiasm for torturing, raping and putting to death crowds of other humans simply because of religious differences. In the comfortable West, more than ever before in history, there are more serial killers either in prison or on the loose; there are more instances of sadistic attacks and murder of the helpless for no reason other than for "kicks." The scent of terror and blood seems to move and excite a greater proportion of "civilized" Westerners than we may wish to imagine or admit.

I wonder how far removed we are from the atavistic impulses which controlled our ancestors—or, indeed, from those murderers in our midst whose sexuality can only operate at a primitive, blood-soaked level. What happens in these warped individuals to inspire their dreadful instincts? Is our revulsion to cannibalism a kind of acquired response, rather than a "natural" one? On the evidence of man's ever-present capacity for inhumanity, could we all become heartless killers—and even revert to cannibalism—given the right set of circumstances?

And H.G. Wells' *Time Machine*: was it a comment not on man's future, after all, but on man's subconscious impulses?

2

Cruelty Amid Chaos

If you were to destroy in mankind the belief in immortality, not only love but every living force maintaining the life of the world would at once be dried up. Moreover, nothing then would be immoral, everything would be permissible, even cannibalism.

Fedor Dostoyevsky, *The Brothers Karamazov*

Cannibal killers are few and far between. While the twentieth century abounds with murderers—and indeed, statistics show that there are now more instances of serial killings than ever before in civilization's history—the crime which, because of its primitive bestiality, evokes the most horror and revulsion in all of us is, thankfully, uncommon. How curious, then, that Germany—a small country in comparison to the USA—has thrown up at least four cannibalistic murderers this century, with three of them operating between the wars, during the 1920s.

After the First World War anarchy reigned, law and order had collapsed, thieves and confidence tricksters abounded and the rest of the people got by as best they could. The economy was at an all-time low and the country was in chaos. There was an atmosphere of godlessness. Streams of refugees roamed through the cities looking for jobs, begging on the streets and sleeping on pavements. A backwards glance at the way Nazism was due to flourish and gain primacy over the next decade or so makes one wonder what exactly was happening to German society during this period which, perhaps, predisposed the population to tolerate the atrocities which were in store. One answer immediately springs to mind. When the population of any species hits rock bottom, the law of the jungle dictates the survival of the fittest. But that does not necessarily mean the survival of the best.

Into this desperate society one morning in 1918 walked a newly-liberated Fritz Haarmann: the prison gates slammed shut behind him and he breathed the free fresh air once more. Recognizing Hanover as being riddled with crooks and villains who exploited those weaker than themselves, Haarmann felt at home. He liked the world he now found himself in. He had been serving a five-year gaol-term for fraud and theft, the latest in a long history of imprisonments imposed as punishment for stealing, picking pockets or indecently assaulting small children. He was thirty-nine in 1918 and had little to show for his life, having spent it as an itinerant hawker and thief, devoted to his mother who had been incapacitated after his birth and remained a lifelong invalid, but filled with hatred for his father, a bitter, miserable railway worker with the revealing nickname Sulky Olle. Fritz's father had beaten him and made his childhood desperately unhappy. As Fritz grew older it became apparent that his IQ was lower than average and he showed signs of the uncontrolled violence which was to make him one of the worst mass murderers of all time. With what turns out in hindsight to have been commendable astuteness, Fritz's father had tried to have him committed to an institution when he sensed the potential dangerousness of the boy, but doctors declared him to be safe and refused Herr Haarmann's request. Had they thought otherwise, a great many lives would have been saved. As a child, Fritz used to enjoy dressing up in his three sisters' clothes—his sisters had drifted into prostitution when they were comparatively young—and as a teenager he was sent to a mental institution for a spell after attacking small children. He escaped to join the Army, but was soon dismissed as an "undesirable" and it was then he devoted himself to a career of theft and sex attacks.

A fleshy man with superficial charm, he was blatantly homosexual and made his mark on the criminal underworld, where he was well liked but thought to be rather stupid, if harmless. Whether he would have been quite so popular had they realized he was also a police informer is something to speculate about, yet this was another string to Haarmann's bow. The police also liked him because of his "it's a fair cop" attitude: he never resisted arrest, appeared to enjoy the discipline of gaol life and joked with them as they pulled him in. The Hanover police nicknamed him "Detective" because he told them of so many crimes and plots that were afoot, and he was even paid a small salary and given a badge—something which provided excellent cover for him to commit his dreadful crimes. Moving among the swindlers at the market in Hanover, Haarmann began gravitating to the nearby railway station where wretched people arrived from all over the country to huddle around stoves in the station's waiting area and beg from passers-by. Among them were scores of homeless youths, some not even teenagers, most of whom had run away from home. They were nameless, untraceable. Over the next five years these boys proved easy prey for Haarmann . . . literally. A smiling Haarmann would flash his police badge and invite a youth to accompany him home. Coupled with his charm and apparent sympathy for their plight, the promise of a good meal tempted these lost and hungry youngsters to return with him to his apartment as easily as the witch persuaded Hansel and Gretel to enter her gingerbread cottage. And Haarmann had exactly the same thing in mind.

The apartment which he shared from 1919 with his young lover, twenty-year-old Hans Grans, was in Hanover's ghetto area, on the third floor of a crumbling block overlooking the River Leine. After getting the youths home, Haarmann would seduce or attack them, use them for his own sexual gratification and then kill them by tearing their throats out with his teeth, after which he would drink their blood and indulge in necrophiliac activities. Then he would drag the body up to his attic where the walls were crimson with encrusted blood. There, sometimes helped by Grans, he would dismember the body and slice it up, transferring the pieces of flesh to buckets. Then Haarmann donned his other vile identity: that of market meat-trader. Taking his buckets of human flesh, he sold it, along with secondhand clothes, at his stall in Hanover's marketplace, telling the hungry German citizens that it was horse-meat. The clothes of his victims also found their way on to his stall. His black-market meat business was highly successful—after all, his prices were lower than anyone else's—and the police, who needed spies like Haarmann to enable them to monitor underworld corruption, turned a blind eye to the illegal trading activities of their paid nark and asked no tricky questions.

Haarmann's first victim among the starving and penniless boys who fell prey to his bribery and charm was seventeen-year-old Friedel Roth, who disappeared in 1918 after being seen with Haarmann. The police investigation led them to Haarmann's door, but their enquiries were half-hearted; Haarmann was, after all, very useful to them. Many years later, when he was finally caught, Haarmann bragged that when police visited his room, "the head of the boy was lying wrapped in newspaper behind the oven." The police did not look too closely on that occasion—or on others. When Haarmann met the psychopathic Hans Grans (who, curiously enough, was a runaway who escaped the lost boys' usual fate) the slim, elegant youth was to incite him to further outrages. Grans, a librarian's son, was Haarmann's social superior and tormented Haarmann with his sarcastic remarks and insults. He selected victims and ordered their murder, often simply because he wanted their clothes. Haarmann sold clothes from victims only days after having killed them and on one occasion, someone saw Grans wearing a suit that he had seen a few days earlier on a boy at the railway station.

Haarmann's neighbours had no idea what was going on, although they were later to recall that they often saw a large number of young men entering the apartment, but never saw them leaving. They heard chopping noises through the walls but thought nothing of it; after all, this man *was* a butcher so it was only to be expected that he chopped up carcasses. Even when one neighbour bumped into Haarmann in the hall when he was carrying a bucket of blood downstairs, she suspected nothing. Another neighbour, meeting Haarmann after he had been butchering a body in his attic, asked him cheekily: "Am I going to get a bit?" Haarmann merely laughed and promised her some meat next time. Occasionally he would supply meat to people in the other apartments. His main problem—disposing of the skulls and bones of his victims—was somewhat solved by giving the bones to the neighbours, who would make soup with them, believing them to be from animals. But eventually, people began to harbour suspicions. These bones were too white, they murmured. What sort of animal did they come from? Haarmann stopped handing the bones out and tossed them, with the skulls, into the river which flowed close by. One customer who bought some meat from Haarmann's market-stall was so worried about it that she went to the police to ask what it was. Pork, she was told.

If the police really suspected the true horror of Haar-

mann's activities—and perhaps one can understand why
such a terrible idea never entered their heads—it was in
their interest to ignore it. Time and again, parents in
search of their lost sons found the trail of clues led to
Haarmann, who had been the last person with whom
their sons had been seen; time and again the police declared themselves satisfied that he was innocent and had
had nothing to do with the youths' disappearances. By
1923, Haarmann was greatly valued by the police and
under their protection. He was helping them to recruit
people for a secret organization trying to combat French
occupation of the Ruhr and had even joined forces with a
prestigious police official to run a detective agency. But
thankfully the newspapers were under no obligation to
protect a killer or draw a veil over police corruption. It
was they who eventually pressured the police into taking
some action by drawing attention to the number of
youths who arrived in Hanover and then instantly disappeared. One newspaper suggested the figure could have
been as high as six hundred in one year. With publicity,
the very name "Hanover" began to induce a chill and
rumours began to circulate that there were such things as
werewolves after all—and that one was at large in the
town, eating the children. The police and the authorities
pooh-poohed such suggestions and dismissed them as
hysteria . . . and then the skull was washed ashore beside the River Leine. It was May 1924 and the frightened
public began harassing the police and demanding action.
A second skull—a small one—was discovered a few days
later, and more were found in the months to come, together with sackfuls of human remains. Dredgers were
brought in to dig in the river-bed; more than five hundred
human bones were found.

The horrified citizens of Hanover were defying their
own disbelief and putting two and two together. Haarmann was their prime suspect. Knowing public opinion
was against him, the chief of police had no alternative but

to have his valued informer watched. At the end of June 1924 in Hanover railway station, Haarmann tried to pick up a boy who then called the police, objecting that Haarmann had sexually interfered with him. Haarmann was arrested and, with him in custody, officers went to search his apartment. They found the bloodstained room, together with piles of clothes, but when confronted with this Haarmann protested. He was a butcher, he said, and a clothes-trader. What did they expect to find? It was the mother of a missing boy, who said her son's coat was being worn by one of Haarmann's neighbours, that prompted the killer's full confession. He instantly implicated Grans in the murders.

At the trial on 4 December 1924, Haarmann, now forty-five, and Grans, twenty-five, were charged with the murder of twenty-seven teenage boys, but this was believed to be an under-estimate. One policeman believed that during the previous year or so, Haarmann and Grans had been killing two boys a week. When asked how many youths he had murdered, Haarmann shrugged carelessly and replied: "It might have been thirty, it might have been forty. I really can't remember the exact number."— and this ghoulish contempt was evident throughout the trial. Fame was his at last and he regarded the court as his stage. Although Grans remained silent throughout, Haarmann behaved like a callous showman, admitting his guilt, showing no remorse but instead making vulgar asides to Grans. Despite there being heartbroken relatives of his victims in court, he interrupted proceedings at will, often making jocular remarks and claiming that he was a selective killer, choosing only to kill good-looking boys and denying three of the charges. One parent whose son was missing showed a picture to the court and Haarmann objected indignantly, cruelly saying: "I have my tastes, after all. Such an ugly creature as, according his photographs, your son must have been, I would never have taken to . . . Poor stuff like him there's plenty

. . . Such a youngster was much beneath my notice."
One distraught mother broke down weeping while testi-
fying and Haarmann, finding this tiresome, interrupted to
ask the judges if he could smoke a cigar. Amazingly, he
was given permission.

The newspapers, which had been so instrumental in
bringing Haarmann to justice, were revolted at the way
he behaved and did not conceal their revulsion. One report described the pitiful scenes "as a poor father or
mother would recognise some fragment or other of the
clothing or belongings of their murdered son . . . And
with the quivering nostrils of a hound snuffling his prey,
as if he were scenting rather than seeing the things displayed, did he admit at once that he knew them." People
in court paled when Haarmann was asked how he killed
his victims and he replied without emotion: "I bit them
through their throats."

He became furious when it seemed to him that Hans
Grans might be found innocent. "Grans should tell you
how shabbily he has treated me," he protested. "I did the
murders—for that work he is too young." But he told
how Grans knocked on the attic door after he had just
finished dismembering one body, and said, on entering:
"Where is the suit?" Cold and unmoved, Grans remained
unnervingly silent, which the crowds in court found
equally horrifying. Haarmann was anxious not to be
found insane and sent to a mental hospital, instead
pleading with the court to behead him in public, on the
spot where he had dealt in his evil trade. "I want to be
executed in the market-place," he demanded excitedly.
"And on my tombstone must be put this inscription:
'Here lies Mass Murderer Haarmann.' On my birthday
Hans Grans must come and lay a wreath upon it." On the
last day of the trial he shouted at the court: "Do you
think I enjoy killing people? I was ill for eight days after
the first time. Condemn me to death . . . I am not mad.
It is true I often get into a state when I do not know what

I am doing, but that is not madness . . . I will not petition for mercy, nor will I appeal. I just want to pass just one more merry evening in my cell, with coffee, hard cheese and cigars, after which I will curse my father and go to my execution as if it were a wedding."

Two psychiatrists declared that Haarmann was mentally sound. He was found guilty of twenty-four murders and beheaded. Grans was sentenced to life imprisonment but was released after twelve years, to walk the streets once more. He may still be alive today.

Haarmann was proof that given the right social conditions, a killer who is careful and cautious enough can get away with his crimes for years and between-the-wars Germany with its catastrophic inflation-rate and mass unemployment evidently provided the right climate in which the usual restraints of civilization were removed and perverts and psychopaths were enabled to flourish. Just as primitive peoples who have practised cannibalism and brutishness abandon this practice when touched by civilization, the reverse evidently applies. Poverty was rife in Germany at this period and self-interest was the dominating motivator, so maybe we should not be so surprised that "dog-eat-dog" became a byword. And it seems in many cases, people ate people, too.

Haarmann had two cannibal contemporaries. George Grossmann, like Haarmann, butchered an unknown number of people during the years after the First World War. Unlike Haarmann, his primary urge for killing was said to be fuelled by mercenary greed rather than sexual deviation, although one might doubt the truth of this, for even the most avaricious villain would blanch at Grossmann's method of getting rich illegally. The *modus operandi* was startlingly similar to Haarmann's. A pedlar, he hung around Berlin's railway station and picked out women who were particularly plump. He took them home, killed them and chopped up their bodies into cuts

of meat to sell to the hungry people of Berlin. With infla-
tion running so high that armfuls of money were needed
to buy so much as a loaf of bread (at one point the
German mark stood at 19 million to the British pound),
Grossmann's cut-price joints proved popular and highly
lucrative. He lived in a Berlin rooming-house and it was
1921 when tenants in adjoining rooms reported hearing
sounds of a struggle coming from his room. When police
burst in, they found the trussed-up corpse of a girl on the
bed, waiting to be butchered by Grossmann. Grossmann
hanged himself in gaol.

Meanwhile, in Munsterberg, Silesia (now Ziebice, Po-
land), Karl Denke ran a boarding-house, offering free
accommodation for the many homeless tramps who
passed through the city during the dire years between
1918 and 1924. They should have known there was no
such thing as a free lunch. Unless, of course, one was
Karl Denke. If one mark of a maniac is a glib exterior
and the ability to charm one's associates, then Denke,
like so many other psychopathic killers, had it. He was
known as "Papa" among his neighbours and tenants and
was regarded as a God-fearing, law-abiding man. Every
Sunday he went to church, where he played the organ,
and his kindness to the homeless was admired.

But as a landlord, he had his tenants at his mercy—and
since many were vagrants about whom no-one asked any
questions, they made easy prey for Denke. Between 1921
and 1924 he killed at least thirty strangers, male and
female, in order to eat their flesh bit by bit. Then, as a
chilling postscript to abhorrent crime, he methodically
entered the victims' names, weight, date of arrival at the
boarding-house and date of death in a ledger before pick-
ling parts of the bodies in brine to eat later. Just before
Christmas 1924, his crimes were discovered. A man who
lived on the storey above Denke heard terrible screams
from the lower floor and rushed downstairs to find a
young man bleeding profusely from a wound on the back

of his head, caused by a hatchet. The man, who was one of Denke's tenants and did not at the time appreciate his luck in escaping from his landlord's clutches, soon lost consciousness, but before doing so, he managed to say that Denke had attacked him from behind. The police, thinking it was a routine assault case, were staggered to find pots of bones and the pickled remains of thirty bodies in Denke's flat. Denke admitted his crime and said he had eaten nothing but human flesh for three years. Soon after his arrest in 1924 Denke committed suicide by hanging himself with his braces in his prison cell.

But if these cannibal-killers escaped justice for so long, the infamous Peter Kurten, who was also busy instilling terror into the folk of Düsseldorf at around this time, outlasted them, managing to avoid detection for seventeen years, from 1913, when he committed his first murder, to 1930. Kurten was inspired by his own madness, rather than anything as mundane as financial expedience during an economic slump. His insanity was portrayed by Peter Lorre in Fritz Lang's movie of 1931 about Kurten's crimes, *M*.

The "Düsseldorf Vampire," as he came to be known, was born in 1883, one of thirteen children of a family steeped in crime and violence. His brothers all served gaol sentences for theft and his father and grandfather were both alcoholics. His father was cruel and violent to both his wife and his children. He would take his violent sexual impulses out on his wife by having brutal intercourse with her as the children watched her pain and indignity, and he regularly raped his thirteen-year-old daughter. Kurten followed his example and raped the girl too.

As a child of only nine, Kurten was drawn into the sordid world of yet another individual who would help with his conditioning into the life of blood and violence which he was to enjoy. The man was the local council's dog- and rat-catcher who had a penchant for torturing animals; part of his sickness was to do it while the young Kurten watched. Kurten found the sight of suffering animals stimulating, and since the rat-catcher also committed sexual acts as part of his attacks, yet again the coupling of sex and sadism reinforced the child Peter's sexual predilections. Kurten soon graduated to committing his own acts of torture, stabbing sheep and other docile farm animals. He particularly found the sight of blood stimulating and often tore the heads off swans to enable him to drink their blood, a taste he never outgrew; when he was an adult and murdered many people, he often indulged in brutal sadism and necrophilia, sometimes drinking the blood of the corpses.

At the age of sixteen he met an older woman whose masochistic tendencies complemented his sadistic desires. During sex, she would enjoy being half-strangled and beaten and she even drew her daughter—who was the same age as Kurten—into their sexual acts. But despite their apparent carnal compatability, the relationship failed. Soon after this, Kurten attacked a girl in a wood and left her for dead, but she survived. Then came an attack on another girl whom he tried to strangle, for which he was arrested and sent to prison for a derisory four years. Altogether, Kurten spent twenty-seven years in prison out of the forty-seven years of his life, during which time he contented himself by fantasizing about performing sadistic acts upon the helpless, or killing schoolchildren by giving them chocolate laced with arsenic. He also obtained sexual pleasure from imagining setting fire to buildings, causing people inside to perish and upon release he began to act out his fantasies for real. Fortunately, no one died during the fires which he caused, but his sadism claimed many victims. Several women and children who were attacked escaped over the years, but just as many were slaughtered.

His violence first exploded into murder in 1913 when he broke into a tavern and raped the ten-year-old daughter of the innkeeper as she lay asleep in bed. Kurten recalled the killing in detail at his trial, showing no emotion, other than enjoyment at the recollection. "I discovered the child asleep. Her head was facing the window. I seized it with my left hand and strangled her for about a minute and a half. The child woke up and struggled but lost consciousness . . . I had a small but sharp pocket knife with me and I held the child's head and cut her throat. I heard the blood spurt and drip on the mat beside the bed . . . The whole thing lasted about three minutes." The day after the murder, Kurten went to a cafe opposite the inn to drink a glass of beer, read about the murder in the newspaper and listen to the shocked locals discussing the crime. "All this amount of horror and indignation did me good," he said.

Called up for the army, Kurten showed himself to be a coward and deserted the following day—presumably the sight of blood and death only held appeal when he was not at personal risk. He ended up in gaol once more for arson offences and volunteered to work in the prison hospital, to enable him to lay out prisoners who had died. Kurten's appearance belied his blood-lust. He was a fastidious, charming, smartly-groomed, well-spoken man with impeccable manners, able easily to persuade his victims to walk with him in a park, or otherwise meet him alone. Children, too, warmed to him and trusted him, which made his grisly acts that much easier to perform— and lends them an added dimension of abomination. In fact, he appeared to be a gentle man to all who knew him —or thought they knew him—including his wife, whom he married in 1921 in Altenburg and to whom he was always kind and loving. When Kurten finally confessed his crimes to her, she would not at first believe him. Within his marriage, Kurten appeared to try to suppress his sadistic instincts, restricting himself to fantasy and exciting himself by reading about Jack the Ripper, who had caused a frenzy of fear in London a few decades previously. He even took a normal job as a moulder in a factory and became an active trade union member—although he did take mistresses with whom his sexual activities became increasingly violent. He enjoyed beating and half-strangling them. But a few years after his marriage he returned to Düsseldorf because he had started a new job. "The sunset was blood-red on my return to Düsseldorf," he told a psychiatrist many years later. "I considered this to be an omen symbolic of my destiny." It was 1925 and from indulging in occasional bloodletting, he began to commit more and more crimes of arson and attempted murder, leading to a campaign of murder so intense that from February 1929 the city was in a state of terror for a full sixteen months until Kurten was caught. Indeed, it was a great irony that Kurten's wife was so afraid of the "Düsseldorf Vampire" that her husband had to accompany her when she came home late at night from the restaurant where she worked.

Men, women and children were stabbed and horribly mutilated in frenzied attacks, their bodies sometimes tossed into the river. Kurten cunningly varied the style of his attacks in order to confuse the police: sometimes his victims were stabbed, sometimes strangled, sometimes bludgeoned to death. All they were certain of was that many, many crimes had been committed by someone who enjoyed drinking the blood of his victims. On occasions he returned to the graves of those he had killed and dug up the bodies. Once when he did this, he intended crucifying the corpse, but then abandoned the idea. "I caressed the dead body . . . experiencing the tenderest emotions that as a living woman she had failed to arouse in me earlier," he was to confess later. As Kurten's defence lawyer said at his trial when trying to encourage the jury to proclaim Kurten insane: "He unites nearly all perversions in one person . . . he killed men, women, children and animals, killed anything he found." And in addition to the murders, there were many more attacks in which the victims, miraculously, escaped.

His last murder victim was a five-year-old girl, Gertrude Albermann, whom he slaughtered with a thin-bladed knife, slashing thirty-six wounds on the child's body—yet he was captured by chance after he inexplicably let a potential victim go. Meeting twenty-year-old Maria Budlik in May 1930, he took her back to his flat for coffee and then offered to walk her home. On the way he dragged her into a wooded area and began to strangle her and try to rape her. Suddenly, he stopped and demanded: "Do you remember where I live, in case you ever need my help?" Smartly, Maria lied, saying she did not remember—which probably saved her life. Kurten escorted her to her tram and she returned to her dwelling, whereupon she contacted the police and led them to Kurten. When Kurten knew that the police were on his trail, he told his wife the truth about his Jekyll-and-Hyde life, urging her to tell the police he had confessed to her, so she could claim the reward which was being offered for his capture. She did so.

At his trial in 1931 he admitted sixty-eight crimes, pleading guilty to nine charges of murder and seven of attempted murder. Standing inside a cage to prevent him escaping, Kurten confessed his crimes in detail, admitting being a sex maniac, rapist, sadist, arsonist, murderer . . . and vampire. Clearly deriving pleasure from the recollections, he described his crimes in depth—even down to his sexual attacks on animals—and admitted drinking blood from the cut throats, hands and other wounds of both his male and female victims. Calmly he told of his repetitive dreams of sex, death and blood, his obsession with Jack the Ripper and of his desire that one day he would deserve a place in a waxworks Chamber of Horrors. He blamed his childhood and his spells in prison for twisting his mind and turning him into a killer—and he also blamed his victims for "asking for it," a notion that is sadly still prevalent today in some male-dominated circles, notably among misogynistic high court judges. "I do feel that I must make one statement: some of my victims made things very easy for me. Manhunting on the part of women today has taken on such forms that . . ." Kurten began pompously to say, before the judge's disgust exploded and, outraged, he silenced the killer. Kurten was found guilty and sentenced to death, which was by the guillotine. As the day dawned, Kurten's perverted bloodlust took on a new twist. He asked his psychiatrist, curiously: "After my head has been chopped off, will I still be able to hear, at least for a moment, the sound of my own blood gushing from my neck?" He added: "That would be the pleasure to end all pleasures."

3.

A Cannibal in New York

There is no better way to know death
than to link it with some licentious image.

Marquis de Sade

It is common knowledge that sex-pests are harmless in-
adequates. When a woman encounters a "flasher" in the
park, discovers someone has stolen her underwear from
the washing-line, hears of a peeping Tom in the neighbourhood or picks up the telephone to hear a heavy
breather whispering obscenities, she knows that her fear
is irrational. After all, haven't we all been told that these
nuisances are no more than that: sad individuals whose
feebleness and undoubted impotence with women means
they are pursuing a fantasy outlet rather than dealing
with reality? Isn't the best advice simply to ignore these
perverts and they'll go away?

Psychiatrist Robert P. Brittain in his classic essay "The
Sadistic Murderer" sounded a note of caution about such
complacency in 1970. When sadistic murderers are finally
caught, he revealed, those with criminal histories have
usually committed sex offences of a non-violent nature,
such as those listed above. "It does not follow that all
who commit such acts are potentially sexual murderers
and many may only be social nuisances; it does follow,

however, that such offenders should be examined most carefully because a proportion, however small, are potentially very dangerous," Dr. Brittain wrote. Those in authority who deal with perverts of the obscene-phone-call variety should, by rights, be aware of research such as Dr. Brittain's and there should be careful monitoring of the offender in case he is one of the few whose crimes escalate into far worse offences. But they are seldom treated very seriously even these days. So, sixty years ago, what chance was there that the New York authorities would guess that the apparently trivial offence for which Albert Fish had been arrested concealed crimes which were so monstrous as to be incomprehensible to most people?

Fish, a harmless-looking, frail old man with grey wispy hair, was arrested in December 1930 for writing obscene letters to lonely widows who had placed advertisements in personal columns of newspapers and magazines, or who had lodged their names with marriage agencies. The letters had been sent over a period of years and his requests to the women were explicit, couched in the most disgusting terms; in essence he wanted the women to beat him or join with him in whipping boys. He was taken to the psychiatric ward of the Bellevue Hospital where psychiatry division director Dr. Menas Gregory, after consultation with his assistant, reported Fish to be "abnormal—a psychopathic personality, with evidence of early senile change, but not insane or a mental defective." Despite a history of masochistic sexual perversion from early on in his life, Fish's behaviour was judged to be "quiet and co-operative, orderly and normal" and he was released. Unknown to them, this elderly man—"sane," "orderly" and "normal"—had, two years previously, abducted and killed a twelve-year-old child in a frenzy of sexual ecstasy, cut her into pieces, put the pieces into a stew with vegetables and eaten her.

* * *

In May 1928, the thin, respectable-looking elderly man who called at the home of Edward and Delia Budd in New York had called himself Frank Howard. His shoes were brightly polished, his hat had a silk lining and his shirt had wing-collars. "He looked like a decent man," Edward Budd was later to recall. He was responding, he said, to a newspaper advertisement which the Budds' eldest son, eighteen-year-old Edward Jr., had placed, seeking summer-vacation work. He claimed to have a farm on Long Island and to be in need of extra help. An arrangement was made for "Mr. Howard" to collect Edward the following week and take him to see the farm. The Budds, being open-hearted people, invited him to come early so he could have dinner with them. And that was how he met little Grace, their second-youngest daughter.

When "Frank Howard" suggested that he take Grace to a children's party, the Budds raised no objection and off they went, the old man and the little girl, hand-in-hand. Grace was wearing her confirmation dress. "She looked real sweet in her grey coat and hat," Edward Budd told reporters six years later. "She was real happy. We didn't see anything wrong. We said she should go, and come home early. We never did see her again." A trusting Little Red Riding Hood walked away with the Wolf towards the subway station.

Is it nature or nurture which turns a man into worse than a beast? The most popular view among psychologists is that environment moulds a person, for better or worse, and in a sense, this absolves them of blame for their later actions. To declare that some people are simply born bad, with their brains containing "a fluke, an accident of internal wiring"—as writer Christine McGuire said of another American sadist, Cameron Hooker, in her book *Perfect Victim*, can draw many a frown from social psychologists. But superficially it might seem that Fish's disturbed background was responsible for his aberrant behaviour. Ham-

ilton Albert Fish was born in 1870 in Washington D.C.
into a respectable family. When he was five his father
died and his mother had to go out to work. She put
Albert in an orphanage and that, according to Fish himself, was to blame for his later abominable crimes. Cruel
treatment was meted out to the children. "I saw so many
boys whipped it ruined my mind," Fish was to say later.
From being an apparently contented child, Albert became a stammering wreck. He wet the bed until he was
eleven and frequently ran away—"every Saturday" he
claimed. And it emerged that among Fish's immediate
family—which included his parents' siblings—there were
disorders of the mind. No less than seven of them suffered from psychoses or had psychopathic personalities.
A couple of them died in mental institutions, another was
an alcoholic and others were looked on as "completely
crazy." Even Fish's mother was regarded with suspicion
by neighbours who reported that she heard voices. It was
an older brother, Fish was later to claim, who sparked his
interest in anthropophagy as a boy by telling him gruesome tales of cannibalism in the Far East. This was hardly
The Waltons, then. And one thing which psychiatrists subsequently discovered was that when one of Fish's teach-
ers spanked children on their bare bottoms, whereas the
other infants cried, Albert Fish enjoyed it. He was only
five years old at the time. Pinpointing the cause of Fish's
twisted mind is, therefore, tricky and blaming it all on
circumstance might be foolhardy.

Fish became a painter and decorator and eventually
married—a marriage which resulted in six children. After
twenty years his wife ran away with the lodger, leaving
the children behind, and it was at this point that Fish
apparently snapped completely, although she later said
of her marriage to Fish: "He was crazy." However, the
abandoned husband raised the children alone, the youngest being three years old at the time, and apparently
never harmed them physically. At Fish's later trial his

daughter, Mrs. Gertrude DeMarco, by then in her thirties, recalled how her father had always said Grace before every meal, frequently read the Bible and regularly attended church. As far as she could remember, Fish had never struck any of the children, she said.

This did not stop him from involving his offspring in his masochistic practices. Not content with self-flagellation, he encouraged his children and their friends to beat him on the buttocks using a paddle which he had made himself, studded with inch-and-a-half nails. He indulged in other, equally bizarre, behaviour, climbing to the top of a hill near their home in Westchester County, New York and baying at the moon, naked, screaming: "I am Christ! I am Christ!" Obsessed with flesh-eating, he served raw meat to his children on nights when the moon was full and collected newspaper articles on cannibalism, which he carried around with him until they turned into yellowed crumbs in his pockets.

Fish became a drifter, travelling through America, settling briefly to work as a house-painter and then moving on. During his sojourns he would write his obscene letters to lonely women . . . and attack children. He had an especial fondness for little boys and claimed to have attacked at least a hundred—"I have had children in every state," he bragged when he was finally arrested for Grace Budd's murder—and the authorities suspected the one hundred figure was an under-estimate. He was believed to have killed at least fifteen children. He would tie them up, beat them and torture them cruelly, usually refraining from gagging them because he liked to hear their terrible screams. He had a penchant for attempting to castrate the small boys—and, according to his own admissions, sometimes succeeded. Frequently he would abduct coloured children; he discovered that the law-enforcers did not look for missing black children as assiduously as they looked for white children.

Fish was the archetypal bogey-man of whom parents

warn their children: tempting them with sweets or stories
of parties, he led them away from safety, strangled them
and on occasions chopped them up and fed on their flesh
and blood. Psychiatrist Dr. Fredric Wertham said after
his first interview when Fish was in custody for the Budd
murder: "He looked like a meek and innocuous little old
man, gentle and benevolent, friendly and polite . . . If
you wanted someone to entrust your children to, he
would be the one you would choose." He was the one the
Budds chose.

There was a full moon on the night of Sunday, 3 June
1928, the ill-fated date when Fish had gone to the Budds'
house for dinner. Some days previously, Fish had gone to
a pawn-shop in Manhattan and bought a cleaver, a saw
and a butcher's knife. On the day of his visit he had
wrapped the weapons in a brown paper parcel and asked
a news vendor to look after it for him. Later, with Grace
by his side, he picked up the parcel and it rested between
them on the train to Greenburgh in Westchester County
—that was where his sister lived, he explained. As they
were getting off the train, Grace hesitated and ran back
inside. She returned with his parcel, handed it to him
with a bright smile and took his hand again as they
walked to a broken-down house with a timeworn sign
declaring it to be Wisteria Cottage. It backed on to a
wood and Fish suggested that Grace go and pick some
flowers while he checked to see where his sister was.

Inside, Fish went into one of the upstairs rooms overlooking the wood, laid out his sharpened weapons—his
"implements of Hell," as he was later to call them,
stripped naked and called to Grace from the window. She
came into the house and when she saw his scrawny, white,
bare flesh, she screamed: "I'll tell Mama!" Sweating and
excited, Fish pounced on the terrified child and strangled
her as she struggled violently. Then in a frenzy, he
hacked the small body into numerous pieces, placed the

head in an outside toilet, dressed again and left the blood-soaked room, taking with him some parts of Grace's body wrapped in a cloth. Once home, he cooked the pieces of flesh with vegetables and ate the stew. For nine days, he made return visits to Wisteria Cottage and returned with more body-parts to eat. As he devoured them—or even when he merely *imagined* devouring them —he would experience exquisite sexual pleasure. At the end of nine days he collected what remained of little Grace Budd's body into a bundle and threw the bundle over a wall at the back of the house. Then, as Grace's weeping parents began their life-sentence of anguish, hoping against hope that their daughter was still alive, "Frank Howard" moved on again.

Why was he not caught? In his life he was—many times— but he was always released. There were frequent arrests and questionings by police over corruption of minors, but Fish served brief sentences, the longest being sixteen months for larceny when he stole money from a store. His offences were not considered to be serious and although he was kept in psychiatric hospitals for short periods in 1930 and 1931, he was released as "not insane" and, after the obscene letters charge, put on probation for a mere six months. In the end, Fish sealed his own fate with his perverted desire to inflict even more pain on the Budd family. The slender hope they nursed that their little Grace was still alive somewhere was snuffed out when, six years after their child's disappearance, an unsigned letter arrived at their home from Fish.

He began by telling of "a friend" who, as a deck-hand, was stranded in China in 1894 at a time of famine:

> So great was the suffering among the very poor that all children under 12 were sent to the butchers [sic] to be cut up and sold for food in order to keep others from starving . . . You could go in any shop and ask for

steak . . . Part of a naked body of a boy or girl would
be brought out and just what you wanted cut from it. A
boy or girls [sic] behind which is the sweetest part of the
body and sold as veal cutlet brought the highest price.

After this nauseating beginning, Fish continued by saying that his "friend" returned to the USA with a taste for
human flesh and captured two small boys whom he
spanked "to make their meat fresh and tender," then
killed and ate them: "I made up my mind to taste [human
flesh]," he wrote and revealed that when Grace had sat
on his lap and kissed him at dinner "I made up my mind
to eat her." Fish then salaciously detailed what had happened in Wisteria Cottage, including Grace's cries and
fear, knowing that each word would be like a scalpel-
blade in her wretched parents' breasts. Finally he ended
the letter, at pains to point out he had not attacked Grace
sexually: "It took me 9 days to eat her entire body. I did
not fuck her tho I could of had I wished to [sic]. She died
a virgin." (This was a lie, he later confessed to a psychiatrist.)

The police went to work on the letter right away, discovering that the envelope in which it was sent had a
monogram design upon it, marking it as having come
from a Manhattan company. Investigations led them to
Fish, living in a New York rooming-house. As some
detectives interrogated him, others went through the old
man's belongings—and found the faded newspaper clip-
pings. There was a bunch, bound together, and they were
all about Fritz Haarmann, the "Hanover Vampire" who,
as the previous chapter outlined, had abducted young
men in the early 1920s, killed them and sold their flesh in
the marketplace. Meanwhile Edward Budd had arrived
at the police-station and instantly identified "Frank Howard." Fish later told his terrible story with obvious relish
and Grace's remains were found at Wisteria Cottage.

"Why did you do it?" asked a disbelieving policeman. "It occurred to me," replied Fish.

Fish confessed to murdering a man in 1910, to mutilating and torturing to death a mentally-retarded boy in New York in 1919 and another boy in Washington the same year. He admitted killing and eating four-year-old William Gaffney in 1927, and five-year-old Francis McDonal in 1934. The police suspected him of many more murders, but began the process of charging him with the killing of Grace Budd. Then they handed him over to the psychiatrists.

The psychiatrists had a field-day with Fish, as one perversion after another was revealed to them as Fish's source of enjoyment for most of his life. "Simple" sado-masochism was only the beginning: an X-ray revealed twenty-nine needles embedded in his body, some of them the enormous needles which are used to repair canvas, and almost all in his pelvic area, around the rectum and near the bladder. They had been inserted through the skin, rather than swallowed and it was estimated that many of the needles had been in his body for years, judging by their erosion patterns. Fish freely admitted that he had stuck needles into his body, near the genitals for many years, usually pulling them out again. "I put them up under the spine," he said. "I put one in the scrotum too, but I couldn't stand the pain." The twenty-nine needles were those which had been put in too far to remove. Fish also said he enjoyed inserting needles into the bodies of children.

"There was no known perversion that he did not practise and practise frequently," said Dr. Fredric Wertham, who made a detailed study of Fish and listed eighteen sexual perversions in which he indulged, including sado-masochism, exhibitionism, coprophagia (eating of faeces), undinism (sexual acts involving urination), fetishism (abnormal preference for a non-genital part of the body such as buttocks, or for inanimate objects), and cannibalism. He also had a castration complex. One of Fish's particular pleasures was to soak cotton-wool in alcohol, insert it into his anus and set fire to it. Wertham proclaimed Fish to be a man of intelligence and cunning, the truth of whose stories could not always be separated from fantasy, but in time he judged himself able to separate fact from fancy and it was to Wertham that Fish revealed the details of Grace Budd's death and the sexual thrill he experienced when eating parts of her body, or when he thought about the murder and the subsequent cannibalism. He took enormous pleasure in describing to the psychiatrist how he cooked and ate a child. "He spoke in a matter-of-fact way, like a housewife describing her favourite methods of cooking," said Wertham.

As if Fish did not have enough deviations which have been categorized above, religious mania can be added to them. In gaol awaiting trial, he regularly fell to his knees in prayer, and in keeping with his children's stories of their naked father shrieking, "I am Christ!" over and over again in the moonlight, Fish told Wertham that God had told him to commit his vile acts on children. Paedophiles tend to be rigidly religious and moralistic, as testified by Fish's daughter when she recalled her childhood, but not all of them claim to have heard voices from angels. Fish claimed to have heard words like "stripes"—which, he explained, meant he was to lash the children. He would quote and misquote the Bible to support his deeds. "Happy is he that taketh Thy little ones and dasheth their heads against the stones," he would say, or, "Blessed is the man who correcteth his son in whom he delighteth with stripes, for great shall be his reward." Claiming to be convinced that God wanted him to castrate little boys, he compared himself to Abraham offering his son Isaac as a sacrifice. On other occasions he saw himself as God making a sacrifice as Jesus was sacrificed.

* * *

Harnessing religion to justify one's wickedness is nothing new. From the witchcraft trials of the Middle Ages to the modern day when people commit the most sickening atrocities upon each other in the name of one religion or another, human beings have always enjoyed having an excuse to sate their appetites for cruelty. As philosopher Blaise Pascal noted: "Men never do evil so completely and cheerfully as when they do it from religious conviction." Hallucinatory "voices from God" sometimes occur in cases of paranoid schizophrenia—for example Herbert Mullin, who killed thirteen people in Santa Cruz during the four months up to February 1973. Under the delusion that God required a certain number of human "sacrifices" every year, he concluded that earthquakes, such as those along the San Andreas fault in San Francisco, only occurred during periods when the murder rate was low. "Murder decreases the number of natural disasters and the extent of the devastation of these disasters," he concluded. Therefore to protect America against the great earthquake, Mullin set out to randomly kill as many people as possible (and since there were no major earthquakes in 1973, he believed he had achieved his mission).

Curiously enough, Fish's belief that he was like Abraham sacrificing his son finds an echo in another incident which happened in a more primitive culture than New York. In August 1973 a thirty-year-old man was tried at a court in Goilala, Papua New Guinea for the murder of his own baby son. A man of limited education and intelligence, there was a history of mental disorder within the family and he had been brought up in a culture whose primitive beliefs had encompassed violence and cannibalism in years gone by. Cannibalism used to be indulged in as a necessity in times of food shortage, as a means of revenge on enemies, or for magical motives, such as to enable one to absorb the virtues of others. In 1973, though, none of these applied—and certainly not to the man in the dock, who had attended well to what Christian missionaries, who are extremely active in Papua New Guinea, had told him. He devotedly read many religious books, including the Bible, and he was particularly taken with the stories about John the Baptist, about Jesus fasting for forty days and about Abraham preparing to sacrifice his son Isaac.

Calmly and earnestly, he told the court that he wanted to help his people and after some thought, came to a conclusion on how this could be effected:

> I decided to kill my child. After I had made up my mind, I fasted for five days. I then took my little boy into the bush and came to the place where I had decided to kill him. When I came to the spot, I prepared a small place for the child to sit and I spread a laplap on the ground for him, then I began to dig a grave. After that was finished, I struck him twice on the forehead with my axe. I then took my knife and cut him in the stomach and upward toward the chest and through the bone. I then took his heart out. I chopped it up and ate some of it. I also made some cuts in my own body and mixed some of my son's blood with this. Then I put the body in the grave. I had brought some glue and petrol with me which I mixed with the remaining cut slices of my son's heart. I tried to boil it but was not successful. I had hoped that the steam and the rest of the mixture would go up to God and he would then send me the power in my dreams to do the right things for my people. The people's heads would also become clear, and they would then do the necessary things to bring about the white man's way of life. God would send many goods to the people and we would find money. Then I lay down in the grave and slept with my dead son. No dream came the first night. On the second, I dreamed that I saw a light go up to heaven. I then covered the grave and returned to my village.

The psychiatrist who reported this case, Dr. B.G. Burton-Bradley, concluded that the man displayed "marked autistic thinking and a delusional state prior to the act" and found evidence of schizophrenia. He warned of the dangers inherent in unthinkingly teaching religion—which is frequently interlaced with symbolism—to a people whose own history might influence their present thinking and create misunderstanding in someone who is mentally unstable and might try, as this man did, to emulate certain aspects of Christian teaching.

Dr. Wertham did not claim that Albert Fish was influenced by cultural, cannibalistic roots when the murder trial began in March 1935, but he did regard Fish to be insane. The prosecutor, Elbert T. Gallagher, insisted otherwise. "He is not defective mentally . . . he has complete orientation as to his immediate surroundings . . . there is no mental deterioration, but . . . he is known medically as a sex pervert or a sex psychopath . . . his acts were abnormal . . . he knew it was wrong . . . he is legally sane and responsible for his acts." Fish's attorney, James Dempsey, opined that Fish had a Jekyll-and-Hyde personality, with one side of his character sweet and gentle and the other side monstrous. He refused to put Fish on the witness stand, saying that he did not believe an insane man should testify. "The story of this man's life is one of unspeakable horror . . . it would disgust and nauseate you," he said.

Dr. Wertham said he believed Fish to be "basically a homosexual" and a paedophile: "Women were just a substitute." He told the jury that the old man read all he could about violence and torture and revealed that as far back as twenty-five years previously, Fish had tried—and failed—to castrate a teenage boy he picked up in St. Louis. He had cut the youth's buttocks with a razor-blade and drunk his blood, but had refrained from killing him, giving him money instead. When Fish had arrived at the Budd house, it had been his intention to take Edward Budd away and castrate him, but on seeing what a strong and powerful youth he was, he thought better of it and selected weaker, more defenceless prey. Dr. Wertham told how Fish had inserted roses into his penis, and would then eat the roses. He spoke of Fish's marriage and declared that Fish's wife was interested to some extent in his sexual perversions. "His relations with her were entirely abnormal," the doctor stated—which was borne out by the woman herself, who had told reporters after Fish was arrested, "The old skunk, I knew something like this would happen."

Fish was undoubtedly insane, declared Dr. Wertham; four other psychiatrists were brought into court to disagree with him about Fish's sanity, one of whom was Dr. Menas S. Gregory who, as head of the Bellevue Hospital, had not exactly covered himself in glory by letting Fish out four years previously and declaring him "abnormal— a psychopathic personality, with evidence of early senile change, but not insane" and displaying "normal" behaviour. He persisted in his view, stating—quite correctly— that many of the assorted perversions enjoyed by Fish were not uncommon. When asked if he considered a man who indulged in such pursuits to be "all right" he replied: "Not perfectly all right, but socially all right. There are men high up socially and financially who unfortunately suffer that way. They know right from wrong. They are successful people."

The jury found Fish guilty and the death penalty was mandatory. Fish was dispatched to Sing Sing Prison to await his punishment. He did not show fear; quite the contrary. "What a thrill it will be if I have to die in the electric chair!" he sighed, "It will be the supreme thrill— the only one I haven't tried." When the moment came, in January 1936, he sat in the electric chair and eagerly helped the executioner to fix the electrodes to his legs. He smiled as other electrodes were placed on his head, and as 3,000 volts shot through his body, he laughed—but he did not die. By a perverse twist of fate, the needles which were still embedded in his body had short-circuited the electric chair. Another charge of electricity had to be put through the body. Finally, as a haze of blue smoke rose from the slumped body, Albert Fish was declared dead.

4

The Man Who Kept Dolls

Doctor: A very pestilent disease my lord,
     They call lycanthropia . . .
       . . . they imagine
     Themselves to be transformed into wolves . . .
       . . . as two nights since
     One met the Duke, 'bout midnight in a lane
     Behind St. Mark's church, with the leg of a man
     Upon his shoulder; and he howl'd fearfully:
     Said he was a wolf: only the difference
     Was, a wolf's skin was hairy on the outside,
     His on the inside.

    John Webster: *The Duchess of Malfi*, Act V, Sc. ii

Oscar Muller was on his way to the shared lavatory on the top floor of his apartment building in Friesen Street, Laar, north of Duisburg, West Germany, when he bumped into his neighbour, an unwashed-looking, brown-eyed, balding little man who, although friendly enough, kept himself to himself. "I wouldn't use the lavatory, if I were you—it's been stopped up," said the small man, whom he knew only as "Uncle Joachim"—because that was what the local children called him when they came to play at his flat. "Stopped up?" said Muller. "What with?" "Guts," replied Uncle Joachim, and went on his way. The smell of his dinner-time stew bubbling gently on the stove drifted on to the landing as the mild little man opened and then softly closed the door of his apartment behind him. Muller smiled at Joachim's odd little joke—for he knew that his neighbour enjoyed jokes —and he went to see what had really happened to the toilet. When he looked into the lavatory-bowl he was appalled to see that the water was red with blood and there appeared to be matter and tissue of some sort floating in the water. Feeling distinctly queasy, Muller ran down the stairs and out of the apartment block as fast as his elderly legs would take him, to find the road outside teeming with policemen. They were making door-to-door enquiries because four-year-old Monika Kettner—a little blonde girl who lived a few doors away—had failed to return home after vanishing from a nearby playground earlier in the day. His sense of horror bordering on hysteria, Oscar Muller took hold of a policeman's arm and anxiously tugged, stammering out what "Uncle Joachim" had said—and what he had found. It took a moment before the distracted policeman realized why, exactly, Muller was complaining to them about his blocked-up toilet.

After a glance into the lavatory bowl, detectives called the police department's medical officer. Between them, they manhandled the porcelain bowl from its mountings and tipped the contents out into a container. What came out was a complete set of internal organs—liver, lungs, kidneys and heart—along with scraps of flesh. They were tiny: about the size one would expect in a four-year-old child.

"Uncle Joachim," who had indeed abducted and murdered little Monika earlier that day, was unflustered when the police knocked on his door to search his apartment. In the refrigerator were pieces of the child's flesh on plates; in the deep-freeze were more body-parts, neatly wrapped. And what of Joachim's stew, boiling merrily in a pan on top of the cooker? Among the carrots, potatoes and gravy was a tiny hand, cooked through.

Joachim Kroll admitted killing a dozen people in the heavily-industrial Ruhr region of West Germany between 1955 and 1976, but he had a poor memory: the likelihood is that these remembered murders are but the tip of the iceberg. For, unlike many sadistic killers who get perverted pleasure out of hearing the news reports about their murders, or of following the police-hunt with a feeling of smugness at having outsmarted the law, Kroll had no interest in his victims after he had killed, raped, mutilated and sometimes butchered cuts of meat from their bodies. While he was undoubtedly sexually motivated in his attacks, his cannibalism was, by his own account, mere expedience: meat was expensive, so Kroll hunted his own.

If this pragmatic motive is correct, this makes him different from, say, Albert Fish, the New York cannibal killer who gained perverted sexual pleasure firstly from eating his victims, and secondly from recollecting his repulsive actions. But then, of course, we only have Joachim Kroll's word for it. True or not, Kroll, who was forty-three at the time of his arrest and working as a lavatory attendant, was not believed to have the above-average intelligence which many psychiatrists associate with sadistic serial killers. On the contrary, Kroll was thought by the authorities to be mentally defective, evidenced by his lack of schooling and inability to read, his apparent unconcern about his crimes, his readiness to confess, his willingness to help the police all he could and his conviction that after his helpful confession, the police would allow him to go back home—perhaps after he had had some sort of operation which would render him harmless to the opposite sex, he speculated.

Such naïveté certainly makes Kroll sound subnormal, but for someone who was mentally handicapped, he certainly showed a surfeit of sharpness and patience in selecting his victims, caution in carrying out his crimes and care not to get caught. Would a subnormal man really be cunning enough to escape detection for twenty-one years? Would he have shown such sly self-preservation and managed to keep his brutality a secret from his neighbours and workmates if he had really been mentally defective? However, as a child he had spent only three years at school in Hindenburg, East Germany—and one of those was a repeat year. He blamed his perverted behaviour on an incident which happened when he was a teenager. He saw some pigs being butchered and this awakened his sex drive, he said. Kroll did not consider that the majority of human beings are not sexually aroused by the sight of animals being slaughtered. When he was in his teens his mother, a widow, moved with her five children to West Germany and when she died the brothers and sisters went their separate ways and eventually lost contact with Joachim.

Kroll kept company with men. His one and only relationship with a woman was, he told police, a failure. As with so many sadistic killers, Kroll was unable to achieve a normal sexual relationship with a living woman. Which was why he murdered them first. He was, however, highly sexed, if deviant; when the police arrested him, they found in his room a well-used rubber sex-doll. Kroll admitted that after several of his regular bouts of carnage— during which he was discovered to have ejaculated twice on some occasions—he would return to his room and seek yet more pleasure with the rubber doll. This was not the only doll in Kroll's apartment, for he had a large collection of children's dollies—used as bait for the little girls he would befriend . . . and also used as practice for strangling children. Sometimes Kroll would masturbate with one hand while strangling a doll with the other.

Many small girls went for walks with Uncle Joachim, hanging on to a doll with one hand and the killer's hand with the other. Almost all of them were unharmed, possi-

bly because Kröll was forbidden by his tenancy regula-
tions to take them up to his room (which did not stop him
from frequently trying to do so), but more likely because
their parents were aware that their children were with
Kroll, whom they regarded as kindly and trustworthy. As
has been remarked upon already, Kroll appears not to
have been as daft as the authorities claimed him to be
and could eaily control his urges when he was obliged to
do so for the sake of self-preservation. His last murder
victim—little Monika Kettner—had been plucked from
the children's playground and taken to his room in secret
without her parents' knowledge. She appears to have
been the only local child to have been murdered by her
friend Uncle Joachim, although one ten-year-old girl,
Gabriele Puettmann, seemingly had a lucky escape in
1967. She was sitting with Uncle Joachim on a park
bench when he said he had something to show her and
produced a book of pornographic pictures. Shocked and
embarrassed, Gabriele put her hands over her eyes and
then felt Kroll's hand on her shoulder. She leapt up and
ran home, saying nothing to her parents because of the
shame she felt. Eleven years later, when Kroll had been
arrested and named her in his lengthy confessions,
Gabriele confirmed the story and shivered as she realised
how close she had come to being listed as yet one more
Kroll victim.

But Kroll usually looked farther afield for his prey to
avoid suspicion. His killing spree began when he was
about twenty-two years old, in 1955. He took a bus or
train to the village of Walstedde, just north of the Ruhr
district and seized nineteen-year-old Irmgard Strehl as
she walked down the main road towards a nearby village.
Her naked body was found several hundred yards off the
road. The abdomen was ripped up and the body had been
raped frenziedly. It was small comfort to her loved ones,
but she had been strangled before these acts had taken
place. Lack of bruising around the genital area proved

that the rape had not been inflicted on the girl when she was still alive—and this was the case with all Kroll's female victims.

When questioned by police twenty-odd years later, Kroll vaguely recollected this first killing, but claimed that his murderous impulses then lay dormant for more than four years, when he recalled slaying a twenty-four-year-old woman called Klara Tesmer in Rheinhausen and, a month later, Manuela Knodt, aged sixteen, in Bredeney. None of the authorities in the Ruhr believes in Kroll's four years of self-restraint for a moment. A man with Kroll's compulsion and his sex-drive is not judged to have been able to remain contented with a rubber doll until 1959 and there are, undoubtedly, other sex killings which were committed by Kroll during this period and remain officially unsolved.

Klara's murder was identical to that of Irmgard, but it was during this killing that Kroll was first known to have practised cannibalism. When he abandoned Klara's body in some woods, he took with him a grisly memento: using a long-bladed folding knife, Kroll hacked pieces of the buttocks and thighs from the body, wrapped them up and took them home for his supper. The police perceived no link between this killing and the one in 1955, and a local man, Heinrich Ott, was arrested and charged with this and several other sex murders which had happened in the region over the preceding few years. Ott hanged himself while awaiting trial. Now, of course, we may look back and wonder whether Kroll was responsible for at least some of those murders—and some of the other murders which were to occur between then and 1961, a period when Kroll claimed that any killing he did had slipped his memory.

The murders of thirteen-year-old Petra Giese in April 1962 and of Monika Tafel, aged twelve, two months later —both in the Bruckhausen region—were the ones which first alerted the police to the possible nature of this killer's crimes. Petra was on her way home from a carnival when she became separated from her friend. Both child victims, in addition to the rape and mutilation, had had pieces of flesh cut from their buttocks and thighs—Petra's left arm was also missing—and the doctors mulled over with detectives why this could have occurred. The pieces were not cut from the reproductive organs or breasts, which is common with sadistic killers. It took a leap of appalled imagination to guess the true, horrific nature of the mutilations. But imaginations were indeed beginning to leap—although not, apparently, enough to link the two crimes, despite their being committed only a matter of miles and months apart. An unmarried fifty-two-year-old man was arrested for the murder of Petra Giese and a thirty-four-year-old man for that of Monika Tafel.

Vinzenz Kuehn was well known locally as a child molester, although he had never physically injured any of the little girls who had been abused by him. Despite his denials, he was nevertheless convicted of raping and murdering Petra and sent to prison for twelve years with an order that he receive psychiatric treatment. He was released six years later. Walter Quicker, suspected of killing Monika Tafel, was not so lucky. Suspicion had fallen upon him because of his fondness for little girls, but it was just that: fondness. There was no evidence to show that he had ever behaved improperly towards any of the children he befriended. Because of this, hard as the police tried, they were unable to make any charges stick and were forced, grudgingly, to release Quicker. A court may not have tried the man, but his friends and neighbours did. His wife, unable to live with "a child molester" any longer, decided to divorce Quicker, and he was persecuted by the community. Shopkeepers even refused to serve him and youngsters would taunt him in the street. A few months after Monika's murder, Quicker went into the same forest where her body had been found and hanged himself. It would be another fourteen years before Kroll's confession absolved both these men of the crimes they were believed to have done.

The next murder which Kroll remembers was that of a man killed for Kroll's convenience. It was three years later, so we may assume that the cannibal had been silently preying elsewhere, undetected, during that period, even if he was not able to recall his victims. He would have used his tried and tested method of trailing girls for days while he planned his strategy before finally pouncing.

The murder of Hermann Schmitz was different—and not just because Schmitz was Kroll's only male victim. For one thing, it was spontaneous, and for another, Kroll was careless enough to almost get caught. Certainly, he left behind a live witness to his crime: the woman whom Kroll had selected as his victim that night in August 1965.

Kroll had been out in Grossenbaum during the evening, searching for a lone female on whom he could slake his appetites when, sexually excited, he ended up spying on a courting couple in a car parked beside an artificial lake, a favourite place for lovers. Watching Hermann Schmitz and his fiancée Marion Veen making love in the front seat of the car, a lust-inflamed Kroll decided on a plan: he would lure Schmitz out of the car, kill him and then, with Schmitz out of the way, he would be able to kill and rape Marion. To this end, he went up to the car and inserted his sharp folding knife into one of the car's tyres. However, Schmitz did not get out of the car. Instead, he drove off—into a dead end—and when he turned the car around, there was Joachim Kroll in the middle of the road, waving his arms. Schmitz, thinking the man was in trouble, got out. Kroll stabbed him repeatedly. Marion Veen, with admirable presence of mind, jumped into the driver's seat and drove the car straight at Kroll, who only just managed to jump out of the way in time. As he

vanished into the undergrowth, the courageous girl
wedged a hair clip into the horn, to make it blast continu-
ously as a desperate Mayday signal, and leapt out to tend
to her blood-soaked fiancé. He was dead.

One might think that here was a good opportunity for
the police to catch Schmitz's killer, but Marion Veen's
description of the unwashed, untidy, insignificant little
man led nowhere. Known peeping Toms were questioned, together with contacts of both Marion and Hermann, but the police drew a blank. After Kroll's next
slaughter—that of twenty-year-old Ursula Rohling in
Marl, forty miles north of Duisburg in September 1966—
there was yet another police bungle, as Ursula's fiancé
Adolf Schickel was hauled in and questioned for a full
three weeks. Schickel was the last person to have been
seen with Ursula—they met for tea to discuss plans for
their wedding—before she set off home through Foer-
sterbusch Park in Marl. When her body was found,
sprawled among some bushes, the pathologist could find
no evidence that she had resisted the rape, and it was this
which convinced the police that Schickel was the guilty
party. However, they could find no proof to uphold their
suspicions and although they still thought Schickel was
guilty, they set him free.

The story is a parallel to that of Walter Quicker: ostracized by his former friends and neighbours who also believed him to be guilty, Schickel was driven out of the
town and less than four months after his fiancée's death,
Adolf Schickel drowned himself in a river. A couple of
weeks before Schickel's suicide, Kroll had killed again,
this time a five-year-old child called Ilona Harke who
lived in Bredeney, the scene of Kroll's third remembered
murder, that of Manuela Knodt. Kroll persuaded little
Ilona to travel on a train with him to a destination twenty
miles south of Bredeney. After killing and raping the
child, Kroll took from her buttocks and shoulders large
quantities of her flesh away with him to eat, wrapping

them up neatly in greaseproof paper. He later told police that he only cannibalized those victims whom he considered to be young and tender. Apart from his final killing, which resulted in his capture, Ilona was Kroll's youngest victim.

In total Kroll confessed to fourteen murders which could be accounted for. He had lost count of the rest. His oldest victim had been a sixty-one-year-old widow, Maria Hettgen, who opened her front door and was instantly strangled by Kroll. Her body was found in the hallway. After another murder, that of thirteen-year-old Jutta Rahn in a town close to Grossenbaum, yet another man had been punished by the community, if not the law, after being charged and cleared of the murder. Peter Schay's blood group matched that of the killer, but there was no concrete evidence to convict him. Nevertheless, Schay was taunted with "murderer" by neighbours until, more than six years later, Kroll confessed to Jutta's murder.

When, by chance, Joachim Kroll's widowed mother had moved her family from East Germany to West Germany thirty years previously, it was providential for Kroll. His mother had inadvertently saved his life, for West Germany did not have capital punishment whereas East Germany did. Kroll was given a life sentence and a place in history as the perpetrator of the longest series of sadistic murders which had ever been known in Germany. Not that the police emerge with much credit, since at the time they were not even aware of the extent of the crime which won Kroll his vile infamy. When they finally captured Kroll, their suspicions extended to only a handful of victims; it was Kroll who supplied confessions to the remainder, often by remarking casually: "I think I murdered someone in that town." When checked out, it was discovered that Kroll's recollections regarding when, where and how matched perfectly with unsolved crimes. But it is truly astonishing that in an area less than fifty miles long by twenty miles wide Kroll could get away with his crimes for twenty years. One might wonder what, in fact, the police were playing at. Not only was the Ruhr region littered with corpses who had died directly at Kroll's hands, but two men had killed themselves because of police blunders associated with the crimes. A further four were sentenced for crimes committed by Kroll.

In the police's defence it must be noted that Kroll confused investigators by deliberately varying his *modus operandi*—and his type of victim. In addition, Germany has always had a high rate of sex murders—for example, for three years until 1956, at the time when Kroll had just begun killing, a twenty-eight-year-old mechanic called Werner Boost was busy in the woods around Düsseldorf attacking courting couples, raping the women and then killing the couple. There were many other sex-killers operating in that area at the time and although no one else devoured parts of their victims, Kroll did not do this on every occasion. The confused police, anxious to reassure frightened townsfolk of their ability to solve such heinous crimes, attributed Kroll's rapes and murders to other people.

And one reason why Kroll escaped for so long is that he appeared to be such an unremarkable little man. He did not look dangerous, and with his soft voice he certainly did not sound like a cruel aggressor. Like the New York cannibal, Albert Fish, he was small and insignificant, gentle in his approach, outwardly far removed from the grinning, slavering monster which we imagine such a ruthless criminal to be. But inwardly . . . ?

5

The Kiss of the Vampire

> He took out a small jewelled knife and put the point to
> my finger. A drop of blood came forth. I would have
> cried out, but something in his expression kept me still.
> "That is the first colour to remember," he told me.
>
> Norman Mailer: *Ancient Evenings*

Mrs. Olive Durand-Deacon had a business plan. It was
1949 and post-war woman was rediscovering glamour,
with role-models like Rita Hayworth and Betty Grable
offering a cinematic ideal. Noting the preoccupation with
sex-appeal and ornamental beauty, sixty-nine-year-old
Mrs. Durand-Deacon was certain there was a market for
artificial fingernails. The elderly widow who had been left
£40,000 by her late husband decided to confide her plan
to the pleasant young man who was a fellow-guest at the
Onslow Court Hotel in South Kensington, London. John
George Haigh was interested. Just by coincidence, he
told her, he was a director of a company in Crawley,
called Hurstlea Products. Why didn't they go there together and see if the managing director would be interested in Mrs. Durand-Deacon's idea? The old lady
eagerly agreed . . . and that was the last her best friend,
Mrs. Lane, ever saw of her.

Mrs. Lane was worried. She knew Mr. Haigh was taking her friend Olive to Crawley and asked him if he had any clue about her whereabouts. Haigh was terribly concerned. It was true he had arranged to drive Mrs. Durand-Deacon to see his boss, but when she failed to turn up for the appointment, he had gone alone, he told Mrs. Lane. "We should inform the police," he said, looking anxious, and the two of them did just that. Haigh couldn't have been more helpful, which was an extraordinary way to behave, for he must have guessed that the police would check out both his story and his life. It took them a very short time to discover that he was not a director of Hurstlea Products, although he worked for them on occasions, but that he did have a considerable criminal record, having been imprisoned on fraud and forgery charges three times since 1935. He took a vain pride in his ability as a master-forger, but unknown to the police, during his periods of freedom he had been committing other, graver crimes.

Investigations led the police to Crawley where they discovered the Hurstlea Products connection. Haigh was using a Hurstlea warehouse in Crawley in return for the work he was supposed to be doing for the company. When the police forced their way into the warehouse they made a chilling discovery: a tank large enough to contain a human being, gallons of acid, a rubber apron and gloves . . . and much blood on the walls. One of the policemen spotted a scrap of paper flapping upon the floor; it was a dry-cleaning receipt for a Persian lamb coat from a cleaner's in nearby Horsham. Following this trail provided them with their next clue: jewellery which had belonged to Mrs. Durand-Deacon had been sold in Horsham by a man answering John Haigh's description. They pulled Haigh in. To their surprise, Haigh confessed almost immediately and regaled the officers with a colourful description of how he had killed Mrs. Durand-Deacon and disposed of her body. "She was inveigled by me into going to Crawley in view of her interest in artificial fingernails," he said and continued:

> Having taken her into the storeroom, I shot her in the back of the head while she was examining some materials. Then I went out to the car and fetched a drinking glass and made an incision—I think with a penknife—in the side of her throat. I collected a glass of blood, which I drank. I removed her coat and jewellery (rings, necklace, earrings and crucifix) and put her in the forty-five-gallon tank. Before I put her handbag in the tank, I took from it about thirty shillings and a fountain pen. I then filled the tank with sulphuric acid, by means of a stirrup pump. I then left it to react.

Mrs. Durand-Deacon weighed 200 lbs. and the effort of getting her body into the tank had exhausted Haigh. While the body was being dissolved, Haigh mentioned as an afterthought that he went to the local tea-shop. "I should have said that, in between having her in the tank and pumping in the acid, I went round to the Ancient Prior's for a cup of tea," he said in the confession which was later read out in court. It had taken several days for the body to break down in the sulphuric acid, which necessitated a few visits to Crawley by Haigh. Why did he commit this atrocity? He had a thirst for blood, he explained, and as the shocked cross-examining officers prepared to leave, appalled yet satisfied with the confession they had obtained so easily, he asked if they wanted to know about the other murders he had committed. They listened with growing incredulity.

The first murder was in 1944 (said Haigh) and the victim was Haigh's friend and occasional employer, a young man called Donald McSwann who ran a pinball arcade in the city. Haigh sometimes worked for McSwann as a mechanic and had invited him to live with him so McSwann could avoid the call-up. McSwann was afraid of dying,

but as events turned out, he should have taken his
chances with the British Army fighting the Germans in
Europe. At least that way he would have known who his
enemy was. The moment he walked into Haigh's basement workshop followed by the man he thought was his
friend, his destiny was decided.

Did Haigh have any motive for killing McSwann when
he smashed an iron bar over the hapless youth's head
. . . apart from a desire to drink his blood? Haigh said
not. He told the police that after biting into the jugular
vein on McSwann's neck, he feasted with delight. But
after satisfying his appetite, Haigh looked at the bloodstained body lying on his basement floor and wondered
what to do next. It wasn't that he felt any remorse for
snuffing out a young man's life so brutally; on the contrary, he was merely plagued with the problem of having
a dead body on his hands. For a whole day he mulled
over how he could dispose of McSwann's body. Then, he
told the police with a triumphant smile, he hit upon the
solution: he would cut up the body and dissolve it with
sulphuric acid. After completing his task, he poured the
sludgy mess, a bucketful at a time, down a manhole in the
basement, which was connected to the London sewage
system. Then he calmly took over the running of Mc-
Swann's pinball arcade and no one asked any questions.

But Haigh was soon beset by a problem. McSwann's
wealthy parents kept writing to their son and sooner or
later Haigh knew that they would become suspicious if
there was no reply. This was where Haigh's forgery skills
became invaluable. He kept Mr. and Mrs. McSwann
away from his door for a whole year by telling them their
son was hiding out in Scotland until the end of the war.
He even travelled up to Scotland every week to post
forged letters to them from their son. Until one day they
received a letter from "Donald," inviting them to visit
him at the home of his friend John Haigh. It was July
1945, almost a year after McSwann's death, when Haigh

bludgeoned McSwann's parents to death and disposed of their bodies using the same method which had been so successful after he had killed his friend. Then, using forged documents, he helped himself to the McSwann estate, which included five houses plus an additional fortune which he transferred to his own name.

The crimes remained undetected and he was delighted with his own cleverness, but the money was not destined to last. Haigh was a gambler and this, together with some bad investments and a lifestyle based on self-indulgence, meant the cash soon dwindled. By 1948 he was on his uppers and he cast around for another wealthy victim. A young married couple, Dr. Archie Henderson and his wife Rosalie, presented themselves. He invited them to look at his new workshop in Crawley. They met the same fate as Haigh's previous victims. When a snag cropped up in the form of Rosalie Henderson's brother questioning their whereabouts, he managed to convince him not only that the couple had left the country to go to South Africa, but that he had lent Dr. Henderson £2,500 and that if the money was not repaid within two months, Dr. Henderson had pledged to give Haigh his house and his car.

There were three other murders, Haigh confessed, but they were just casual strangers, killed to enable him to drink their blood, because the need had come upon him. He neither knew their names, nor cared, he said flipping his hand in disdain. Haigh told his stories with such obvious relish that the police began to wonder whether they were the truth, or whether they were the result of the over-active imagination of a madman. The supposed murders were so bizarre. How could Haigh have avoided detection for so many years? Could they really believe his stories of blood-drinking?

In the psychiatric literature could be found stories of others who had had the same deviant bloodthirsty desires. For instance, there was the man who had been a stretcher-bearer during the 1914-18 war and had enjoyed feeling the blood of the wounded drench his clothes. He had told his psychiatrist that he would wear his underclothing stiffened by the blood for a long time afterwards. He was a hypochondriac and his habit was to go to slaughter-houses to drink a glass of warm blood as a therapeutic measure. He had previously murdered a woman, cut up and eviscerated her and cannibalized her body. This gave him such sexual satisfaction that he would attain an orgasm. But Haigh claimed no sexual motive. His blood-lust was fired, he said, after he had a recurring dream. He would dream he was walking in a forest of crucifixes which turned into green trees, dripping blood. One tree would assume the shape of a man who held a bowl in which he would collect blood from one of the trees. He would then offer it to Haigh. But as Haigh tried to take it, the man would move away. Only after Haigh began killing, he said, did the man come within reach and in his dream Haigh was able to drink the blood, just as he drank the blood of his victims in real life. In total he had killed nine people, he claimed, and in each case he had cut open their necks to drink a cupful of blood from each one, to quench "the desire that demanded fulfilment," he said. He would drink "for three to five minutes, after which I felt better."

After regaling the policemen with these tales of blood-drenched reality and nightmare, Haigh smiled a wolfish smile. "Of course, you can never prove it," he told them. "There's no evidence." This was true: there was no trace of the victims' bodies—if indeed there were any victims, for Haigh's confession was so fantastic that some officers wondered whether it was really true or whether it was fuelled by fantasy. Forensic experts were dispatched to Crawley where, outside the warehouse, the spot was found where Haigh emptied the acid tank. An undissolved bone, a gallstone, a red plastic bag which had belonged to Mrs. Durand-Deacon and an almost complete set of dentures were discovered, which, the widow's dentist confirmed, belonged to the old lady.

Haigh's case bewildered the lawyers. In six of the nine cases of self-confessed murder, a motive might have been found in Haigh's greed for money or for acquiring their property by fraudulent means. Mrs. Durand-Deacon had little money, but Haigh was not to know that—and he was certainly hard-up; a cheque he had given to the manageress of the Onslow Court Hotel had bounced. The killing of total strangers who yielded him nothing other than their life-blood was a little more difficult to explain in terms of a sane man with a greed-motive. He confirmed this himself: "There are so many other ways of making easy money, though illegitimately," Haigh said.

Before Haigh's case came to court he had been questioned by psychiatrists who could find nothing in his family background to explain his crimes, neither the fraud offences nor the murders with their alleged associated deviant behaviour. Haigh was an only child of middle-class, God-fearing parents. They were members of the Plymouth Brethren and demanded strict conformity from their son. As a schoolboy he was an organist and chorister at Wakefield Cathedral and displayed good character until he was twenty-five, when he served the first of his prison sentences. Could the submersion in religion have caused his abnormality? Could he have been rebelling against the suffocating piety of his childhood? Possibly— and yet there are many other children raised by strict religious parents, and parents who treat their offspring in far worse ways than demanding that they go to church regularly; very few such children turn into bloodthirsty killers. In any case, his childhood did not tally with the psychological profile of the man he had become. Apparently he had been a generous boy, made friends easily and was kind-natured, adoring animals and hating cruelty and violence. Yet, he revealed, even as a very small child he liked blood and would lick scratches or cut himself to suck his own blood. His dreams were filled with images of injured and bleeding people and he was fascinated by the Church's Holy Communion in which supplicants were obliged to imagine they were drinking the blood of Christ. He even dreamed of the bleeding figure of Christ and the crucifixion, sometimes imagining that blood came from the cross over the altar in the cathedral.

It was a dream in 1944, when he was thirty-five, which prompted his first murder, he said. Earlier in the day he had accidentally injured his head and blood had dripped into his mouth. That night he dreamed his mouth was "full of blood, which revived the old taste" and he knew he would have to drink some blood to satiate himself. Before each of the killings he would have the series of dreams about the forest of crucifixes dripping blood. They would begin during the week and end on a Friday which, as psychologists have since noted, was the day of the Crucifixion. "Being led by an irresistible urge, I was not given to the discovery of the distress this might cause to myself and others," he said, thinking of his parents, to whom he felt bonds of affection all his life. Indeed, he had good friends who remained to support him even after his conviction. A marriage at twenty-five had broken down and Haigh had no apparent interest in sex thereafter. No one had suspected he was capable of such heinous crimes.

No, this was not the psychodynamic profile of someone who could be guilty of the actions to which he had confessed, decided psychiatrists. His childhood character conflicted with his later life and his identity seemed inconstant. To reconcile this, it was suggested that Haigh had a Multiple Personality Disorder—the most serious and complex of all the psychoses. Why else would a skilled swindler and forger suddenly change his criminal tack and become a killer and a "vampire"? This opened the door to an "insanity" plea, which Haigh readily made, through his lawyers. He was dubbed "The Vampire

Killer" by British newspapers, but the judge and jury refused to accept this as evidence of insanity. Haigh knew he was doing wrong, they decided, therefore he was sane and guilty. It took them a mere seventeen minutes to find him guilty and sentence him to death by hanging. Haigh, it seemed, was not afraid to die. He asked for a rehearsal of the hanging before the event, in case anything went wrong on the day, and even bequeathed some of his clothes to Madame Tussaud's waxworks museum, so his wax model would look its best in the Chamber of Horrors.

Insane? Since Haigh's death there has been much controversy in psychiatric circles about Haigh's mental state and whether or not he was faking his abnormality. But psychiatrists R.E. Hemphill and T. Zabow made a study of "clinical vampirism" in 1983 and concluded that Haigh was indeed a vampirist. Noting that vampirism has been reported in the medical literature for more than a century they classified this rare condition as not only the sucking of or craving for blood, but also an abnormal interest in death or the dead. The condition cannot be placed in any pigeonhole of psychosis, they say, because it "is not a primary symptom of any other psychiatric or psychopathic disorder, and its specific motive distinguishes it from other blood-related aberrations. The condition is not likely to be discovered except in criminal cases . . . Some of our patients who carry out self-mutilation cut themselves in order to suck blood . . . Vampirism, although specifically psychopathic, is not necessarily associated with general or violent psychopathic disorder and, conceivably, might occur in persons not recognized as abnormal, for example, Haigh."

The essential characteristic of the vampire—both mythical and in reality—has always been that he drank blood "specifically to satisfy a need." Haigh easily fits this model, say the psychiatrists. He ingested his own and others' blood, and after taking a cupful achieved "a warm, relaxed feeling, with calm and disappearance of the craving." Additionally, he was attracted by death and spent time with his decomposing victims. His identity was changeable. "Haigh appeared to develop satisfactorily to adulthood; he fluctuated thereafter, and the fastidious, socially acceptable young man cannot be recognized in the callous, revolting murderer . . . Vampirism and psychopathy developed in spite of favourable influence and no possible causes for either were discovered." Hemphill and Zabow concluded that vampirism is a clinical entity on its own, not necessarily associated with other disorders such as sado-masochism where a desire for cruelty or self-punishment is a primary aim. But, they warn, "Vampirism is thus a possible cause of unpredicted repeated murder which is likely to be overlooked. The vampirist may show no obvious signs of mental disorder. It is a disturbing thought that a pleasant person, like Haigh, unsuspected, may be a vampirist liable to a periodic craving for blood."

Or was he? It has not gone unnoticed that the only claims regarding Haigh's vampirism came voluntarily from Haigh himself. Herschel Prins, a British professor of clinical criminology, challenged Hemphill and Zabow's assertion that Haigh was a vampirist. "Haigh attempted to simulate insanity," reports Prins. "Part of this simulation was to claim to have drunk the blood of his victims and to have drunk his own urine." This view is supported by the revelation by the prosecuting lawyer at Haigh's trial that Haigh had asked a police officer what the chances were of anyone being released from Broadmoor Hospital (one of Britain's major institutions for dangerous killers who are considered "mad, not bad"). That piece of evidence certainly helped to convince the jury to discount Haigh's insanity plea.

As for the suggestion that vampirism is a clinical entity, while acknowledging Hemphill and Zabow's suggestion that the phenomenon may be more common than has hitherto been supposed, Professor Prins points out that vampiristic activity "is not infrequently seen in association with serious sexual offending where biting and perhaps the ingestion of blood may be a fairly common phenomena" and, noting that it takes place in people functioning at a very primitive mental and emotional level, finds it unsurprising that it is "not infrequently" associated with schizoid, schizophrenic or the "borderline" disorders. However, most clinicians who have explored the vampirism phenomenon relate it to sexuality of one form or another: that it satisfies oral-sadistic needs, for instance. Hemphill and Zabow were at pains to point out that Haigh was uninterested in sex, "and blood evoked no sexual feeling, in contrast with a very rare form of sadomasochism in which drinking a partner's blood is said to cause sexual arousal and orgasm."

Haigh's explanation, given just before his execution in August 1949, was that he was "impelled to kill by wild blood demons, the spirit inside me commanded me to kill." And in a book about the Haigh trial, Lord Dunboyne wrote: "No other reported case traceable seems to suggest that a murderer drank the blood of the murdered as an end in itself, unassociated with any sexual perversion."

But barely thirty years after Haigh's execution—in January 1979—the trial began in Sacramento, California, of another man who initially seemed readily to fulfil Lord Dunboyne's criteria. His reason for drinking human blood was, he said, "therapeutic." He believed that he was dying and his only cure was to drink blood, which was why he had slaughtered six people, including a twenty-two-month-old baby, had cut open bodies, scooped out blood by the potful and taken it home with him to drink.

Richard Trenton Chase said at the murder trial that he had begun drinking blood after watching medical shows on television. He started with birds then moved on to

rabbits, dogs and cows before he graduated to killing
humans. Which explained why there were so many missing dogs and cats in Sacramento County in the late 1970s
—and provided an answer for Chase's neighbours who
had often puzzled about the number of puppies and cats
he carried into his apartment and which were never seen
again. Then the day came, just after Christmas 1977,
when Chase took his .22 handgun and went after people
instead.

His first victim was Ambrose Griffin, a fifty-one-year-
old engineer who was casually gunned down as he carried
the groceries into his house from his car. He died in
hospital. Two days earlier one of his near-neighbours had
been rather luckier. Dorothy Polenske had been in her
kitchen when she heard a pop, the kitchen window shat-
tered and she felt something pass through her hair. Police
later found a .22 calibre bullet embedded in a shelf. It
was from the same gun which was to kill Ambrose Griffin. Almost a month later, Chase struck again—and this
time he was to satisfy his thirst for blood. The victim was
Teresa Wallin, twenty-two years old and three months
pregnant. She had been carrying a sack of rubbish to the
front door when it opened and Richard Chase, standing
there, fired three shots. Then, picking up an empty yogurt
carton from the rubbish-sack, he dragged her body to the
bedroom where he tore into her body with a knife and
dragged out the intestines. As the pathologist was to later
report, the killer "tampered with" the viscera by carefully
displacing the kidneys and "explored the innards of the
deceased."

When the police, led by Lt. Ray Biondi, turned up to
survey the horror, they saw that Teresa's underclothes
had been pulled down around her ankles, but, Lt. Biondi
said in a book he wrote about the case, [1] that did not
necessarily mean she had been sexually assaulted. "Some

---

[1] *The Dracula Killer* by Lt. Ray Biondi and Walt Hecox, 1992.

sexually deviant killers, I knew, pulled down clothing and elaborately positioned bodies so that their victims would be found in such humiliating poses," he noted—and his assumption was correct in this case. There was no evidence of sexual assault. (In fact, it is interesting to note that although some authorities might interpret murder using a firearm as being Freudian sexual symbolism— replacing penetration and ejaculation with the penetration of a bullet from that phallic symbol, the gun—this is rare in sexually-inspired serial killings. The sexual motive usually demands that the murder involves violent physical contact, which is how such killers obtain satisfaction and the stimulation of the feeling of power.)

Other discoveries at the murder-scene where Teresa Wallin's torn body lay bewildered the police. A crumpled yogurt container, smeared with blood inside and out, lay beside the body. On the wooden floor alongside were "bloody, ringlet-shaped stains," Lt. Biondi reported. "I have never seen anything like them and couldn't imagine what the ringlets were." That was because the answer defied imagination. Four days later those ring-shaped bloodstains would be recalled with a chill of horror by Lt. Biondi and other homicide officers.

On that day, Richard Chase had called at the home of Evelyn Miroth, a thirty-eight-year-old single mother who had two sons, Vernon aged thirteen and Jason aged six. On 27 January 1978 she was baby-sitting David, the twenty-two-month-old baby of her friend Karen Ferreira. If the policemen had been shocked by the scene of carnage at the Wallin home, the sight that met them at Evelyn's house was enough to move some of them to tears. Evelyn's body, naked except for a necklace, was on the bed, attacked in exactly the same way that Teresa had been, but with extra mutilations. One eye had been carefully gouged out by severing the muscles around the eyeball and a butcher's knife and a carving knife lay bloody at her side. A family friend, Daniel Meredith, lay on the

living-room floor with a bullet in his head; he had been
shot at point-blank range. On the other side of Evelyn's
bed was the small body of six-year-old Jason Miroth, also
shot in the head. Jason was dressed in his best clothes,
ready to go out on a day-trip with neighbours that day.
The pathologist arrived at the scene and, examining Evelyn Miroth's body, noted that there appeared to have
been little bleeding. Unlike the Wallin murder, there was
evidence of sexual assault: the woman was later discovered to have been sodomized and also penetrated anally
with a knife. But like the Wallin murder, there was an
unusual clue. "There is a series of rings in the carpet next
to her body," the pathologist reported—and he guessed
they were made by human blood contained in a bucket or
pan. The pathologist's later post-mortem report was
compared to the results of the autopsy on Teresa Wallin.
In both cases, the same organs had been cut and pulled
from the abdomens of the victims. This, said the pathologist, would "facilitate getting at blood in the abdominal
cavity." His guess was correct: Chase had used a vessel
for that very purpose, to enable him to take the blood
home with him.

But there was even worse to come. The police found
baby David Ferreira's crib—empty, but with a bullet-hole
in the blood-soaked pillow. The baby's body was nowhere
to be found. Richard Chase had taken that away with
him, too. To what end, the investigators could not bring
themselves to imagine. Could their killer really be so
depraved as to snatch babies from their cribs and prey
upon them, like a wild beast?

Using the tactics which have been proclaimed successful by the FBI's Behavioural Science Unit at Quantico
and made famous by such films as *Silence of the Lambs*,
Lt. Biondi and his men set about trying to formulate a
psychological profile of their murderer, using clues to his
behaviour and personality which could be found at the
scenes of the crimes. They concluded he was a white male

in his twenties, probably schizophrenic, a loner and unmarried, probably unemployed (the murders took place
in the daytime) with limited social skills, and that he had
recently been released from a mental institution. "In
short, we had profiled a weirdo," said Biondi. But profiling alone does not catch a murderer; it is the laborious,
and infinitely more dangerous, work of police officers to
do that. The hunt for the "weirdo" was stepped up.

Richard Chase was twenty-eight and had been in and out
of psychiatric hospitals for years. In one he earned the
nickname "Dracula" from fellow-patients because he
used to kill birds and drink their blood, and he had a
preoccupation with blood, talking only about killing animals. More than once in the past he had been found
naked in a Nevada field covered with the blood of a cow
he had slaughtered. But the doctors did not consider him
to be dangerous and he was repeatedly released, usually
to the care of his mother Beatrice.

Where did the roots of Chase's perversions lie? Somewhat unusually, his early childhood had been happy, giving no hint of the monster he was to become, but at the
age of ten he began killing cats in the neighbourhood and
burying their bodies in the garden. His teenage years
were overtly normal, but although popular, Richard
proved to be impotent with girls, which was obviously a
source of great trauma to him. So much so that when he
was eighteen he visited a psychiatrist and told him of his
problems. He left home and began acting irrationally,
becoming obsessed with his health. He told people his
stomach was turned around the wrong way and that his
heart often stopped beating. Once he believed he had
had a heart attack and called the emergency services. He
saw a doctor and said his heart and kidneys had stopped
working, his pulmonary artery had been stolen and his
blood had stopped flowing. He said he had a hernia and
that his entire body was numb. The doctors said there

was nothing physically wrong with him, but diagnosed chronic paranoid schizophrenia and kept him in the psychiatric ward for three days. Then, declaring him not to be dangerous, they freed him.

Over the years, he sought medical help again and again as his behaviour became more extreme. On occasions he claimed his mother was trying to poison him and he threw meals on the floor when she had prepared them. He convinced her she should buy an oxygen tent and then claimed she was controlling his mind. He moved in with his father and, unknown to Mr. Chase, he began buying rabbits and butchering them, but because he had stopped complaining about physical illness his father thought he was getting better. Then he became sick. It was caused, said Richard, by having eaten a rabbit that had eaten battery acid. It was this which had seeped through the walls of his stomach, he said. He drank rabbits' blood "to help his weak heart," he claimed. Again he was admitted to a mental hospital and again he was judged to be a paranoid schizophrenic. Again, they let him out after a short time, the psychiatrist saying he had developed "good socialization" and a "realistic view of his problems." That was the year before Richard Chase began killing people and drinking their blood.

Buying the gun had been easy. In California, the only preamble to buying a weapon is producing one's driving licence and signing a form to say one has never been convicted of a felony, one is not a mental patient and one has never been judged to be dangerous because of a mental disorder. It was simple—which explains why deaths caused by shooting are increasing by the year in America, where there are more than 13,000 hand-guns per 100,000 head of population. Small wonder that law-abiding American citizens sleep uneasily in their beds, when men like Richard Chase can purchase a gun as simply as they might hire a car. And after shooting up the puppies and kittens he had acquired through the small-ad columns of newspapers, Chase moved on to bigger things. That was what Ambrose Griffin had been for Chase: just target practice.

The police captured Chase within days after an old school friend of his reported a chance meeting she had had with Chase. She had been shocked at his odd behaviour, and how skinny and dirty-looking he had become. Her response to a "wanted" poster led to Chase's arrest. In his pocket was Daniel Meredith's wallet, together with pictures of Evelyn and Jason Miroth. Chase denied everything, except the killing of some puppies. He said he cut up one dog with a machete "because it was mean." (Chase was later to express regret about killing cats and dogs, although this remorse did not extend to the people he had murdered, even after his eventual admission of guilt.) His confidence only shook on one occasion. When the nurse at the police station took a blood sample from him, his terror was so great he had to be held down.

Meanwhile, Chase's apartment was being taken apart. The first thing to invade the nostrils of the police as they opened the door was the stink. The sight that met their eyes was even more sickening. Everything was bloodstained, from the walls and floors to an unwashed plate and drinking tumbler. On the wall were pictures of human anatomy and among Chase's books were various medical volumes about the internal organs of the body, psychological data and health topics. The drains in the sinks and bath were found to contain blood and tissue samples. The tissue was later identified as human brain matter. Bits of bone were found scattered around the kitchen and a filthy, bloodstained electric blender emitted a foul stench. Of baby David Ferreira there was no sign.

Chase was adamant in his denials. Then, for some reason, he decided to confess to a cell-mate as he was held in custody. The other prisoner was serving a sentence for repeated drunken driving—and he was revolted at what Chase had to say. "I don't remember how I drank the blood. I just sucked it," Chase told him.

> I had to do it. I have blood poisoning and I need blood. I was tired of hunting and killing animals so I could drink their blood. I thought about it for several weeks and decided I would kill humans for their blood.

He told the other man details about the murders which tallied with what the police knew, and added that he had shot the baby because it was screaming. "I took it home, where I drank some of its blood. When I was through with it I took the body out and placed it in the garbage." There was more that Chase did not reveal. When the police eventually found the baby's decapitated body, two months later, they discovered the infant had been shot and repeatedly stabbed. Chase had also cut open the child's skull and removed the brain.

While primitive rituals made much of drinking blood to maintain health or cure the sick, was there the faint possibility that Chase *did* need blood? In view of his mental state, no there was not, but as mentioned earlier, Canadian chemist Professor David Dolphin drew attention to the genetic condition of porphyria which, he surmised, could have given rise to the vampire myth because it affects the production of heme, the red pigment in the blood. A modern way of alleviating symptoms of this genetic deficiency is to inject the sufferer with heme, but the same effect could be achieved by ingesting large quantities of blood. Professor Dolphin contends that in less enlightened times, "blood-drinking vampires were in fact victims of porphyria trying to alleviate the symptoms of their dreadful disease." Even the folklore concerning garlic as a "weapon" against vampires has an explanation, in that one of the constituents of garlic—dialkyl disulphide—may contribute to the destruction of heme in the body. "This suggests that garlic might increase the severity of an attack of porphyria . . . Can you imagine a more powerful 'talisman' against vampires than this?" asks Professor Dolphin.

Perhaps John George Haigh's defence lawyers might have been fascinated by the idea of porphyria in 1949, but despite Richard Chase's pale, undernourished appearance, such a notion would have found no sympathy with Ronald W. Tochterman, the assistant chief deputy district attorney who conducted the prosecution of Richard Chase in Santa Cruz in 1979 and had no doubt that vampirism was very much linked to sexuality. His research showed that some sexual sadists claimed therapeutic justification for their ingestion of blood merely to conceal their sexual predilection for mutilating and—literally—erotic bloodthirstiness. It even has a name: haemostodipsia. Those with this condition desire blood both during sex and at other times, when the act of blood-drinking or watching the flow of blood offers the sole means of sexual gratification.

One psychiatrist concluded that Chase was not schizophrenic but a "paranoid antisocial personality" with "a well-developed sense of right and wrong." Chase told another psychiatrist how he had collected animals' blood in a cup to drink, but admitted that it had not helped his illness. He said he enjoyed watching operations on television and the sight of a heart pumping blood was fascinating. He thought that drinking human blood would be "therapeutic." The psychiatrist reported to the court: "He (Chase) believed that drinking blood was a possible solution to save him from certain death." But, he added, "he understood that he was killing people and that it was wrong to kill people."

Chase was judged sane and, therefore, culpable. He was capable of choosing not to kill people, said the psychiatrists, although, of course, Chase claimed insanity as a defence and did not deny the crimes. He admitted shooting baby David Ferreira, taking him away and decapitating him to drink his blood, but said he "thought the baby was something else." Although the FBI's Behavioural Science Unit cites Chase as a classic example of a disorganized offender, Mr. Tochterman drew attention to the killer's organization in going prepared for his crimes, carrying them out with care and then evading detection. He was equipped in advance for his bloody work with rubber gloves, he attacked particular organs and in the case of Teresa Wallin, after sating his thirst washed his hands and the knife, returning it to the rack in the kitchen. He related the other revolting murder-details, including those relating to little David Ferreira's death. The murders, said Tochtermann, were caused by Chase's "sheer sexual sadism motivated by a literal blood lust." The trial took four months, at the end of which the jury declared Chase to be sane and guilty of six counts of first-degree murder. His pleas for mercy were discounted —"You have to be the most naïve optimist, a Pollyanna ten times over, to believe that Mr. Chase has the possibility to be a decent human being. He is a dangerous person . . . a time bomb." said Tochterman.

Recently, as he reflected on the case, Lt. Biondi put it more baldly: "He was crazy as a loon—but he did have the choice to kill or not to kill. The FBI consider him a classic example of a disorganized killer, but he was cagey enough to get away from each scene without being caught."

Chase was sentenced to die in the gas chamber, but he "jumped ship." He committed suicide in San Quentin Penitentiary on 26 December 1980, after taking an overdose of tablets he had been prescribed for depression.

6

Do Mothers Make Monsters?

They fuck you up, your mum and dad.
They may not mean to, but they do.
They fill you with the faults they had
And add some extra, just for you.

Philip Larkin: *This Be The Verse*

What would be the result if one crossed Norman Bates, mother-obsessed murderer from the movie *Psycho*, with "Buffalo Bill," the serial killer of women who removed sections of his victims' skin to fashion his own suit in *The Silence of the Lambs*? Throw a little of Hannibal "the Cannibal" Lecter—the sinister anti-hero of the latter film and book—into this foul brew of human psychopathy, and you have Edward Gein.

Ghoulish Gein is thought to bear the dubious distinction of inspiring the creation of at least two screen monsters, even without taking his cannibalistic tendencies into account. But unlike several of the other killers discussed in this book, Gein was no glib charmer with a superficial normality. Gein was not one of those Jekyll-and-Hydes whose crimes, when they come to light, cause enormous amazement because they had presented such a well-balanced façade to the world. No, Ed Gein was not really like that. Ed Gein was a strange, eccentric little

man with pale, icy eyes and a reserved manner, not given
to idle chit-chat with his neighbours. People in rural
Plainfield, Wisconsin, USA would have admitted that, in
retrospect, he always had been a bit of a weirdo. But no
one could possibly have imagined just how very weird
Gein was until the day in November 1957 when the police
arrived at Gein's farmhouse to check out the disappearance of Bernice Worden, the mother of a local store
owner . . . and made discoveries so unspeakable that
some of the officers felt their stomachs heave.

No one could ever have guessed the depths of deprav-
ity enjoyed by someone who had lived within this small,
700-strong community all his life. Someone who had run
the 160-acre family farm on the outskirts of Plainfield
alongside the overpowering presence of his mother and
his only brother Henry, until they both died, leaving him
completely alone. Someone who, thanks to federal subsi-
dies, did not need to farm his land any longer so abandoned it to do odd jobs for residents of the township,
which earned him a little extra cash and alleviated his
loneliness. Someone who was living off the fat of the land
in more ways than one. But, of course, no one really knew
what Ed Gein was like, even though he lived among
them. His mother had seen to that.

Gein was born in 1906 and he and brother Henry were
completely ruled by their dominant, possessive, man-hat-
ing mother Augusta who preached hell-fire scriptures at
her sons but hated her alcoholic husband George so
much that she used to kneel in her children's presence
and pray that her husband would die soon. Saying she
feared that her boys' morality would be sullied by contact
with the outside world, the austere and unloving woman
kept them isolated and refused to allow them to make
friends, all the while quoting from the Bible. All men are
sinners, she warned—but in particular she was suspicious
of other women and advised both boys against getting

involved with girls. Women are scheming and cunning, she would tell her sons and she took pains to ensure that any relationship which looked like developing—with people of either sex—was brought to a sharp end.

In 1940, Augusta's prayers were answered and George Gein died. When old Mrs. Gein died of a cerebral haemorrhage five years later, after being nursed for a year by her sons, Henry and Ed were bereft. They came to depend upon each other as they had once depended on their mother. When Henry died in a forest fire, Ed was left alone in the enormous farmhouse set amid 160 acres of land which stretched as far as the eye could see. He began to act oddly. First he sealed up his mother's bedroom, the drawing-room and five more upstairs rooms, living in only one room and the kitchen. Then he began buying books and magazines about human anatomy and spent hours poring over them. He became fascinated by the atrocities committed by Nazis during the Second World War. In particular he devoured information about the concentration camp medical experiments performed on Jews.

Soon, second-hand experiences were not enough and Gein began robbing graves to fulfil his necrophiliac needs. In this he was helped by an elderly, feeble-minded associate called Gus. He convinced Gus that he needed the bodies for "experiments" and the couple would sneak into far-flung Wisconsin cemeteries to steal complete corpses. On other occasions Gein took only the body-parts which particularly interested him. Gus helped Gein to store the bodies in a shed at the back of his farmhouse and, it seemed, never questioned Gein too closely about what happened to the cadavers. Later Gein was to confess that he had believed himself to be a transsexual and that reading about the sex-change operation of Christine Jorgenson—a sensational story at that time—had made his desire to become a woman even more urgent. No doubt this desire was part of the twisted emotional legacy left to him by a mother who swamped his own male personality. But, he explained, this was why he wanted to study female reproductive organs. Gein would dissect the bodies and keep some parts—heads, sex organs, livers, hearts and intestines. He would eat the dead flesh of the corpses and make ornaments and decorations for the house from body parts. Painstakingly he sewed himself a belt out of carved-off nipples and he upholstered a chair with human skin. A table was propped up by human shinbones. A tom-tom drum was created out of a coffee-tin with human skin stretched across it and half a human skull became a soup-bowl. The four posts on Gein's bed were topped with skulls and a human head hung in his house in the way most people would position an attractive plant. On the walls were nine death-masks—the skinned faces of women—and he made decorative bracelets out of human skin.

In his study of sadistic murderers, Robert P. Brittain notes that such a killer might hide in his house a mask, cloak or objects such as "a hood of the Ku Klux Klan type . . . a child's doll, a life-sized model of a woman . . . or . . . the place itself might be made to represent an execution chamber." In Gein's case, this was no representation: by the time he was caught, it *was* an execution chamber. Dr. Brittain remarks that some sex-killers may also be transvestites, although their predilections are somewhat different from the usual desires of a "normal" transvestite.

> Many dress up in female clothing at times . . . unlike certain other transvestites, they do not usually wish to be seen by others when dressed as women and no one may know that they do this. When they start the practice they most commonly use clothing belonging to their mothers or sometimes to sisters . . . There may be a large mirror in which they can watch themselves transvested,

while they indulge in various sexual fantasies and they
may even kiss their own reflection.

Even Dr. Brittain, hardened as he was from studying
sadistic killers, might have raised an eyebrow to learn the
lengths to which Gein went in satisfying his perversion.
Gein made himself a mask from a woman's face and a
waistcoat out of female skin, complete with breasts. He
would skin bodies and wear the skin as if it were a shawl
or fashion it into leggings. The female sex organs which
he had hacked out of corpses and from the bodies of
those he subsequently murdered, were toys to him: he
would play with and fondle these rotting pieces of tissue,
saying later that this gave him "inexplicable thrills," and
he even filled a pair of women's knickers with excised
female genitalia, which he would then put on. Crazed
Gein would, on certain nights, dress up in his macabre
costume and dance around in the light of the moon or
admire himself in a full-length mirror. This ghoulish behaviour stimulated him because, claim Jack Levin and
James Alan Fox in their book *Mass Murder*, it enabled
Gein "to recreate the form and presence of his dead
mother."

But as happens with sadistic murderers, it became necessary for Gein's fantasies to intrude upon reality in a
more fatal way. When Gus became too old to farm his
land and moved into an old people's home, Gein decided
it was too much trouble—and too much hard work—to
dig up corpses on his own. It was but a short, conscience-
free step for Gein to move from acquiring already-dead
bodies for his "experiments" to acquiring live ones . . .
and then swiftly rendering them dead. In the middle of a
snowstorm one winter night in 1954, Gein waited outside
Hogan's Tavern, a bar in the nearby town of Pine Grove,
until all the customers had gone. Then he walked up to
the saloon-keeper Mary Hogan, a tough and dominant
fifty-one-year-old woman who bore a striking resem-

blance to Gein's mother, calmly placed the muzzle of a
gun against her head and shot her dead with a single
bullet. Then he hauled her body outside and strapped it
to a sledge he had brought with him. It took him many
hours to drag the sledge home through the snow.

How many other victims did Gein claim in a similar
way? There were the scattered remains of an estimated
fifteen bodies found at Gein's house when he was eventually arrested, but Gein could not remember how many
murders he had done. He did, however, remember eating
the flesh of the cadavers and of those women he had
killed and he was able to recall, with undisguised pleasure and no sense of shame, the times when he would
dance naked around his kitchen or bedroom, cavorting
with his gruesome mementos. Clearly, he thought that
this was normal behaviour. The police believed—but
could not prove—he could have been responsible for the
disappearance of several missing local females over the
decade until 1957 when Gein was arrested, including an
eight-year-old who had gone missing on her way home
from school one day in 1947 and a fifteen-year-old who
had disappeared while babysitting one day in 1953. Her
bloodstained clothes were found later, but again, there
was no body to be found.

Gein's perversions were brought to an end after the
murder of his next, and last, known victim. Like Mary
Hogan, she was a middle-aged woman similar in looks to
Ed Gein's dead mother. On the morning of 16 November, 1957, the deer-hunting season began in the county,
providing the cue for the men of Plainfield to don their
warm jackets, boots and deer-stalker hats and, leaving
their womenfolk behind in the town, take off into the
wild yonder for a spot of bloody slaughter. Ed Gein had
something similar in mind when he wandered into town
that day. In Frank Worden's hardware store he found
Frank's mother Bernice minding the shop, as Gein had
known she would be when he had heard Frank talking

about the deer-hunting trip earlier in the week. He used the pretext of wanting to buy some anti-freeze and while an unsuspecting Mrs. Worden wrote out the sales-slip, Gein casually took a .22 rifle from a rack on the wall and shot her once in the head at point-blank range. Then calmly locking up the shop and putting the cash-register under one arm, he dragged Mrs. Worden's body out the back way, put it into her own delivery van and drove to a forest where he had left his own car. He transferred the body to his car and drove away fast; home to his house of death.

During that day several locals saw Gein. One man called on him to apologize about shooting a deer on Gein's land. Gein was busy working on his car and waved aside the apology. Later, two teenage neighbours called to ask Gein to run them into town and he emerged from his house with his hands red with blood. He told them he was dressing a deer, but broke off to give the youngsters a lift and was rewarded with an invitation to stay to supper with one of the families, who ran a grocery store. He accepted. Meanwhile, the men who had gone on the hunting trip were arriving back in town.

When Frank Worden returned from his day's sport, he found the store deserted, the cash-register missing and a pool of blood on the floor, with a trail leading to where his delivery truck had been parked that morning. The truck was gone and a neighbour told him he had seen it shoot out of town that morning. His feeling of sickness and horror grew as Frank remembered that his mother had no deliveries to make. But something was nagging at his memory . . . what was it? Frank, who was deputy sheriff of Plainfield, suddenly remembered: Ed Gein had ordered some anti-freeze and had told him he would be calling at the store to collect it that day. Frank raced back into the store: on the counter was the half-written receipt for anti-freeze.

He immediately told the sheriff of his suspicions and

the police set off for Gein's home. Meanwhile, other officers found Gein having supper at the grocery store. Could he account for his movements that day? they asked him.

"Somebody framed me," declared Gein immediately.

"Framed you for what?"

"About Mrs. Worden," Gein replied.

"What about her?" asked the officers.

"Well, she's dead, ain't she?" said Gein.

The police hauled him in. Gein was securely locked in a police cell as the sheriff's men descended on his isolated farmhouse. Since there was no electricity, the place was in darkness, so, using flashlights, they began searching. What they found in the barn repelled them. Mrs. Worden's headless body was hanging upside-down from a pulley attached to a block and tackle and hoisted to the ceiling. The corpse had been gutted and hung in just the way, said one of the policemen on the case, that a deer might have been trussed up. With her head cut off at the shoulders, Gein had slit the skin on the back of her ankles and through the cut tendons he had inserted a wooden rod, three and a half feet long, by which she was suspended.

Could the police make any discovery more gruesome? They could and did. Mrs. Worden's head was found with two hooks in the ears, ready for hanging on the wall. The house was filthy, littered with old newspapers and the rotting remains of meals. As if stuck in a time-warp, it appeared to have been untouched since the death of Gein's mother twelve years previously. The remains of Mary Hogan were found in a house which was like an abattoir. In the basement parts of human bodies hung from hooks on the walls and the floor was thick with dried blood and tissue. In the kitchen, four human noses were found in a cup and a pair of human lips dangled from a string like a grisly mobile toy. Decorating the walls were ten female heads, all sawn off above the eyebrows, some with traces of lipstick on the cold, hard lips. The refrigerator contained frozen body parts. A human heart —Mrs. Worden's—was in the pan on the stove. And there was an armchair . . . with real arms.

When the sheriff returned to town with his men, they were at first too shocked and sickened to tell what they had found, but gradually they began to reveal the full, unbelievable horror of the Gein house. Gein was unperturbed and at first denied everything. Then he began talking and confessed his gruesome cannibalistic practices together with the two murders. There were probably more murders, he said, but his memory did not serve him well. Bizarrely, Gein was most angry at the accusation that he had stolen the cash register containing $41 from the Worden shop. This was not the case, he raged; he only took the cash register to see how it worked—much as he had done with the bodies he had dug up and eviscerated. "I'm no robber!" he protested . . . although when it came to stealing corpses, this was another matter. He freely admitted his grave-robbing and said that his practice was to note when there was a funeral in town and go that night to the graveyard to dig up the body. They were always the bodies of women and he always left the grave "in apple-pie order," he declared with some pride. "I had a compulsion to do it," he admitted. "It all started after my mother died in 1945. I felt I wanted to change my sex and become a woman. I used to skin the bodies and wear the skin. I'd make a mask from the face, then I felt I was really like the woman I wanted to be. I liked to wear women's hair, too. I'd wear a scalp like a wig. I enjoyed cutting up bodies and sorting out the inside parts." When police checked out the graves which Gein remembered robbing they found them to be empty.

The people of Plainfield were horrified when news of their lonely neighbour's crimes and obsessions began to spread. Okay, they said, so Ed Gein was always a little strange—becoming even odder after his mother's death

—and you might warn your children to give him a wide berth, but no normal person could ever have dreamed of the vileness of his acts. Many shuddered with sickened disgust to remember that Gein had sometimes given them gifts of "venison," and after Gein was taken away, his farm, which was due to be auctioned, was set on fire and burned to the ground. No culprit was ever found by the town's police.

The psychiatric report on Gein concluded that he had schizophrenia. He told the psychiatrists that as a child he had watched his mother killing a pig, cutting open its stomach and eviscerating it with her bare and bloody hands, and when Gein eventually appeared in court charged with the murders of Mary Hogan and Bernice Worden, his plea of "guilty but insane" was backed up by the doctors. Gein was sent to the state mental hospital for an indefinite time. His repeated requests for parole were turned down (the last was in 1974) and one of American history's most revolting cannibal killers died ten years later, still in captivity in the psychiatric ward at Mendota, aged seventy-eight. He was buried in Plainfield cemetery, next to his mother.

In their 1985 book, *Mass Murder*, James Fox and Jack Levin claim that Gein, although little known outside Wisconsin, came to the attention of Hollywood's horror film industry. Long after he had been incarcerated for life, *The Texas Chainsaw Massacre* was released. The promoters claimed that it was based on fact, but, say Fox and Levin, no carbon-copy crime had been found. However, the film contained "numerous elements reminiscent of Gein." Another film called *Deranged* bore an even closer resemblance, with a serial killer known as "the butcher of Woodside" at one point dressing in the skin of one of his female victims, just as Gein did. But when Fox and Levin wrote their book, the closest celluloid parallel to Ed Gein was Norman Bates, the psychotic motel-owner in Alfred

Hitchcock's classic film *Psycho*, adapted from the novel by Robert Bloch. It was the chiller of its era with the late Anthony Perkins giving a mind-numbing performance as the man who was so obsessed with his dead mother that he held conversations with her, dressed up as her when carrying out his murders, and kept her dead body in a rocking-chair in the cellar—complete with wig—in an effort to bring her back to life. In the same way, say Levin and Fox, Gein used female body parts in an effort to "symbolize and resurrect" his mother. He too used to converse with his mother "and both struggled with strict moral constraints that had been enforced by their dominating and sickly mothers." Another writer, Brian Marriner, suggests the opposite, concluding that Gein did not want to replace his mother but that he gained satisfaction from mutilating dead female bodies as a "symbolic form of revenge on his cold and unloving mother." He points out that both Mary Hogan and Bernice Worden resembled his mother: ". . . middle-aged, overweight and dominant. Was he killing his mother over and over again?"

In 1991 Hollywood provided yet another monster who appears to have been inspired by Gein. Thomas Harris wrote *The Silence of the Lambs* in 1988 as a sequel to *Red Dragon*. The principal character in both books was Dr. Hannibal Lecter, a psychopathic psychiatrist who cannibalized his victims. In the Oscar-winning film version of *The Silence of the Lambs*, Lecter (played with sinister charm by Anthony Hopkins) was in an escape-proof psychiatric institution, but was asked by the FBI for help as they tried to capture a serial killer nicknamed Buffalo Bill. The killer's "trademark" was that he flayed his victim's torsos. As the story progresses we learn that Buffalo Bill is a twisted transvestite who is tailoring his own female outfit, sewing the pieces of skin together to make a complete woman's skin. At one point a naked Buffalo Bill, with his male genitals strapped down between his legs, prances and pouts in front of a mirror, clearly convinced he looks like a woman. The parallel with Ed Gein, dancing in the moonlight wearing his "suit" of women's skins is too obvious to be coincidental.

Are mothers at the heart of such perversions? Rejecting and cruel or suffocating and dominant—mothers are often blamed for creating monsters. In the next chapter we may speculate on this further, with yet another cannibal killer.

7

"Few and Evil Have the Years of My Life Been"

I will kill thee and love thee after.

Othello, Act V, Sc. ii

If I kiss her, I would have to kill her first.
Edmund Kemper, murderer, aged seven

Ed Gein and Ed Kemper could not have been more different in appearance. While Gein was small and insignificant, Kemper was unusually tall—6′ 9″—and powerfully built, weighing twenty stone. Ed Gein was certainly a monstrous weirdo, but as to the finer points of sexual sadism, Gein's prime motivator appears to have been his necrophilia, rather than, as Kemper enjoyed, observing the suffering and fear of his victims and avenging himself on women in a world in which he felt he was an outsider. Finally, the two men's lives and lifestyles bore little relation to one another: Kemper's family were city-based, in Santa Cruz, California, whereas the Gein family led a life of isolation in small-town Plainfield and until Gein's arrest, at the age of fifty, no one had any inkling of the secret disturbances of his mind. But there were plenty of early indications that Kemper was abnormal, for his sadism manifested itself when he was very young. It was just that no one put Kemper away for good before he could do any harm to his fellow human beings. Which he ultimately did with a vengeance.

Inside their troubled heads, Gein and Kemper had lots in common. Necrophilia and the inability to have a normal sexual relationship with a live woman, a penchant for eating parts of human bodies . . . and a problem with a dominating mother. Repeated studies of sadistic killers throw up parental influences as possible factors in "making" monsters like Kemper and the other serial killers contained within these pages. Robert P. Brittain, whose study of the sadistic murderer has been mentioned more than once in these pages, could have been using Kemper as his archetypal case when he described the type of person for whom the police should search after the discovery of a particularly brutal crime involving mutilation. Brittain's profile of such a criminal, formulated after twenty odd years' work in forensic pathology and psychiatry, lists characteristics of lifestyle, past experience and personality which are displayed, to a greater or lesser degree, by sadistic murderers. Kemper, like Gein, matched the profile closely, especially with regard to his mother. Brittain noted a sadistic killer's

> strong, ambivalent relationship to his mother, both loving her and hating her. He is often known as a particularly devoted son, emotionally very closely bound to her, bringing her gifts to a degree beyond the ordinary. He is a "mother's boy" even when adult. There is also a deep hatred of her, not superficially obvious and not always acknowledged even to himself. He sometimes kills his mother and all male matricides should be examined with this psychopathology in mind. He often tells of having, as a child, seen his mother undressed . . . In some cases, the father is known to have been very authoritarian and punitive.

In addition, rape is commonly thought to be "a symbolic attack on the aggressor's own parents—particularly the mother."[1] So what of Edmund Emil Kemper III who, after being born into an apparently normal family, the second of three children, went on to rape, murder and sometimes cannibalize his victims—fourteen in all? Brittain says of the typical sadistic murderer: "The seeds of his abnormalities would seem to be planted at a very early age and a careful history will often show clear evidence of some manifestations of his perversions even before puberty."

So it was with Kemper. His youngest sister recalled much evidence of Ed's "spooky" childhood behaviour. There was a fascination with staging pretend executions when he would make her blindfold him, then pull an imaginary lever and he would writhe around as if dying. There was the time when he took her new doll and she later found it with its head and hands cut off—something which Kemper would later do to his victims. She also remembered teasing him about a teacher he had a crush on. "Why don't you go and kiss her?" she joked. "If I kiss her, I would have to kill her first," replied the seven-year-old boy. If that was a strange remark from a small child, even more bizarre were the fantasies he nursed before he was an adolescent. Apart from an occasion when he stood outside his teacher's house one night and envisaged what it would be like to kill her and then make love to her, he also imagined killing his neighbours, having sex with corpses and killing his mother. Being a self-confessed "weapons freak" (yet another typical characteristic of the sadistic murderer, according to Brittain), he later admitted to psychiatrist Donald T. Lunde that on numerous occasions as a youngster he had gone into his

[1] "Rape: An Analysis," *The Evening Star* (Washington DC) 12 November 1971.

mother's bedroom carrying a weapon and had thought about killing her.

After his arrest, Kemper told why he hated his mother, and of his resentment that his father was not around very much when he was young. His parents separated when he was seven, and his mother moved from California to Montana, which resulted in Ed hardly ever seeing his father. Kemper blamed his mother utterly for the non-presence of his father and also claimed that his mother frequently punished and ridiculed him "to make him a man." In addition "she used to tell me how much I reminded her of my father, whom she dearly hated, of course." Kemper alleged the strictness of discipline included moving his belongings out of his bedroom one day when he was an eight-year-old at school. When he returned home he was told he must sleep in the cellar thereafter, because his huge, bulky presence was, according to Clarnell Kemper, making his sisters feel uncomfortable. In later life Ed Kemper remembered the dark store-room where, he believed, goblins and demons lurked. When Kemper's father heard about this some months later, he was angry and put a stop to it, threatening his ex-wife with legal action. "There was only one way out—someone had to move the kitchen table and lift a trapdoor," he said. But isolated thus, and with his high intelligence and fertile imagination, Kemper's fantasies were given free rein, and they were all murderous—a combination of revenge, mutilation, power, possession and sex. And he was not yet out of short pants. His mother, Clarnell Kemper, explained her harshness on one occasion when she looked back on her son's childhood and remarked: "I was deeply worried during the years about the lack of a father relationship, and so I tried everything I could to compensate for that."

Perhaps Clarnell Kemper was, as her son alleged, over-punitive—and excessive parental punishment has been shown by many psychiatric researchers to result in abnormal aggression in children. [2] Alan R. Felthous concluded that parental brutality could predispose a child to aggressive behaviour, including cruelty to animals and—perhaps interesting as we look at Kemper's case—added: "The combination of parental brutality and absence of a stable and emotionally available father-figure may increase the likelihood of a boy showing cruelty to dogs or cats." Kemper certainly showed such cruelty when young, but while it is convenient and somewhat gratifying to try and apportion blame to parents in these labelling exercises, it is also worth remembering that although parents who abuse and neglect their children are likely to have a negative effect on them, made more probable if the parents also have some sort of psychological disturbance, this does not necessarily mean that their offspring will always be criminals. Indeed, many children who suffer at their parents' hands in much the same way that Kemper claimed to have suffered—and some who endure much worse cruelty—turn out to be normal, and sometimes valuable members of society. They may carry long-term effects of their trauma, but this is not always expressed in law-breaking, and in still fewer cases, in murder. Likewise, some criminals come from devoted families with responsible, caring parents. The outdated behavioural psychologists' view that the newborn child is a *tabula rasa* —a blank slate—whose personality is solely dependent upon the life events and influences which are written thereon is fairly comprehensively debunked by those two contradictory facts.

This is not to say that a sexual sadist's early life does not offer useful insights into the likely personality of the man. In Ed Kemper's case these were numerous, the most obvious indicator of his psychopathy being torture of animals, to which he graduated when he tired of cut-

[2] Hollenberg and Sperry, Sears and others, Gluecks, Bandura and Walters, Eron and others, Duncan and others, Sattin and others.

ting up his sister's dolls. Says Robert P. Brittain of sadistic killers:

> Their sadism is manifested in various ways. They are excited by cruelty whether in books or in films, in fact or in fantasy. There is sometimes a history of extreme cruelty to animals. Paradoxically they can also be very fond of animals . . . the only animal which seems to be safe is one belonging to the sadist himself.

Not, it seemed, in Kemper's case. He was thirteen when his mother noticed that the family cat had vanished. Unknown to her, it was only the latest feline victim of Ed's cruelty; he had been killing the neighbourhood cats for a long time previously, sometimes burying them alive, then putting their heads on poles and muttering incantations over his "trophies." Once he killed a cat in jealousy because it showed a preference for his sister over him: he sliced off the top of its head with a machete. On other occasions, he kept body parts of the cats in his wardrobe. Ed's mother found their cat in the dustbin. It had been decapitated and cut into pieces—which is, frighteningly, exactly what Ed was later to do to his murder victims . . . including Clarnell Kemper herself.

Also at thirteen, Kemper was suspected of shooting a pet dog belonging to a neighbour and he was ostracized by other boys of his age. Kemper was an awkward and oversized child, much bigger than his peers, which increased his isolation. The assertive Clarnell Kemper was busy with her own life and her own marital relationships —which were legion. One of Kemper's step-fathers warmed to Ed and took the boy under his wing, taking him fishing and shooting—the sort of masculine role-modelling of which he had been deprived. Yet his kindness was not rewarded—eventually Ed, armed with an iron bar, tried (but failed) to pluck up the courage to attack the man, after which, he planned, he would steal his car and drive to California to see his real father.

In the nineteenth century, there was the belief that people were born criminals—people such as Italian criminologist Cesare Lombroso even believed that they could be identified by their physical and facial features—and the notion of "born killers" rose again in the 1960s when the XYY hypothesis was explored. During research which related the male sex hormone testosterone to aggressive behaviour, speculation began that people with an extra Y (male) chromosome would be unusually aggressive. Some studies showed a higher incidence of violent crimes among XYY individuals and there is a higher percentage of XYY people in prisons and maximum security hospitals (however, statistics show that many did not commit violent crimes). The XYY syndrome might be evidenced by an exaggerated male appearance and Kemper might be thought to fall into this category, being unusually tall, above average intelligence and exceptionally violent. Was he really a "born killer" with an extra "criminal chromosome"? Was this the reason for his later aberrant behaviour? No, it was not. The XYY theory is judged to be inconclusive in general and particularly so in Kemper's case: his chromosomal pattern was entirely normal.

But his size and his manner did mark him out from the other boys. He became a loner, reading science fiction and books about the occult, playing with his guns and knives and indulging in a violent fantasy life which often spilled over into reality, when he would feel obliged to go out and chop up a cat. At thirteen, Kemper ran away from home to his father's house, hoping to be allowed to stay, but his father refused and sent him back to his mother. Clarnell Kemper was finding her son increasingly hard to handle and was at a loss as to what she should do with him. Her ex-husband solved the problem: he would be sent to live with his paternal grandparents who had an isolated ranch in northern California. Clarnell expressed some anxiety about this course of action. "You might wake up one day and find they've been killed," she warned, but her husband dismissed her fears and began to make plans. Ed objected strongly to this "punishment," as he saw it, but his protests were swept aside and he was packed off to live on the mountain-top ranch with his grandparents.

Soon, he transferred his murderous fantasies about his mother to his grandmother, who was an equally dominant woman. One day a year later, when his grandfather was away, he took a .22-calibre rifle and shot his grandmother in the back of the head. He fired two more shots into her as she lay on the ground and then, his excitement mounting, he stabbed her over and over again in a frenzy. When his grandfather returned home, Kemper shot him before he could get into the house and discover his wife's corpse. Then he locked his grandfather's body in the garage and ambled back into the house to telephone his mother and tell the shocked woman what he had done. Immediately, she told him to ring the police, which he did. Then he sat on the step and waited for them to come and get him. He was fifteen years old. Why had he done this terrible thing? Ed Kemper didn't really know. "I just wondered how it would feel to shoot Grandma," he shrugged. Psychiatrist Dr. Lunde had another theory. "In his way, he had avenged the rejection of both his mother and father," he hypothesized in his book *Murder and Madness*.

Kemper was handed over firstly to the California Youth Authority where psychiatrists examined him and, as well as judging that his IQ was above average at 136, also discovered his violent hostility towards his mother. If this individual is ever released, they warned, he should never, ever be placed in his mother's custody. Then, because the Youth Authority's detention facilities were inadequate to meet the seriousness of Kemper's crime, he was put into Atascadero maximum security mental hospital where he spent four of the following five years, but received little in the way of treatment. He was, however, a model patient. At twenty-one he was transferred back to the CYA and came up for parole. The parole board did not contain any psychologists or psychiatrists and they chose to ignore the limited psychiatric reports they had regarding the 6′ 9″ youth towering in front of them. They said he was cured, ordered his release and sent him home to his mother.

By now, she was living in Santa Cruz and working as an administrative assistant at the University of California. It is clear that in many ways Clarnell Kemper tried to make life easy for her troublesome son: she obtained a parking sticker for him so that he could park his car on the campus, and as the months passed, she also fought to have his juvenile record sealed, so he could begin life anew without a blot on his character. But at the same time, she continued to nag and find fault with her son, sometimes, according to those who knew them, reducing him to tears with her accusations of idleness and inadequacy. He told people that the arguments were unimportant, that they were both expressive, explosive people, but very close, and to prove it, he showered his mother with gifts. "I kept trying to push her toward where she would be a nice motherly type and quit being such a damned manipulating, controlling vicious beast," he said later. "She was Mrs. Wonderful on the campus . . . when she comes home she lets everything down and she's just a pure bitch."

As the arguments between them began to escalate, his violent fantasies were re-awakened. He began preparing for his killing spree. He developed an image of himself as a gentle giant, and adopted an easy, friendly manner with women, so they would feel comfortable with him. Meanwhile, he adapted his car so that the door on the passenger side could not be opened from the inside and he took pains to learn all the back lanes in the local road system. He began collecting knives again. His favourite knife—which he was to use for killing—he called the General. ("The sadistic murderer has strong feelings about [weapons], may have special favourites and he can even have 'pet' names for these," notes Brittain.) Then Kemper began travelling around, looking for girls to pick up and finding his campus parking sticker most useful to lure students into his death-trap car. This was what earned him the nickname of the Co-ed Killer.

His first murder, in May 1972, should, by rights, have failed. He picked up two hitch-hiking college girls, Anita Luchese and Mary Anne Pesce and attacked them with "the General," but panicked when things did not go as smoothly as he had hoped. At one point he found himself locked outside the car with the two girls inside. Amazingly, Mary Anne Pesce opened the doors to him. He made Anita climb into the boot of the car while he handcuffed Mary Anne and put a plastic bag over her head. The frightened girl tried to reason with him, but he was impervious to logic: he stabbed her many times in the abdomen and back before cutting her throat. He killed Anita in the same way and then took their bodies home with him where he decapitated and dissected the corpses, had sex with them and took some Polaroid pictures during the whole bloody procedure. This was an act he had fantasized about many times while at Atascadero—and now he was doing it for real. He disposed of the torsos in the Santa Cruz mountains, but kept the heads . . . his hunting trophies.

His second victim four months later was Aiko Koo, aged fifteen, who was hitch-hiking to a dancing class. He drove her into the mountains at gunpoint and taped up her mouth. Then he suffocated her by blocking her nostrils with his fingers, before raping her. He was fulfilling his own childhood fantasy which he had related to his sister: "If I kiss her, I'd have to kill her first." Kemper threw Aiko's body in the boot of his car, drove off—and stopped for a few beers on the way home. On returning to the car, he opened the boot to look at his handiwork "admiring my catch—like a fisherman," he recalled later. Then he took the teenager's body home and mutilated it as he had with his earlier victims, keeping the decapitated head in the car with him for several days.

Three more young women aged between fifteen and twenty-three fell prey to Kemper's murderous savagery during the following year. His *modus operandi* rarely differed. The act of killing alone often induced orgasm: sex killers usually indulge in frenzied stabbing or beating of a victim because they need to continue the attack until they have completed ejaculation. The sadism provides a sexual release which normal intercourse fails to do. After killing his victim by shooting or stabbing her, Kemper would take the body home and, as he had done with his sister's doll all those years ago, he removed the head and hands before having sex with the lifeless and identity-free torso, often devouring the flesh before chopping the remainder of the body up and burying the pieces in the mountains the next day.

The act of decapitation caused Kemper great sexual excitement and he would wrap the heads of his victims in cellophane to keep them in his closet. Later he would perform sex-acts on the severed heads, on one occasion burying a head in his yard, facing his bedroom, so he could imagine it "looking at him" and he "could talk to it at night." The significance of the head, Kemper later said, was that it was a trophy: "the head is where everything is at, the brain, eyes, mouth. That's the person . . . you cut off the head and the body dies."

A psychoanalytic theory of the sadistic man is that he has a castration complex and inflicts pain to assure himself of his power and masculinity. In particular, beheading a victim is said to be part of such a castration

complex and thought to have its roots in a jealous Oedipal fantasy of the son to destroy the father. Castration
was common among our primitive ancestors, when men
emasculated their enemies to prevent them using their
sexual power, and symbolic castration—robbing a victim
of power by decapitation—can be found in the mythical
methods of destroying vampires. But other researchers
suggest that *mothers* are the true target: blood symbolizes
"an unobtainable object" or "forbidden fruit," and this
forbidden fruit, Freudians would say, is the sexual con-
quest of the mother. Blood-letting and -drinking is therefore symbolically obtaining the unobtainable mother.
Could maternal deprivation mean that a cannibal or vampire killer has a need to be nourished which was never
fulfilled? Vampiristic and, by the nature of the act, cannibalistic, impulses are to be found in individuals who are
retarded at an infantile Oedipal stage of development
and regard the mother's body as the object of genital and
oral impulses, while at the same time experiencing aggressive and controlling desires. This can be exacerbated
if there is poor or dysfunctional masculine identification
during this time, perhaps because the father is absent, as
in Kemper's case. Certainly, part of Kemper's stimulation
came from associating his acts with his mother. On one
occasion, she came home just as Ed had put a body in his
wardrobe. He behaved entirely normally with her, but the
next morning he committed sex acts with the body, took
it into the shower and used an axe to cut it up before
disposing of it in his usual way. He took particular pleasure in talking to his mother while he had the body of a
dead woman in his car and sometimes went to visit her
after a murder because of the thrill this gave him.

As the absences of the students began to be realized
and the buried body parts were uncovered in the mountains, the Santa Cruz police realized they had a serial
killer on their hands; one whose perverted brutality knew
no bounds. In spite of Kemper's previous record, suspi-

cion never fell on him for a moment—presumably, the murder of his grandparents was regarded by those who knew little about Kemper's mental state as a one-off, the specificity of his victims making it a crime he was assumed to be unlikely to repeat with strangers. But Kemper was absorbed with his own behaviour and since the police did not come to visit him to talk about his crimes, he decided to go and visit them. He began to go to the Santa Cruz bars where he knew they gathered and joined in their conversations, plaguing them with questions about the Co-ed Killer. Since talk revolved around each latest ghastly killing and the identity of the murderer, Kemper was able to satisfy his own desire to relive every grisly episode and, at the same time, enjoy a feeling of smug superiority as he rubbed shoulders and drank beers with the men who wanted him behind bars, laughing up his sleeve at them as he asked about their progress in solving the crimes. Then he went home and watched television programmes like *Police Story* for tips on how to avoid detection—something at which he excelled. On one occasion, Kemper picked up a female hitch-hiker and her twelve-year-old son, intending to kill them, but as he drove away he spotted the woman's friend writing down the number of his car's licence-plate. Instead of killing his passengers, he delivered them to their destination in a gentlemanly way and returned to the city to search for an alternative victim. Another time, he drove calmly past guards at the entrance to the campus with two dying girls in his car, blankets thrown roughly over them.

Kemper's killing spree reached its gruesome, and many would say, entirely predictable finale on 21 April 1973. It was Easter weekend when after some thought Ed decided he had to fulfil what he believed was his destiny —"It's something hard to just up and do," he said later, as he recollected events, "but I was pretty fixed on that issue because there were a lot of things involved." His mother was asleep at five o'clock in the morning when Ed

Kemper, acting out yet another fantasy from his childhood, entered her bedroom with a hammer in one hand
and "the General" in the other. But this time he did not
restrict himself to imagination. Ferociously he brought
the hammer down on his mother's head time and again,
then turned her on her back and carefully lifting her chin,
slashed her throat. When she was dead he decapitated
her and removed her larynx, throwing it down the waste
disposal unit. "This seemed appropriate," he said later,
"as much as she'd bitched and screamed and yelled at me
over the years." But when he switched on the machine, it
would not work properly and the grisly piece of tissue
flew out again. "Even when she was dead, she was still
bitching at me," he was to complain as he recalled the
incident. "I couldn't get her to shut up." He propped his
mother's head on a hat-box and used it as a dartboard
before sexually attacking her headless corpse and dumping the body in a closet. Then he went out for a drive and
met an acquaintance who owed him ten dollars. Kemper
was in a murderous mood. His friend paid him the money
he owed and this, Kemper declared later, "saved his life."
But his blood-lust had not abated and he needed to kill
again. Returning home, Kemper telephoned his mother's
best friend Sarah Hallett and invited her round for dinner. When she arrived, he recalled, she said, "Let's sit
down, I'm dead." And, said Kemper, as if the murder was
a sickly black joke, "I kind of took her at her word there."
He strangled and decapitated her, too. He slept in his
mother's bed that night and the next morning decided to
leave Santa Cruz, using Sarah Hallett's car, dumping it
later and renting another. Before he left his home, Kemper wrote a taunting note to the police, saying: "5:15 a.m.
Saturday. No need for her to suffer any more at the
hands of this 'murderous Butcher.' It was quick—asleep
—the way I wanted it. Not sloppy or incomplete, gents.
Just a 'lack of time.' I got things to do!!!"

Kemper rented a car and drove non-stop to Pueblo,

Colorado, listening to radio reports in excitement as he imagined the nationwide hunt for the Co-ed Killer. He heard nothing. In Pueblo, Kemper bought newspapers, expecting splash headlines about the massive man-hunt. Again, to his growing dismay, nothing. After three days he telephoned the Santa Cruz police and confessed that he was the Co-ed Killer. The police dismissed it, thinking he was just another crank. Kemper had to call three times and repeat his story before they began to take him seriously. He patiently waited in a public telephone booth for the police to arrive and arrest him. When they took him in and returned him to Santa Cruz he admitted his crimes at once and confessed to cannibalizing two of his victims. He said he had taken flesh from the women's legs and had frozen it, later making a casserole with it. He also admitted having other "keepsakes" of his victims—teeth or pieces of skin. When he was asked why he had eaten the flesh of his victims, Kemper said: "I wanted them to be part of me—and now they are." He also said that he had killed his mother to spare her the embarrassment of discovering that her son was a murderer, for, after a policeman had visited him to check up on his gun licence, he began to believe that it would only be a matter of time before he was caught.

Kemper stood trial on eight counts of first-degree murder in April 1973. He proved to be an intelligent and articulate defendant and suggested to the court that he was a Jekyll-and-Hyde character. "I believe very deeply there are two people inside me," he said. Psychiatrists were called to verify Kemper's mental state and one declared that Kemper would kill again if he had the opportunity. Kemper was found guilty but legally sane and despite his request that he be executed, he was instead sentenced to life imprisonment. At present he is in the California Medical Facility at Vacaville. "He has been through therapy and is trying to work through his problems," said a hospital spokesperson in 1992. But a magazine interview in recent years showed Kemper is still fantasizing. It was reported that during the interview he interrupted his own lucid and reasonable discourse with a burst of excitement. "Sudden thought," he declared. "A guy could kidnap a number of good-looking women, put them on a ship for who knows where, and sell them to some sultan. You could get away with it! There are no Kojaks out there."

Maternal failings, especially their sexual misdemeanours, are frequently to be found in the histories of sadistic killers like Kemper and Gein and, indeed, are offered by them as reasons for their crimes. Overpowering and rejecting mothers, suggest psychoanalysts, can result in sexually-repressed sons who have castration-anxiety and who feel unable to express normal sexuality because of this negative, destructive mother-complex. Another aspect of the maternal conflict, according to Professor Richard Ratner, a psychiatrist at George Washington University, is that the individual feels hate towards the person whom he believes has hurt him—his mother—but at the same time is extremely dependent upon her, and comes to bitterly resent that dependence, which is why it explodes in adolescence when the resentment is no longer containable. Gein's mother was smothering, intense and oppressive; Kemper's mother was over-strict and critical. They would seem to support such theories—but let us not lose sight of the fact that thousands of men suffer similar maternal failings . . . without becoming cannibal killers.

8

Cannibalism as Art?

I would my love could kill thee; I am satiated
With seeing thee live, and fain would have thee dead.
I would earth had thy body as fruit to eat,
And no mouth but some serpent's found thee sweet.
I would find grievous ways to have thee slain,
Intense device, and superflux of pain;
Vex thee with amorous agonies, and shake
Life at thy lips, and leave it there to ache;
Strain out thy soul with pangs too soft to kill,
Intolerable interludes, and infinite ill;
Relapse and reluctation of the breath,
Dumb tones and shuddering semitones of death.

Ah that my lips were tuneless lips, but pressed
To the bruised blossom of thy scourged white breast!
Ah that my mouth for Muses' milk were fed
On the sweet blood thy sweet small wounds had bled!
That with my tongue I felt them, and could taste
The faint flakes from thy bosom to the waist!
That I could drink thy veins as wine, and eat
Thy breast like honey! that from face to feet
Thy body were abolished and consumed,
And in my flesh the very flesh entombed!

Algernon Charles Swinburne: "Anactoria"

While some readers may be shocked at the sexual sadism
and cannibalism contained in the above poem—the work

of one of Britain's acclaimed poets of the nineteenth century—it comes as no surprise to anybody who has glanced into the life of Swinburne. Like Baudelaire before him, who also placed the rotting fruits of his corrupt imagination into his literary work, he idolized the Marquis de Sade. Sade's writings, he declared, showed the aesthetic perfection which was the stamp of genius. But the truth behind his admiration was that de Sade's preoccupation with the sexual satisfaction to be derived from cruelty was reflected in Swinburne's own deviant interests in pain, punishment and dying. He revelled in stories about death and sadism and in his writing these obsessions were frequently laid bare, as can be seen in poems such as the one quoted above. In one poem "Itylus," he tells the story of a man who rapes his sister-in-law and cuts out her tongue to ensure her silence. In revenge for her sister's mutilation and suffering, his wife kills their child and serves it to him for dinner. In another poem, "Dolores," Swinburne writes:

> By the ravenous teeth that have smitten
> Through the kisses that blossom and bud,
> By the lips intertwisted and bitten
> Till the foam has a savour of blood.
> By the pulse as it rises and falters,
> By the hands as they slacken and strain,
> I adjure thee respond from thine altars,
> Our Lady of Pain.

For "Our Lady of Pain" was what Swinburne truly worshipped in his life. He may not, in reality, have indulged in the vampirism and cannibalism which poems like "Anactoria" perversely celebrated in words more customarily used to express romantic love, but his sexual thrill certainly came from sado-masochism, from being beaten or from watching others being flogged or hurt. He never had a normal sexual relationship with a woman—in

Elderly house-painter Albert Fish, accused murderer of ten-year-old Grace Budd, waits in the White Plains, NY county courthouse in 1935. (*AP/Wide World Photos*)

Edward Gein, the rural Wisconsin handyman, after being sentenced to an indeterminate term at the Wisconsin State Hospital for the Criminal Insane in 1958. Gein provided the inspiration for two film monsters: the mother-obsessed Norman Bates in Alfred Hitchcock's *Psycho* and the women's flesh-wearing serial killer "Buffalo Bill" in *The Silence of the Lambs*. (*AP/Wide World Photos*)

Edmund Kemper is found guilty of eight charges of murder in Santa Cruz, California in 1973. Known as the Coed Killer, Kemper ended his gruesome spree with a brutal attack on his mother. (*AP/Wide World Photos*)

Issei Sagawa, a former graduate student in Paris accused of murdering and consuming body parts of a young Dutch woman, is seen returning to Japan in 1984 for psychiatric treatment. Sagawa was found unfit to stand trial for the 1981 murder in 1983. (*AP/Wide World Photos*)

Andrei Chikatilo faces the court from a metal cage in Rostov-on-Don, Russia. Chikatilo is on record as the world's worst serial killer, having been convicted of murdering 53 people over a span of twelve years. (*AP/Wide World Photos*)

Chikatilo, the "Rostov Ripper," languishes in his cell after his conviction in 1992. (*AP/Wide World Photos*)

Jeffrey Dahmer, who confessed to killing and dismembering eleven people in his Milwaukee apartment, in his 1977 high school yearbook photo (*left*) and in 1982 (*below*). (*AP/Wide World Photos*)

Dahmer sits in Milwaukee County Circuit Court.
(*AP/Wide World Photos*)

fact, when his friend, the poet Dante Gabriel Rossetti, bribed a woman to invoke some sign of sexual arousal in Swinburne, she eventually admitted the seduction had been a failure and gave back Rossetti's money, telling him that she had been unable to persuade Swinburne that intercourse might be more pleasurable than biting. Swinburne turned to his poems, including "Dolores," to sublimate his lustful desires. It is in this work that he elevates a bruised and cut body into something which in his perversity he perceives as beautiful:

> The white wealth of thy body made whiter
> By the blushes of amorous blows,
> And seamed with sharp lips and fierce fingers,
> And branded by kisses that bruise . . .

and the question arises: can such writing, devoted to something which stirs Swinburne's malignantly sadistic senses and is the fuel of his fantasies, yet is distasteful to the vast majority of the population, be seen as true art? When, in 1866, Swinburne's *Poems and Ballads* was published, containing "Dolores" and other outrageous offerings, there was a Victorian backlash (to use a singularly apposite word) and the writer was dubbed "Swine-born" by *Punch* magazine. There was similar public shock in America, but since human nature is unchanging, evidenced today by the enormous popularity in both these countries of salacious tabloid newspapers which people outwardly profess to despise, the book was a sell-out. Disregarding this hypocrisy, again we might ask, is it art? Swinburne's masterly use of language and his evocative phraseology may show literary skills which applied to other topics would be very beautiful, but should these eclipse the unsavoury messages contained in these poems? Is it right that we should believe someone like Swinburne to be an artistic genius, superior to the mass of humanity, when he celebrates in words the sexual psychopathy exhibited in the deeds of cannibalistic murderers like Edmund Kemper, Jeffrey Dahmer, Albert Fish, Ed Gein?

And Issei Sagawa. If there is one cannibal killer who would in all likelihood applaud the beauty of Swinburne's poetry together with the notion that you can eat someone to prove you love them, Sagawa would probably fit the bill. He, too, is an artist and he particularly admires tall, generously-proportioned, beautiful girls. He enjoys painting them, reproducing the tones of their flesh and the plumpness of their buttocks on the canvas. Now in his early forties, the tiny Japanese artist says he contents himself with such depictions to fulfil his fantasies. But in Paris in 1981 he did not restrict his sensuous pleasure to the external beauty of the female form. Unlike Swinburne, who restrained the most shocking desires of his imagination within his writing, Sagawa allowed his frighteningly deviant fantasies off their leash. His longing was for soft flesh and hot blood, for complete, exploratory knowledge of those big, beautiful women—and in Paris he found satisfaction with a 25-year-old Dutch woman, Renee Hartevelt, with whom he fell in love "at first sight." But as in "Anactoria," the Swinburne poem which opened this chapter, Sagawa's love and passion bore no resemblance to that of a normal human being.

Renee was beautiful, blonde and well built, a serious-minded, independent woman who spoke three languages and was in Paris studying for her PhD in French literature at the Censier Institute. She supported herself by teaching languages and encountered Sagawa when he asked her to teach him German and offered to pay her handsomely. The son of Akira Sagawa, the wealthy and influential president of Kurita Water Industries, a prestigious Tokyo company, Issei had been a precocious child, enjoying Impressionist paintings from the age of five and being a prodigious reader from an early age. Like Renee, Sagawa was an intellectual, also working on his doctorate

—in comparative literature—at Paris University. He already had his MA in Shakespeare Studies. When he sat next to Renee Hartevelt in a classroom one day, he saw in her the living stuff of his fantasies. "I couldn't keep my eyes off her. Out of her short T-shirt I could see her white arms," he wrote later in his book *In The Fog*, in which he described what he called his Parisian "affair." He and Renee talked about literature together. They went to concerts and dances. Issei wrote her love-letters. She should have been suspicious when he spoke of his love of raw meat, but she evinced no surprise. When he held her to dance, he envisaged her nude body with its "white flesh." So far, not an uncommon normal male fantasy, one might think. But Sagawa was no normal male. In fact, he was wildly abnormal in enjoying the dark avenues down which his imagination took him. "I admire very much beautiful girls, especially Occidental girls who are healthy and tall. On the other hand, I also have this aspiration, this strange desire for cannibalism," he calmly told reporter Peter McGill in the British newspaper the *Observer* in 1992, as if it were for all the world just a quirk of taste, an antisocial habit. He recalled the childhood nightmare which he blamed for his "strange desire." He and his brother were boiling inside a pot. "It was my first nightmare of cannibalism, first, not to eat someone, but to be eaten." By the age of fifteen, the child was regularly fantasizing about cannibalism. "In my case it is just sexual desire. Sexual fetishism," he explained to McGill. "For Japanese girls I haven't any sexual desire. I am feeling as if she is my own daughter, no, sister, so it would be incestuous. For Occidentals though, I have a big adoration. The style, physically, I find very sexual . . . I prefer big women, but they are also repulsive."

Sagawa had studied for his degree in English literature at Wako University in Tokyo. While he was there he attacked a German woman, who, like Renee, was teaching him German. "In my head there was always a fantasy of cannibalism, and when I met this German lady in the street, I wondered if I could eat her," he explained to McGill. With "a mischievous smile" he related how he had climbed through the window of her ground-floor apartment on a summer's afternoon. "She was sleeping and almost naked. I wanted to attack her with an umbrella, but I was a little scared, and when I got close to her, she woke and screamed. She was stronger than me. I fell down, and tried to escape. I couldn't tell people it was because of cannibalism. I was too ashamed." After the attack, he saw a psychiatrist who declared that Sagawa was "extremely dangerous," but the incident was hushed up and in the late 1970s Sagawa, supported by the wealth of his father, went to live in Paris. He at once bought a rifle—as self-protection, he would later tell the police. There were, he explained, many murderers in Paris.

Renee apparently liked Sagawa. She wrote to her parents telling of her friendship with "a brilliant Japanese student" and invited the slightly-built, strange-looking oriental man to her room to discuss literature and have tea with her. He was not a threatening-looking man: less than five feet tall, weighing only six stone and with a limp, he was soft and rabbit-like. His lisping voice was gently plaintive and feminine: his hands and feet were tiny and childlike. Renee would tease him about his French, saying that it was so execrable that she would have to teach him French as well as German, and when, in turn, he invited her to visit him in his apartment to continue their discussion of literature, she willingly went. He served tea and his own special whisky brew. The two were kneeling on the floor, facing each other Japanese-style when Sagawa told Renee he loved her and asked her to go to bed with him. She dismissed his declaration of love and told him she would not sleep with him, for she saw him as a friend—that was all. Sagawa appeared to take her refusal placidly, nodding and indicating his assent. Standing up, he reached for a book of poetry and asked Renee to read it aloud to him. While she was preoccupied with this, he fetched his rifle and shot the girl in the back of the neck.

Sagawa told what happened next in *In The Fog*, the book he wrote when he was incarcerated in a French mental hospital and in whose pages he enthuses about eating human flesh. But before Sagawa dined on Renee's corpse, he indulged in what to him was a little foreplay: after undressing he had sex with the body. Then he cut off the tip of Renee's nose and part of a breast, which he devoured raw. "I touched her hip and wondered where I should eat first. After a little consideration, I ate right in the centre of the abundant, bouncing part of the right hip . . . I took a meat knife, and when I stabbed it went right in . . . When I started cutting, I could see some corn-like yellow stuff. I thought it was probably a white woman's own peculiar thick and soft fat. Beyond that I could see a red colour, it looked like beef, red meat . . . a little came out and I put it into my mouth . . . it had no smell or taste, and melted in my mouth like raw tuna in a sushi restaurant. Finally I was eating a beautiful white woman, and thought nothing was so delicious!"

With an electric carving knife, Sagawa cut up Renee's body carefully, removing strips of flesh to store in his refrigerator, and keeping the other parts he wanted to eat later. Some pieces he ate raw, others he fried with salt, pepper and mustard. Those parts in which he had no interest he cut into pieces small enough to be easily discarded. In between his butchering, Sagawa took photographs of his handiwork. He also took time off to go and watch a film with his friends. After a supper of raw flesh, Sagawa went to bed to sleep well in preparation for the busy day ahead. The next morning he went out and bought a luggage trolley and two large suitcases, together with a carpet-cleaning machine. He placed the remains of Renee Hartevelt in black plastic bin-liners and then put

them into the suitcases, called a taxi-cab and tried to find
a suitable place to dispose of the suitcases. He failed.

In fact, he made three attempts to get rid of them, but
there were always too many people about. It was the
following day when he finally dragged his wheeled trolley
to a pond in the picturesque Bois de Boulogne where he
intended to dump the cases in the water. It was hardly
surprising that he was spotted by passers-by. Sagawa was
such an unnaturally small, slight person that the suitcases
weighed more than he did and dwarfed him. Diners at a
restaurant watched with interest as a little Japanese man
puffed and panted his way across the grass with his heavy
load. He was about to push them into the pond when he
saw a couple watching him. Sagawa panicked and ran
away, leaving the cases. Curiously, the couple approached the cases. They were heavily bloodstained, but
what horrified them more was the hand which protruded
from one . . .

The police were greatly puzzled when they found the
butchered female remains, together with Renee's clothes
and shoes, in the suitcases. The purpose of this dismemberment seemed only to be to make the body fit into the
cases. Most murderers would mutilate a body in order to
prevent identification, yet here were the young woman's
head and hands almost intact, apart from the missing
nose-tip, and together with her belongings this would
make it easy to find out who she was—which they discovered within days. And they were soon to solve their murder mystery. A taxi-driver remembered collecting Sagawa
from his apartment and the police closed in on him
within forty-eight hours.

The 33-year-old man greeted the officers pleasantly
and confessed freely to the murder, but claimed he had a
history of mental illness. When the police opened the
refrigerator door and discovered Renee Hartevelt's
breast, one of her lips and both buttocks on the shelves—
and when Sagawa said he had eaten the other missing

parts of her body "sliced thin and raw" and that it was as satisfying as he had always imagined it would be—they were inclined to agree that they were dealing with a madman.

While waiting for his trial to begin, Sagawa was confident that his influential father could do something to help him. He expressed no regret for his victim, but he did say he had learned a lesson from his experience of murder. He was quoted as saying: "I know now what to do when killing a girl, how not to be arrested." It was 1983 before a judge decided that Sagawa was mentally incompetent to stand trial, that criminal charges would be dropped because Sagawa was in a "state of dementia" at the time of the murder and that he should be placed in a secure mental hospital—the Paul Guiraud asylum in a Paris suburb—indefinitely. Hospital psychiatrists said that he was an untreatable psychotic.

And there the story should have ended. Unhappily ever after for Sagawa. But that is to disregard the curious appeal that this man held for the Japanese people. Sagawa had described Renee Hartevelt's raw, dead flesh as tasting "like raw tuna in a sushi restaurant," and those Westerners whose stomachs turn at the Japanese predilection for sushi—raw fish—can only feel even more disgust at what happened next to "insane" Issei Sagawa: he became a star. No sooner had he arrived at the Paul Guiraud hospital than a Japanese film company was looking at his story in just the way Sagawa had regarded Renee: in terms of consumer-appeal. This could be a hit, they told Japanese playwright Juro Kara, who immediately began exchanging letters with Sagawa, which were then published in the form of a fictional novel called *Sagawa-kun kara no Tegami (Letters from Sagawa)* in 1983. In it, with a distasteful—and entirely inappropriate—picturesqueness, Kara described French women as having huge breasts "swinging to and fro like monsters, with blue veins running through them like Martian rivers." The book was a sell-out and won a literary prize for its "interesting intellectual approach." The Rolling Stones wrote a song about the case, called "Too Much Blood," and recorded it on their album *Under Cover*. Meanwhile, Sagawa was writing his first of five books, *Kiri no Naka (In the Fog)*, which contains lavish and intricate descriptions about the murder and cannibalization of Renee, written in a way which reveals the erotic fetishism which dominated Sagawa's psyche. The blurb on the cover includes a quotation from Sagawa describing Renee as "the most delicious meat I ever had" and the book was an instant success in Japan, where the newspaper *Tokyo Shimbun* declared it to be "beautifully done, and outstanding among recent Japanese literature, which has become boring." Sagawa also began making plans for directing a film of his experience, with himself in the starring role.

One would think that these offerings and plans were proof enough that Sagawa was a hopeless and dangerous case of a sexual deviant who should remain incarcerated until the breath has left his body. As Dr. Bernard Defer, one of Sagawa's psychiatrists in France, remarked in 1991: "Sexual desire, especially perverse desire, is something lasting, something permanent. It forms part of the personality. He can still have the desire to eat a woman. It is preferable that he still be in an institution." But Issei Sagawa is not still in an institution. Following approaches from his father shortly after his hospitalization, within a year Sagawa was removed from the French hospital and taken back to Tokyo where he was placed in the Matsuzawa Hospital "by the agreement of his parents," rather than being officially committed. Fifteen months later, in 1985, Akira Sagawa decided that his son should leave the hospital. Unable to object, they let Issei Sagawa out, whereupon he became an exciting celebrity with a story which combined sex, violence and fetishism and commanded untiring fascination. He was feted by the popular press and on television, a real-life Hannibal Lecter to whet the strange appetites of the Japanese masses. One interviewer fawningly told Sagawa: "Human beings like you are very rare. You act as a prism. You are Sagawa, who ate a human being." Sagawa was featured on the gourmet page of a magazine, eating barbecued food at a restaurant.

The Japanese, more than most nationalities, have always shown a peculiar appetite for the bizarre, especially if there is a macabre element of suffering or pain to spice up the entertainment value. Arguably the most successful Japanese writer of all time, Yukio Mishima, who died in 1970, was a homosexual sadist who was stimulated by the sight of blood and only joined the army in order to be able to observe blood, agony and death at first-hand. His dreams, according to his biographer Henry Scott Stokes were of "bloodshed—massacring youths, preferably Circassian [white] on large marble tables and eating parts of their bodies." Obsessed with strong young male bodies, Mishima himself was unattractive, short in stature, weak and thin—something which may find an echo in what we know of Issei Sagawa—and later in his life he became obsessed with bodybuilding to improve his physique. Yukio Mishima was his pen-name; he was originally named Kimitake Hiraoka and was a descendant of the *samurai*. His fascination with their ritualistic suicide tradition, *hara kiri*, was unsurprising since one of his favourite erotic images—seen graphically time and again in his work—was of a knife being thrust into an abdomen, which was then ripped asunder.

In the 1960s he became a right-wing political activist. He and his Imperialist sympathizers would swear allegiance by dripping blood from a cut finger into a cup, which would then be passed around for drinking. His public behaviour became more and more bizarre. He appeared in a trashy film and posed for a series of narcissistic photographs, one of which depicted him as St. Sebastian during his execution, his flesh pierced by many arrows. Death, he declared, was "the only truly vivid and erotic idea" and in November 1970 the stuff of his erotic imagination entered into reality. He and his small army stormed the headquarters of the Eastern Army in Tokyo and took the commander hostage. After notifying the media of his actions, he emerged from the building to speak out against democracy, but receiving only jeers he went back inside, knelt down, drove a dagger into his own abdomen and ripped it sideways to disembowel himself. He was forty-five.

Issei Sagawa grew up during a time when Mishima's genius was being lauded and Mishima's pervertedly "erotic" act can be compared with Sagawa's attempt to bestow artistic values upon his act of murder and his unstable sexual proclivities. He likes to speculate about whether the murder of Renee was one of exquisite and pure love, of crime redeemed by art. In the world of normal sexuality, the debate over where erotica ends and pornography begins may be argued by defining the erotic in the beauty or expressiveness of words or images, where coarseness or exploitation is absent. But this argument concerns images of "normal" sexuality: What of the abnormal—and what of "flawed genius"? There are those who say that with true genius also comes instability—that creativity cannot co-exist with normality—which is why many of the world's greatest artists and writers have displayed mental, emotional or sexual trauma in their lives. So what if the talented artist—like Mishima or Swinburne—can bring all his wonderfully positive literary or expressive devices to bear in his creation of "erotica," acknowledging that for him, the erotic is that perversion which he finds most arousing, but disgusts the normal human being? Deviant desires like sadism, murder, necrophilia, cannibalism? Is it still art?

Issei Sagawa clearly regards himself as an artist. Under

an assumed name, he now lives in a third-floor apartment in a suburb of Tokyo where the walls are hung with his own oil paintings—mostly of Western women, with particular attention paid to their fleshy pink buttocks. He is unsupervised, despite the fact that Dr. Tsuguo Kaneko, the superintendent of the Japanese hospital where Sagawa was kept prior to his release, believes that he is a dangerous psychopath who should be prosecuted for his crime. "I think he is sane and guilty. Maybe he is a danger to foreign females. He must be in prison," Dr. Kaneko is reported as saying. Instead, Sagawa has become an established media figure, a role in which he delights and for which he is prepared to do and say just about anything. In 1989 he was announcing his intention to open a vegetarian restaurant in Tokyo; by 1992 he was planning his autobiographical film with Juro Kara and wondering who to choose to play the victim.

There is a complete absence of moral concern from both the media and Sagawa himself. He now says he is "no longer a cannibal," that he was sick during his Parisian period, but has recovered and would not repeat his crime. But the books he has written about cannibalism have all been best-sellers—an anthology of short stories on cannibalistic fantasies he describes as "a little bit comical"—and he writes regular articles for pornographic magazines, repeating in gory detail the story of his cannibalistic exploits. He writes film reviews for another magazine, revealing that he thought *The Silence of the Lambs* movie lacked psychological depth but he liked very much a German film called *Trance* "about the very beautiful girl who kills her boyfriend when he wants to leave her, and ate him up." In 1992 there was much outrage—particularly from the Netherlands embassy in Tokyo—when the Japanese authorities issued Sagawa with a passport to enable him to travel to Germany to appear on a chat show and talk about how he killed and ate Renee Hartevelt.

Contrasting with the shocked disbelief with which most Westerners regard Sagawa's celebrity status, there is, in addition to the tabloid-and-TV support he receives, a nucleus of intellectuals in Japan who, astonishingly, sympathize with Sagawa, regarding him as an anti-establishment outsider who should be admired for the fulfilment of his fantasy and for his "artistic insanity." High-flown debate rages in respected artistic circles concerning the "artistry" of Sagawa: whether he showed the purest form of love by devouring his girlfriend or whether it was simply a bizarre fetish. Morality does not enter into it. The artistic circles claim Sagawa's "crime" had to be committed, otherwise his "art" would have suffered. Detached, they speak philosophically about Sagawa's enjoyment of Renee Hartevelt's body, for all the world as if this was an imaginary learning experience rather than a real horrific sex murder. "Eating human flesh is the same thing as assimilating yourself to the body you are eating," coolly explains psychologist Shu Kishida. "In the Western world there are many historical cases in tribes, that you eat the flesh of the man you respect. In Sagawa's case it is an extreme form of the inherent admiration of every Japanese for the white race. His admiration of the white race took the extreme form of killing and eating that white woman's flesh."

Yasuhisa Yazaki, the editor of a magazine which carried a flattering article about the cannibal killer describes him as "a human being who has undergone a very special experience." He elaborates: "We have to say that in this world some human beings want to eat the flesh of other people. We have to admit their existence and accept it in the future." Other magazines carry pictures of his paintings. Sagawa believes he is artistically stimulated by "tall and robust" Western women and declares: "I'm essentially a romantic." Some women have been persuaded to pose nude for him. One of them, a young Dutch model, Ingrid, whom he contacted when he saw her photograph in a magazine, returned to Holland without ever knowing his real name or anything of his past. A British reporter, Joanna Pitman of *The Times*, actually went and took tea with Sagawa—not unaccompanied, of course—and was alarmed when he handed out cups of the special tea-and-whisky brew he had given to Renee before killing her:

> He welcomed us to his cramped and dingy home with fawning hospitality, displaying an ominous and hair-raising delight at the sight of a foreign female visitor. "I still adore the sight and the shape of young Western women, particularly beautiful ones," he said, his wolfish eyes staring out from behind dark glasses. "I was a premature and unhealthy baby, I am ugly and small, but I indulge in fantasies about strong healthy bodies."

Most alarmingly, Sagawa still talks with enthusiasm about cannibalism being an "expression of love" and seems unwilling to admit to the perversity of his peculiar passion. "Cannibalism has been my obsession since I was very young, it is a pleasure lying deep in the human spirit," he says. In magazine interviews he outlines his various sensual aims. "My long-cherished desire is to be eaten by a beautiful Western woman," he said on one occasion—and then admitted that he still fantasizes about eating a woman's flesh . . . although, he hastened to add, without murdering her and only with her consent. Such irrationality is evidence of the unbalanced mind of Sagawa, who is basking in the Japanese limelight thanks to his heinous deeds. But how will he react when the limelight fades? One of his former friends said she was afraid of what may happen when the media loses interest in him. "It's like a protective wall for him," she says. "He lives now in a type of world that he knows really well how to work."

And although he tries to make clear that artistic fantasy now substitutes for his very real desires, Joanna Pitman observed his "disturbingly carnal" paintings and said: "One of the most distressing aspects of this solitary man is the fact that he believes he is normal." Sagawa told her: "My time in the mental ward was like hell. Everyone else in there was crazy, but the doctors saw that I was not like them, that I was cured. I am normal. I eat an evening meal with my parents every day and spend my spare time painting and writing." In a magazine article entitled "I Ate Her Because of Fetishism" he explained that he recognized that he was sick in Paris, because he had allowed himself to become consumed by his fetishes and fantasies. "I think everyone has a curious fantasy. But they can't realize it, that's all. My fantasy of cannibalism is not crazy. Everyone has fantasies. The special thing about me is that I acted upon mine."

9

"Do As Thou Wilt
Shall Be The Whole of the
Law." [1]

He has an awful lot of love for me . . . He always
wanted to do things for me. He's a boy who likes things I
like. He loves flowers, roses. He doesn't hesitate to show
his love for me.

A doting grandma is describing her grandson, a man who
has just been arrested for an abominable series of crimes.
The man's stepmother is talking to a British journalist
and says: "If you could meet him he would wring your
heart out. He is such a sad person, he brings out all your
maternal instincts." "Sit down and talk with him," says
his lawyer, "and you'll say he's as nice a young man as
you could meet." The man's neighbour recalls: "We used
to hear sawing coming from his apartment at all hours
. . . I said [to my husband] one night at about two in the
morning, 'What in the world is he building at this
hour?' " And . . . "He seemed like a regular guy," says
the frightened individual who narrowly avoided becoming the regular guy's eighteenth victim—and supper.
Tracy Edwards had fled the man's apartment in panic

[1] Aleister Crowley, black magician, citing Satanic commandment.

after being drugged, handcuffed and threatened with a knife. He gibbered out his story to two passing bored police officers—who sighed deeply and offered to check out his tale, all the time assuming it would be just a routine rapping of the regular guy's knuckles.

Their first glimpse of Jeffrey Dahmer certainly would not have indicated that he was anything other than a normal, somewhat serious young man. The good-looking 31-year-old who opened his front door to them on that night in July 1991 was skinny and blond, with a gentle, unhurried manner and a calm voice. Perhaps this makes it more understandable why three other police officers, two months previously, had returned to Dahmer a 14-year-old boy who had escaped his murderous clutches and, bruised, bleeding, naked and near-catatonic, had wandered out on to the street where the policemen found him after being called by a neighbour. Dahmer had turned up and, in pacifying tones, had explained that the young man was a friend who was staying with him and had had too much to drink. The officers had been convinced. They had allowed Dahmer to take Konerak Sinthasomphone back into his apartment, where the uncomprehending boy had watched the door close on his last chance of survival.

But in July these police officers, Robert Rauth and Rolf Mueller, knew nothing of that incident as they asked Jeffrey Dahmer if they could look around his apartment, having received complaints from Tracy Edwards, the 32-year-old black man who stood at their shoulders, that from being a friendly, normal guy one minute, this man had suddenly become crazy and tried to kill him the next. Dahmer quietly acquiesced and offered to go and fetch the key to the handcuffs from his bedroom. Edwards loudly told the officers that Dahmer's knife was in the bedroom, so Mueller went to search instead. What he found jolted and revolted him. In a drawer were gruesome Polaroid pictures of bodies at different stages of mutilation and dismemberment, photographs of skulls and skeletons . . . and a picture of a severed human head. As soon as the horrific importance of his discovery dawned on Mueller, Dahmer was handcuffed and arrested and Mueller showed Edwards the awful picture of the severed head. "This could have been you," he told him grimly with barely controlled revulsion. Edwards, in a state of high excitement by now, remarked to Mueller that Dahmer had freaked out when he had gone to open the refrigerator earlier in the evening. "Maybe there's a head in there?" he cried. Mueller smiled nervously at this outlandish idea—fuelled, no doubt, by Edwards' hysteria. "Yeah, maybe," he laughed, pulling open the door. There was a head in there. In fact, there were three heads in there.

Mueller screamed.

The question everyone wanted answering was: what turned Jeffrey Dahmer into a monster who cannibalized the bodies of those he murdered? And the answer is simply: nobody knows. People who like to claim that early environment—perhaps an unhappy childhood, severity of punishment or being starved of affection—is to blame for a man's later heinous crimes, would scratch their heads over Dahmer, who fails to fit any bill of deprivation. Born in 1960, Jeffrey was the elder son of Lionel and Joyce Dahmer, who led a comfortable middle-class life in Bath, Ohio. Lionel Dahmer told a reporter that Jeffrey was an ordinary little boy. He recalled how his son would become excited when his grandparents came to visit, just like any normal kid. He denied a story, which was circulating at the time of Dahmer's arrest, that his son had been sexually abused by a neighbour when he was eight years old—as, indeed, did Jeffrey Dahmer himself. And although another journalist turned up a schoolteacher's report which said that the 6-year-old Jeffrey Dahmer seemed to feel neglected after the birth of his brother David, this is a common enough occurrence in families. There seems little in the way of childhood trauma to explain adequately why this small boy grew up to be a sick cannibalistic serial killer who would shock the world. One psychiatrist suggested that it might have been because he had had a hernia operation at the age of four; a suggestion born, one feels, of desperation rather than real in-depth analysis. The home was not without affection; Jeffrey was adored by his grandmother in particular. True, there were problems between his parents and soon after David's birth they moved into separate bedrooms— friends even claimed that Lionel Dahmer had a string of bells outside his room to warn him of his wife's imminent arrival—but the couple stayed together for the sake of their sons until Jeffrey was eighteen and David twelve. Jeffrey Dahmer would later tell a probation officer that if there was anything he would have liked to change about his childhood, "it would be the way my parents behaved towards each other," but again, thousands of children from broken homes endure far worse. But while David developed normally, Jeffrey's peculiar interests and fantasies began to evolve early. The child was only eight when his interest in dead bodies began to manifest itself. He was fascinated by the insides of bodies, the bright colours, Dahmer's lawyer was to tell the court at his trial —when it was also revealed that Dahmer preferred to have sex with the viscera of the young men whom he had killed.

Lionel Dahmer, a chemist, may have thought his son would follow in his footsteps when he bought little Jeffrey a chemistry set. The worst use to which most children put their chemistry sets is creating flashes and bangs. Jeffrey's experiments were more sinister. His early interests lay with insects which he preserved in jars, but later he moved on to mammals, impaling cats and frogs on sticks. He would collect animals which had been run over and skin them, using the substances in his chemistry set. Dried-out animal skins and their decapitated heads impaled on spikes were scattered around the woods at the back of his home and he was fascinated with the innards of animals, cutting them up to see how they worked. Dahmer later told the police that when he was young he and a friend would drive around looking for dogs which were walking along the road, and run them over. He recalled hitting a beagle puppy and relished the look of terror on its face as it hit the windscreen of the car.

At age fourteen, he said, he had his first homosexual experience and confessed that he regularly fantasized about using a corpse for sex. Necrophilia became an obsession and like other sadistic killers he had a fertile imagination. As his lawyer Gerald Boyle was to remark after Dahmer's imprisonment, "When you're fourteen and you want to make love to a dead body, you've got a hell of a problem." Schoolmates cast back their minds and described the teenage Dahmer as an isolated, lonely individual with a peculiar sense of humour. One girl remembered, "I felt uncomfortable around him because he was so weird and so emotionless," and another recalled that he had an established drink problem by the time he was sixteen, which led to him drinking neat Scotch during class. Gerald Boyle said that by this age Dahmer was "a desperately lonely person with no friends" and claimed, "If Jeffrey Dahmer had gotten help when he was sixteen he'd be a free man today."

Dahmer's home life was obviously far from perfect at this time, but it was not until he was eighteen—an independent adult, according to the law—that his parents sorted out their divorce, which involved a wrangle over custody of Jeffrey's younger brother, then aged twelve. Lionel and Joyce accused each other of neglect and cruelty and Lionel alleged that Joyce should not be awarded custody of David because of "extreme mental illness." However, Joyce did win custody and a month later, in

August 1978, she left Jeffrey in the family home and took off with her younger son to settle firstly in Chippewa Falls, Wisconsin and later in Fresno, California. Lionel, robbed of his regular meetings with his younger son, applied to the court again for custody—and this time it was granted. Meanwhile, throughout all these family battles, during that summer of 1978 Jeffrey was left very much to his own devices.

The month before his parents' divorce hearing, Jeffrey Dahmer murdered the first of his seventeen victims. "One night," Gerald Boyle was to tell a packed Milwaukee court, "he is driving around and he sees a hitch-hiker, and the hitch-hiker doesn't have a shirt on, and Jeffrey Dahmer wants his body." Boyle was to pause before repeating significantly: "His *body*." Dahmer picked up 18-year-old Steven Hicks, who was hitch-hiking from a rock concert, took him home, got drunk, had sex with Steven and then killed him, hiding the corpse in the crawl-space beneath the house. "The guy wanted to leave and I didn't want him to leave," he said later. Then, as he had done with the animals ten years previously, Dahmer dismembered Steven Hicks' body with a kitchen knife, placed the pieces in plastic bags and carried them around in his car with him. Much later he scattered Steven Hicks' remains around the wood at the back of his home. The murder was not to come to light until thirteen years later when Dahmer made a confession to Milwaukee police, although he could remember the hitch-hiker only as Steve. When shown a photograph of Hicks, he said: "Yeah, that's him," displaying no emotion at all.

But back in 1978, Dahmer's family had no clue to the teenager's unspeakable fantasies or his awful secret. Jeffrey went off to Ohio State University to study business but dropped out after one term, his drink problem increasingly hard to handle. In December that year Shari Jordan married Lionel Dahmer. Jeffrey was eighteen and she remembers him as "practically an alcoholic." Like his father, she was to express bewilderment at Jeffrey Dahmer's dreadful crimes. "None of us know why, out of two children with a similar upbringing, one should become a killer," she said. Dahmer enrolled in the army where he was to spend the next two years. The following July he was posted to Baumholder, West Germany, as a combat medic. Unlike many soldiers he did not join in the "buddy culture" and remained a loner, on the periphery of his fellow-soldiers' social interactions. Occasionally he drank heavily and hurled racist abuse at black soldiers and in the course of duty it seemed he was squeamish. He was afraid of needles and could not bear to take anyone's blood—which makes it even more curious to consider that, only a year after his discharge for alcohol abuse, he got a job at the Milwaukee Blood Plasma Centre, doing exactly that.

But his first job on leaving the army was in a Florida sandwich bar where he worked for a time before moving back to the home of his father and stepmother. Lionel Dahmer, unable to cope with his son's heavy and frequent drinking at the local bars, decided to send him to his grandmother's house to live, on the grounds that Catherine Dahmer and Jeffrey had always been very close. It was true that there was a loving bond between the two of them. But a stable home life over the next five years did not alter Dahmer's lifestyle. At the end of this period he was working at a chocolate factory during the daytime and in the evenings he cruised around the gay bars. He was arrested a couple of times for exposing himself and masturbating in public, and on one occasion he was accused of drugging people at a gay bath-house, but predictably enough no man wished to stand up and be counted by pressing charges against Dahmer. There was nothing and no one to stop Dahmer. Towards the end of 1987, and still living with his grandma, he began his killing spree in earnest.

Steven Toumi, one of the few white males who became

a Dahmer victim, shared a hotel room for a night with Dahmer after meeting him at a gay bar in Milwaukee. Dahmer claimed in his later confession that he woke up the next morning to find Toumi dead and bleeding from the mouth. Experts, puzzled as to why he should give graphic accounts of other murders but insist he remembered nothing of this one, are inclined to believe that for some reason he has blocked out all memory of the events that night. However he clearly recalled his actions the following morning: he bought a big suitcase, put the corpse inside and took it back to Catherine Dahmer's house where, after having sex with the body in his basement room, he mutilated the corpse and then dismembered it, putting the pieces into the dustbin.

Two months later he repeated his actions with a 14-year-old boy, James Doxtator, whom he had picked up outside the same club. This time, Dahmer avoided the cost of a hotel room by bribing the boy with cash in return for posing naked for him, and taking him straight home. After having sex with James, Dahmer gave him a drink with some sleeping pills in it—a technique which was to become a routine part of his killing method. When the drugs had the required effect, Dahmer strangled James and dismembered his body, throwing it out with the rubbish as he had done with Toumi. The scenario was repeated after another two-month period of abstinence. This time the victim was Richard Guerrero, aged twenty-five.

Dahmer did not keep any "mementos" of these three victims, unlike later in his killing career when he began preserving their heads, genitals, bones or other organs. At his later trial, Dahmer's attorney Gerald Boyle said Dahmer viewed the act of mutilation as "just making a human being disappear"—as if he was driven to dispose of his victims in this way by sheer expedience. That was certainly not the case towards the end of his murderous spree—and judging by what we know of Dahmer's per-

verted childhood interests, it was probably not his prime
motivation at the time of these murders. His behaviour
with corpses was, however, going to become more and
more extreme to meet his necrophiliac desires. Eventually he demanded greater stimulation to gain the same
sexual satisfaction, and would achieve it in a number of
ways, including cannibalism.

Jeffrey's drunken behaviour was becoming as intolerable for his grandmother as it had been for his father. In
summer 1988 she asked him to move out and he found an
apartment in Milwaukee. Almost immediately, he inter-
cepted a 13-year-old boy on his way home from school
and offered him fifty dollars to go home with him and
pose half-naked for photographs. The boy obliged and
Dahmer made homosexual advances to him, kissing him
and touching his penis. He also gave the boy some
drugged coffee, but perhaps he misjudged the quantity of
drug required to knock out the teenager because, although dopey, the youth did not fall asleep. Instead he
went home where, after behaving in a disoriented way, he
eventually passed out and his family took him to hospital.
The drugs were discovered, the story was told and
Dahmer was soon under arrest.

His family rallied round. Catherine Dahmer took her
grandson into her home again and Lionel Dahmer put up
bail and hired a top lawyer, Gerald Boyle, to defend him.
At first Dahmer denied the events, explaining away the
drugging as an accident—because, he claimed, when he
took his sleeping tablets, he always drank them from the
cup which he had given to the child. Obviously, he said,
there must have been some residue left in there. But
when the case was heard the following year, he pleaded
guilty to second-degree sexual assault and to enticing a
child for immoral purposes.

While on bail, Dahmer was seeing a psychologist from
the probation department. These consultations had, declared one report, been most useful. Dahmer was more

amiable and relaxed and more willing to talk about himself, the report said optimistically. The probation department did not know that Dahmer had been busy during those months when it was supposedly monitoring him. A matter of weeks before he was due to be sentenced, he picked up 20-year-old Anthony Sears at a gay bar, took him home to his grandmother's house for sex and killed and disposed of him in his customary way. This time, he kept a souvenir: Anthony's head, which was to be discovered when police raided Dahmer's apartment two years later. After boiling the head to remove the skin, he painted the skull grey, so it would appear to be like a medical model such as doctors or medical students might use. Later he would admit that he enjoyed masturbating in front of this skull, and other skulls.

In court for sentence on the enticement charge, the Assistant District Attorney Gale Shelton pleaded that Dahmer be imprisoned for many years—on the grounds that although he was superficially co-operative he had "deep-seated anger and deep-seated psychological problems." Two psychologists agreed with her, between them offering opinions that Dahmer was manipulative, had problems with his sexuality and was a schizoid personality who needed intensive treatment. His defending attorney Gerald Boyle, unaware that the man in the dock had already killed five people, the last one only weeks previously, pleaded for lenience, citing Dahmer's sense of responsibility in holding down a job and his belief that Dahmer was "semi-sick"—that he had not reached the stage where he was a chronic offender. "I believe that he was caught before it got to the point where it would have gotten worse—a blessing in disguise," he said and added that as far as he was aware, there had been "no recurrence of this type of conduct." In an ironic sense, this was true; Dahmer had made sure that things were different with his most recent victim Anthony Sears, giving him such a hefty dose of drugs that he was too sedated to get up and leave Dahmer's room to blow the whistle on him.

But Dahmer was the very model of contrition in court, blaming alcohol for his misdemeanours, saying he had never before done anything as awful as this assault on the boy and that it had shocked him out of his bad behaviour pattern. He pleaded that the court allow him to continue his job. "Please don't destroy my life," he begged piteously, knowing all the time that he had destroyed five other lives more completely than this court could ever hope to damage his. But the judge was convinced of Dahmer's wish to reform. He sent Dahmer to a correction centre for a year, with day release so he could continue his job, and gave him suspended prison sentences on both the charges, together with a five-year probation order and an order to get counselling and treatment for his drink problem. Three years later, Gerald Boyle was to say that this sentence was appropriate at the time, no one having had any idea of Dahmer's dark secrets: "He fooled a lot of people." When Dahmer was released from the correction centre ten months later, he moved into the apartment which was to become the most infamous in Milwaukee. In only a matter of months Dahmer turned it into a human abattoir.

In just over a year, Dahmer murdered twelve people in that apartment, typically luring them there for sex, photographic sessions or to watch homosexual videos, with the promise of payment. The murders were part of his weekend entertainment; before he left to cruise the gay bars and select a victim, he would shift the furniture to make more room to carry out the murder when he returned later. He was preoccupied with the horror film *The Exorcist III* and would often play the video of it to his potential victims. He would sedate them, strangle or stab them, have anal and oral sex with the corpses and then dismember them, always doing this in the nude to avoid messing up his clothes. Before dismemberment he would frequently wait until the bodies were stiff with rigor mortis, then he would stand them up, cut them open and take Polaroid pictures, which he put in an album. He would remove the genitals, preserving them in formaldehyde and would decapitate his victims, usually boiling the heads to keep as trophies and sometimes painting them grey. He saved the penis of one victim and painted it a "natural" flesh-colour. Dahmer told police he disposed of six victims' torsos by soaking them in acid until they became "slushy" and then flushing them down a toilet.

Dahmer ate the flesh of three victims and performed sex acts on two of the severed heads. He admitted experimenting with various culinary seasonings in order to make the flesh taste better and kept human-meat "patties" in the freezer.

During his later confession to the police, he was reluctant to give details about which victims he ate, but admitted to cutting flesh from one man's thigh and eating it, to saving a heart in his freezer "to eat later" and to frying and eating the biceps of 24-year-old Ernest Miller "because they were big" and he "wanted to try it." Ernest Miller, a dancer, evidently held many attractions for Dahmer—he also flayed this man's body, removed the flesh from the bones and discarded it, saving the skull and skeleton, which he hung in his apartment. A photograph was found of the skeleton hanging in the shower.

As time went on, even this horrific behaviour became inadequate to satiate Dahmer's lust. He began to perform experiments on his sedated victims. Testimony at his sanity trial showed Dahmer drilled the skulls of some unconscious victims and poured acid into the drill-holes in a crude attempt to lobotomize the men and create zombie-like sex partners for himself. Needless to say, the experiments failed. Sometimes, in a further twist of cruelty, Dahmer would anonymously telephone the families of his murder victims and tell them their sons were dead and that he had killed them.

The majority of Dahmer's victims were non-white, which makes their murders at the hands of Dahmer unusual in terms of serial murder statistics. FBI profiles of serial killers show that they usually only attack people within their own ethnic group—and serial killers are almost always white. Dahmer also was unusual in that he didn't have a car and killed most of his victims at his home. Since Dahmer's arrest, many people have come forward to declare that Dahmer was a racist who frequently made anti-black remarks. At Dahmer's trial, however, Dr. Frederick Fosdal, a forensic psychiatrist hired by the state, said that in his interview of Dahmer he found no evidence that the killings were racially motivated, although he established that Dahmer was homosexual.

All Dahmer's known victims were gay—a fact which Dahmer was keen to point out at the time of his confession, as if he thought it might exculpate his murders. Why should he draw attention to this when he was himself gay? There are clues to be found to this puzzle. All the time that Dahmer was committing these dreadful crimes, he was turning up—fairly regularly, at least—for his monthly appointments with his probation officer Donna Chester, who noted his depression and his problem with his sexual identity. He admitted being gay but said he felt guilty about it. This attitude is borne out by a 21-year-old single mother who, in 1992, under banner headlines of "The Only Woman Who Loved Hannibal the Cannibal" told a British newspaper, *Today*, about Dahmer's hatred for homosexuals and his preoccupation with God and religion.

She met Dahmer in 1988 when he was living with his grandmother before his arrest on the indecency charge—about which the young woman knew nothing until Dahmer's atrocities were made public—and they became friends. She even helped him to choose the apartment in which he later butchered countless victims. The young woman would sit in Dahmer's room for hours and he would sometimes recite the Lord's Prayer or preach passages from the Bible to her. Sometimes, she revealed, he would ask her what she thought about homosexuals and he made plain his own opinion. "He couldn't stand them," she said. "He said sex between men and men or women and women was wrong . . . that they were committing a sin."

Dahmer's antipathy towards homosexuals is interesting in that it provides a possible shred of insight into his behaviour. This knowledge tells us that he must necessarily have been filled with self-disgust at his own homosexual desires and, possibly, wishing to deny the homosexual act in which he indulged, he projected this disgust on to his partners. By eradicating them, in some twisted way he may have believed he was attacking himself and destroying the evidence of his "shameful" actions. However, while this internal conflict might offer a "reason" why a person with a severe personality disorder would wish to kill, it fails to explain why they would indulge in the sordid cannibalistic and necrophiliac activities which so delighted Dahmer.

In May 1991, two months before the full horror of what had gone on in Jeffrey Dahmer's apartment was discovered, the police had a telephone call from Sandra Smith, one of his close neighbours who, with her mother, Glenda Cleveland, was alarmed to see a naked boy, his legs covered with blood, running down the street, having fled from Dahmer's apartment. By the time officers Joe Gabrish, Richard Porubcan and John Balcerzak arrived, so had Dahmer, on his way back from a bar. Dahmer had already had oral sex with 14-year-old Konerak Sinthasomphone while the drugged boy was inert and unconscious and he had left his flat only briefly to buy some beer, relishing the thought that his next blood-sacrifice was drugged into oblivion and would be there when he returned to do with as he pleased. Instead his plan was going wrong, for he was alarmed to see this boy standing stark naked in the company of three police officers. But Dahmer was gratified to observe that the drugged coffee *had* taken effect: the boy was dazed and incoherent. Having summoned up a surge of strength and courage to run, he now slumped into glassy-eyed silence. In the glib, manipulative way which Dahmer had practised before and was to display again, he quietly told the police that their charge was a 19-year-old friend who was staying with him and had had too much to drink. The three officers were clearly fooled by Dahmer but decided to check out his apartment anyway. There they found Konerak's clothes neatly stacked on a chair with no apparent sign of any struggle. Konerak sat on the sofa and said nothing, no longer trying to escape, and the officers put the incident down to a lovers' tiff. Had they investigated a little further, they would have discovered the decomposing corpse of Tony Hughes spread out on Dahmer's bed, where it had been since Dahmer had killed him three days previously. Sure, the police officers noticed the appalling, blocked drains-type smell in Dahmer's apartment—as did everyone else who visited it—but they had no reason to conclude that this was because the pleasant, polite, sandy-haired chap before them had several rotting corpses in a fifty-gallon container in his bedroom. As Balcerzak said later: "Dahmer was a straightforward, calm, convincing person who voluntarily came forward with information with no hint of stress and no hint that he didn't want us to continue with our investigation."

Nevertheless, they were glad to leave the stench of the room and the squalor of the Milwaukee building and be on their way. In flippant mood they radioed in to HQ "The intoxicated Asian naked male was returned to sober boyfriend," Balcerzak reported amid much laughter, adding, "my partner's going to get deloused at the station" as a graphic comment on the unsanitary conditions of the Milwaukee apartment. As soon as the police had gone, Dahmer is said to have drilled into Konerak's head and poured acid into his brain in one of his attempts to create a zombie sex slave. Then he strangled Konerak, sexually violated his corpse and dismembered it, taking photographs and keeping the boy's skull.

When Dahmer was eventually arrested and tried for murder, the details of this bungled incident emerged and the three officers found themselves "in the dock" too. As Janie Hagen, the sister of victim Richard Guerrero said: "Jeffrey Dahmer will get what he deserves—life in prison. The three police officers are next." Joe Gabrish and John Balcerzak were fired almost instantly; Richard Porubcan was suspended. In retrospect it is easy to blame these officers for failing to carry out their duty to the hapless Konerak and no one doubts that they should have been more suspicious of Dahmer. But Dahmer, as a psychiatrist was later to declare, was "a formidable liar." He had already shown, at the indecency trial where he had deceived everyone from his attorney to the judge, that if you're smart enough, you *can* fool all of the people all of the time.

Tracy Edwards, the man who lived to tell the tale of his encounter with Milwaukee's most infamous murderer—and who put a stop to his slaying of young men—claimed that there was no mention of homosexuality when he went back to Dahmer's apartment with him on 22 July 1991 (although Dahmer claimed that Edwards was there for a "photo session") but that he went merely for a drink. However, he told the court at Dahmer's trial, he suspected that his rum and Coke had been drugged when he began feeling dizzy. In the bedroom, where the walls were plastered with pornographic pictures of gay sex acts, Dahmer handcuffed Edwards and pulled out a knife. The horrified young man saw a large bloodstain on the bedspread and later said that there was a human hand sticking out from under the bed—although he does not appear to have mentioned this to the police at the time they rescued him. Dahmer, claimed Edwards, told him he intended to eat him. "You'll never leave here," he said and pulled a skull out of a filing cabinet saying: "This is how I get people to stay with me—you will stay with me too." Then he listened to the terrified Edwards' heart beating and announced, "Soon it will be mine. I'm going to cut your heart out." (It must be noted that doubt has been cast on Edwards' claims regarding these threats; such killers do not usually announce their intentions in advance, say some psychiatrists.) Seizing an opportune moment—when Dahmer was rocking manically back and forth and chanting, "It's time, it's time"—Edwards said he punched and kicked him and fled the apartment to flag down officers Rauth and Mueller, who exposed the bloody slaughterhouse which was Jeffrey Dahmer's home. The remains of eleven victims were found there. Most were identified by dental records.

Meanwhile, officers investigating his past discovered other unsolved murders in places where, coincidentally, Dahmer had lived. While Dahmer was in the army and stationed in Baumholder, Germany, there were five unsolved murders involving mutilation of the victims in the area. The Baumholder connection was abandoned as theoretically unlikely because there were females among the victims. When Dahmer left the army he lived for a time in Miami. Four months after his arrival, a 6-year-old boy called Adam Walsh was abducted in Hollywood, Florida and two weeks later his head was found in a canal 120 miles away. No other remains were found. Dahmer refused to admit any involvement in this murder and police appear to have ruled out any connection.

Dahmer confessed to killing seventeen young males, sixteen in Wisconsin and one in Ohio, but when he came to trial on 13 January 1992 he was only charged with fifteen. One of the Wisconsin murder cases was aban-

doned because of lack of evidence and Dahmer's first
victim, Steven Hicks, was killed in Dahmer's home town
of Bath, Ohio, where he was due to stand trial separately.
Dahmer pleaded guilty but insane to the fifteen murders.
When the jury was selected, Dahmer's attorney Gerald
Boyle cautioned that the trial would include "human carnage, killing, mutilation, cannibalism—everything you
can possibly imagine." Two women who said they
couldn't endure it were excused. After the trial the jury
were offered counselling to help them cope with the
gruesome details they had heard.

Jurors had to decide whether Dahmer suffered from a
mental illness which stopped him knowing his crimes
were wrong or which made him unable to stop himself
from committing them. District Attorney Michael Mc-
Cann reminded them that the case was about Dahmer's
state of mind when he killed, not about the carnage surrounding the deaths. "This is about responsibility for killing fifteen men," he advised. "Not responsibility for
dismemberment. Not responsibility for having sex with a
dead body." Dahmer sat silently during most of the jury
selection, looking at the floor or at the judge, although he
occasionally looked at potential jurors with sideways
glances. If found insane, he would be sent to a mental
hospital and could petition for release every six months.
If judged to be sane, he would receive a mandatory life
prison sentence for each murder. Wisconsin has no death
penalty.

One of the officers who had taken down Dahmer's
confession described to the court how calm and com-
posed the killer was as he talked for hours about how he
had mutilated his victims, smoking cigarettes and drinking coffee as he went over the details. Detective Murphy
said that Dahmer told the police he "would have preferred that the victims stayed alive. However, he felt that
it was better to have them dead than to have them leave,"
he added. "He became more relaxed as conversations

went on. At the beginning there was no eye contact. Toward the end he would look at us and occasionally smile." Officer Murphy said he was like someone who had been caught doing "something wrong and was a little embarrassed about it." He said Dahmer told him of taking the bicep of one of his victims and frying it, using meat tenderizer on it and then eating it. "He said it tasted like beef."

Gerald Boyle argued that Dahmer's craving for sex with dead bodies and his fear of loneliness escalated into a killing spree that he couldn't control. Dahmer's acts were not those of a normal man, he said, but a man who was caught up in the "personification of Satan." Dahmer's early dabblings in necrophilia had involved an attempt to dig up a body from a cemetery but he had failed because the ground was frozen, said Boyle. He said that although Dahmer had tasted blood while working at the plasma clinic in Milwaukee in 1983, he didn't like it and had never tried it again. However, later in his killing spree he did perform acts of cannibalism. There were two occasions confirmed, but up to ten reported by Dahmer, it was said. Boyle expanded on the idea that Dahmer was "keeping" his victims with him to prevent them abandoning him—a grisly attempt to fulfil a need for human contact. "He ate body parts so these poor people he killed would become alive in him," said Boyle, claiming that the fact that Dahmer's victims wanted to leave drove him to kill them to keep them with him out of loneliness and out of his desire to have their bodies and enjoy them sexually in numerous ways. Dahmer could not perform sexual acts with men when they were awake, so he would drug them and then kill them. He said that after sex Dahmer missed feeling the heartbeats of his partners— and that was when he began experimenting with lobotomies to turn his victims into "Zombies or sex slaves . . . people who would be there for him." After Dahmer had drilled holes in the skulls of his unconscious victims, he

injected muriatic acid into their brains. Some died instantly, but one victim, Jeremiah Weinberger, walked
around for two days after being "lobotomized."

One clinical psychologist, Dr. Judith Becker, revealed
that Dahmer had planned to build a magical shrine which
would enable him to receive "special powers." Dahmer
had drawn a picture of this shrine, which featured a black
table and chair, incense burners and the skulls and skeletons of his victims. He had already bought the base of the
table and planned to illuminate it with blue lights di-
rected on to a backdrop curtain featuring a goat. Dahmer
had also bought a statue of a mythical monster, the griffin, which—like the goat—is sometimes used in Satanic
ceremonies. Dahmer told the psychologist that the griffin
captured the way he felt, in that it represented evil.

Throughout the terrible evidence offered during the
trial Dahmer's father and stepmother listened intently,
sometimes hugging relatives of Dahmer's victims. "They
knew that we were hurting too," Lionel Dahmer told
reporters and Shari added: "It's tragic. And what do we
say to those families out there who don't even have the
child to bury in many cases?" "I don't think I'll ever come
to terms with it," Mr. Dahmer said. "Nothing will ever be
the same again."

Dahmer spoke at the end of the trial, issuing an elaborate apology to the families of his victims and begging to
be forgiven for his "holocaust" of evil. "I hope God can
forgive me," he said. Lionel Dahmer, a religious man
who could never have imagined that when he bought his
small son his first chemistry set all those years ago, it
would one day lead to this horror, listened in sorrow,
saying later that Jeffrey would willingly have chosen
death as punishment. But Dahmer was not to get his
wish. He was declared to be sane and sentenced to fifteen
consecutive life sentences and was sent to the Columbia
Correctional Institution at Portage, about eighty miles
north-west of Milwaukee, where he lived in an isolated

glass cage reminiscent of that which contained Hannibal the Cannibal in the movie *The Silence of the Lambs*. The high-tech equipment and design made it one of the most secure and safe prisons in the country, but it ultimately didn't save Dahmer, who was killed in 1994 in an attack by fellow inmates.

Those people who had seen *The Silence of the Lambs* realized, watching Dahmer, that charming, powerful psychopaths like Hannibal Lecter exist mainly in fiction. The courtroom crowds in Milwaukee may have been disappointed to see, not the wild-eyed Devil incarnate, but an untidy, somewhat insubstantial young man who kept his eyes downcast and remained passive throughout the trial. His manner changed only once, to display a grisly sense of humour. The day that the case went to the jury, he brought into court a copy of a supermarket tabloid with his picture on the cover. The headline read: "Milwaukee Cannibal Kills His Cellmate." The story said Dahmer also ate the cellmate. Dahmer flashed the paper around in disdainful amusement. "Isn't it amazing what they come up with?" asked the man who may not have eaten his cellmate but *had* killed and partially eaten seventeen other people. The irony of his words was lost on him.

10

"The Stubborn Beast Flesh Grows Back"

Did he live his life again in every detail of desire, temptation, and surrender during that supreme moment of complete knowledge? He cried in a whisper at some image, at some vision—he cried out twice, a cry that was no more than a breath—"The horror! The horror!"

Joseph Conrad: *The Heart of Darkness*

Andrei Romanovich always stayed close to his mother. He knew what could happen to small children who wandered too far from home. Terrible stories were told, of wolves in the wild land, just waiting in the undergrowth, their yellow eyes glittering, waiting, waiting. Waiting for a boy like himself who had strayed away from the safety of his village, who had chased foolishly after a thrown stone or to investigate a sudden fluttering in a bush. Waiting for a loyal blanket of dusk to conceal their stealthy advance on a village to find that lone, straggling boy idly humming as he scrawls in the dust with a stick. They pounce. Showing no mercy, they gobble him up. Andrei Romanovich knew. His mother had warned her sweet-faced boy.

And he had heard tales of other monsters: dragons with fierce teeth that ached to tear into the tender flesh of little children; witches who would wheedle children into their houses and, hurling them into cages, would keep and fatten the boys, then would chop them into little pieces and eat them all up. Andrei Romanovich shivered with a thrill of exciting horror at such stories. Other boys might scoff at tales of werewolves and witches, other boys might laugh at him and call him names for clinging to his mother's skirts, just as they jeered at his inept responses at school when he failed to give correct answers, even though the words he needed were there, on the blackboard. The other children could not know how bad Andrei's eyesight was, how the chalk writing became a blur as he gazed as hard as he could to no avail. They could not know what he knew about the true savagery of the world. That was why, timid and shy, he never strayed far from his mother. For he knew that along with the dragons and witches, there were real human monsters out there who could perform worse acts than the wolves he sometimes heard howling at night. His mother had told him.

He knew what had happened to his brother Stepan, only a few years before he himself had been born in 1936. Stalin's regime had caused widespread famine. Thousands of Soviet citizens in the southern republics were being starved as Stalin tried to force private farmers into collectives. The people of Andrei's village, Yablochnoye in the Ukraine, struggled and suffered, along with the rest of the Soviet Union. But no one he knew had sunk to the level which, it was said, some had. Little Stepan had wandered too far from home, his mother had told Andrei time and again, her eyes filling up with tears every time she repeated the tale. And Stepan never returned. The child was captured, killed and eaten, by hungry people. His mother wept as she told Andrei and his sister Tatyana the full horror of what had happened to Stepan. It was an awful warning. Andrei was appalled. The story haunted his mind. As he grew older, his passive reserve caused him to be isolated from the other boys. He lived in terror

of them discovering his other secret: that although he was
a big boy now, he still had a small child's problem in bed
at night. He could not understand why so often he woke
up wet in the morning—but he knew he could not bear
the ridicule if his schoolmates found out. Andrei re-
treated into the world of his imagination. Into his mind,
again and again, would come terrifying images of what
had happened to his older brother, the brother who
would have been united with him against the taunts of
the other children. Now they scolded him with taunts of
"Traitor!" hissing the word as he passed. He was
ashamed. His father was to blame. A Soviet soldier, he
had been captured by the Nazis during the war and
placed in a prisoner-of-war camp. On his return to the
Soviet Union, he was arrested again, an enemy of the
people for allowing himself to be captured, was placed in
a work camp far from home and was regarded as an
outcast because of it. His family suffered their neighbours' spite because of this . . . and the boy bore it
badly.

And as Andrei Romanovich approached adolescence,
the images developed more richly. The terror, the
screams, the blood. The feast. Instead of revolting him,
the fearsome fantasies came to evoke in him a response
of another sort. The boy was turning into a man—his
bodily responses to his fantasies told him that. Yet his
only attempted seduction of a girl had ended in humiliating failure, and the stirring in his groin only occurred
when he was held in the thrall of his extraordinary
dreams. The sex-talk which caused lewd merriment in the
other boys, the crude pictures they would pass round, all
these things left him cold and disgusted. No, the source
of Andrei Romanovich Chikatilo's stimulation was rather
more disturbing . . .

As she checked herself over in the mirror, Fayina wondered whether she would care for Tatyana's brother. If

Tatyana was to be believed, Andrei Romanovich sounded like quite a catch: twenty-seven years old, shy, gentle and well educated. Tall, too, which was always an attraction as far as she was concerned, being on the large side herself. It was 1963. In Britain, the Beatles were inducing hysteria in teenage fans; in America, John F. Kennedy was planning his fateful Dallas trip; and in Novoshakhtinsk, Fayina, twenty-four-year-old daughter of a pit-worker, hummed as she prepared for the meeting with Tatyana and Andrei which was to change her life.

As she had expected, she liked Tatyana's brother. He was good-looking, in a soft sort of way, and although his shoulders sloped in a manner which was perhaps unmasculine, for it gave his neck the appearance of being elongated, Andrei was otherwise powerfully built and treated Fayina with such reverence and respect that he captivated her. As their relationship progressed, she realized that Andrei was shy and insecure, so shy that he never even kissed her, but this added to his appeal, for although she was not head-over-heels in love, Fayina liked so much about him: he did not drink or smoke, he was quietly spoken, subdued in his dress—he was no flashy fly-by-night. Ordinary, that was what he was. Some might call him boring, with his drab clothes and quiet reserve. He might never be very rich or very famous, but she didn't care: she liked his ordinariness. They were married that same year.

The first night, Fayina knew there was something wrong. Andrei's shyness was embarrassing. His attempts at love-making were painfully inept and she seemed unable to arouse his passion. They gave up. For a week, Fayina tried to persuade Andrei to try again and finally, using all her skills of seduction and patient dexterity, the marriage was consummated. As the couple's life together continued, it became clear that sex was an ordeal for Andrei, that he was almost repelled by intimacy with the female body. He performed perfunctorily, without emotion, passion or variation, very seldom, and only managed to complete the act with a great deal of manual help from his wife. But the infrequent sex was enough to produce two children—Ludmilla in 1965 and Yuri in 1969—and the relationship was successful in other ways. Andrei was determined to better himself and studied at home, eventually gaining degrees in Russian literature, engineering and Marxist-Leninism. He was a faithful, almost fanatical, Party member and wrote articles for newspapers on Soviet patriotism and morality. Eventually he got a job as a teacher. Sex wasn't everything, thought Fayina. Andrei was a good father and never became angry with the children. Fayina was proud of her hard-working, non-flamboyant, clever husband teaching the Soviet children of tomorrow at his school.

What he was teaching them was another matter. Not many years passed before Andrei Chikatilo was caught molesting little girls at his school. He discovered he liked their fear after grabbing one girl who screamed and pushed him away. Such resistance gave him pleasure. Was there a subconscious link there between his act and the seizure of struggling little Stepan forty years earlier? Who knows? When his sexual peccadilloes were uncovered, he eventually lost his job. But there was no official inquiry, no charges were brought, so Fayina remained in ignorance. He took another job, an inferior one at a mining school, and moved into a school-owned house in Shakhty. Fayina also got a job at the school. And unknown to his wife, Chikatilo bought another house in Shakhty as well: a run-down, three-roomed shack in the shabbiest part of town. Here, he was to bring a succession of prostitutes in an effort to overcome his impotence. With his odd, prudish morality, they were forbidden fruit. Unlike his good, pure Fayina to whom he looked up so earnestly, these women were low creatures: loose and promiscuous. They were prepared to perform sexual acts which he would never have dreamed of suggesting to

Fayina. So he brought his despised whores to this place. He also brought small girls to the filthy, broken-down hut, where he would sexually assault them, but, in a community where secretiveness was second nature, never so seriously as to bring the law down upon him. This house was to be the place where, almost by accident, he first discovered the true nature of his own terrible desires.

It was 1978 and little Lena Zakotnova was nine, the same age as Chikatilo's son Yuri. Chikatilo spotted her at the tram-stop in Shakhty. In her red coat and brown fur hat, she was on her way home from an after-school skating trip when Chikatilo began chatting easily to her. He talked of school, her friends, her interests; he knew how to talk to children, for he had been communicating with them for years in his work. Lena was dancing from foot to foot and confided in this pleasant, grandfatherly man that she badly needed the toilet. "I only live round the corner," said the man, smiling. "You can go there." It was as easy as that for Andrei Chikatilo.

As soon as he had Lena in the squalid little house, he threw her to the ground and tore at her clothes, silencing her screams with an arm on her throat. Unable to stand the look of reproach in her eyes, he blindfolded her with her own scarf and tried to rape the child, but he could not sustain an erection. Seized by a sudden impulse, he took out his knife, which he carried for self-protection, and thrust it into the child's lower abdomen, the unflinching steel substituting for his limp penis. As if transformed into a wild, carnivorous beast, he revelled in the blood and gore. He thrust the knife again. And again. And, miraculously to him, there was no mistaking the sexual relief his terrible act drew from him.

Chikatilo marvelled as he realized how simple his needs were, after all. And how simple, too, it would be to pluck victims from the streets; helpless people like this small girl whose life-blood was still pumping stickily out of her tiny body. Such people would give him the sexual satisfaction that had eluded him all these years. And it had taken him until now, at forty-two, to know what was necessary to arouse and satiate him: blood. Emerging from his monstrous reverie, Chikatilo looked absently at the body of the child and knew that he must dispose of it speedily. Tucking it beneath his arm, as if it were a doll, he left the house quickly and hastened to the banks of the nearby Grushevka River, tossing the little body in, with Lena's school satchel after her. Then, feeling a warm glow which could have been stoked by the fires of Hell, he hurried home to Fayina.

Lena's body was not swept far from Shakhty, as Chikatilo had hoped, but remained close to the house where he had murdered the child. The police inquiry should, by rights, have put Chikatilo under grave suspicion. They had evidence that he had frequently taken children and women back to the house; a neighbour had reported that, unusually, that night the light had been left on overnight although the house was empty; there was blood on the road outside; most importantly of all, they had an eye-witness, a woman, who had seen Lena leave the tram-stop with Chikatilo just before her disappearance. She gave a police artist an excellent description of the tall, bespectacled man with sloping shoulders. They also discovered the child molestation complaints which had been lodged against Chikatilo in the past and learned that a man answering his description had been seen hanging around the girls' toilets at local schools. But the sketch alone was enough to identify Chikatilo and he was pulled in for questioning. He hung his head in shame and admitted his "sexual weakness" where interfering with little girls was concerned, but insisted that it was in the past; his interest in sexual matters had declined. Fayina, who went with him, would have seconded that—and she swore that her husband had spent the entire evening at home. The police let Chikatilo go, but kept his file open.

Then they had what they believed to be a big break in their hunt for the murderer.

Only yards from the place where Lena's body was found lived a man called Alexander Kravchenko who had served a prison sentence for the murder of a teenage girl eight years previously and was just making a new life for himself with his wife and family. But with astonishing self-destructive misjudgment, a month after Lena's death, Kravchenko was in trouble with the law again. He indulged in some petty theft, was caught red-handed with the stolen goods and was hauled into the police station. Having discovered that Kravchenko had the same semen type as that found on Lena's body, the police used all the means at their disposal—some of them dubious, to say the least—to break his alibi for the night of her death. Eventually they succeeded and Kravchenko confessed to Chikatilo's crime. Later he denied his confession, but his denials were disregarded. No one bothered asking the eye-witness who had been the last to see Lena alive to identify Kravchenko as the man who had accompanied the child. And no one visited Chikatilo again. Five years later, Kravchenko, still protesting his innocence, was executed for Lena's murder.

After his first murder, it was almost three years before the beast within Chikatilo rose up to feast again. By this time he had changed jobs once more: now he was a supply clerk for an industrial firm, which, conveniently for Chikatilo, involved travelling farther afield to collect and deliver goods, often with an overnight stay. When he was not required to stay on somewhere, he invented a reason —"business," he would tell his fellow delivery-man. On 3 September 1981 he found himself in Rostov where, as in any large city, there was a large population of itinerants, vagrants, homeless runaways and wretched, unhappy young women who would do almost anything for the offer of a meal. One such was Larisa Tkachenko, aged seventeen, whose red jacket caught Chikatilo's attention as she stood at a bus-stop. Red, the colour of his fantasies. They chatted, and Larisa indicated that she was prepared to have sex with Chikatilo in exchange for a little supper. Together they set off for the overgrown badlands on the other side of the River Don, a place popular with young lovers. But of this ill-matched pair, only one was to walk back over the bridge.

As soon as they were out of sight of passers-by, Chikatilo became a monster. Despite seizing Larisa roughly to feed his domination fantasy and violently ripping off her red jacket and her other clothes, his potency still failed him. This time he knew exactly what he needed: suffering, screams and, most of all, blood. Strangling Larisa to near-unconsciousness, he tore into her with his teeth, biting her neck like an animal deranged by the smell of blood, bathing his face in it. He bit off part of her breast and swallowed it, then mutilated her genitals, discovering anew that this taste for blood guaranteed him orgasm. Perhaps he justified his actions by telling himself that Larisa was a depraved, loose woman who deserved her fate. With the extraordinary primness which had commanded him to be celibate until marriage, and then to respect his wife as a Madonna figure, this contradictory logic is a probability, particularly since he was, after his arrest, to describe his victims as "degenerate elements" whose "right to life" was questionable. Before he left the scene of carnage, he cleaned the blood off his face and hands with Larisa's clothing, with her red coat. He planned to change his clothes as soon as possible; in the bag he always carried with him there was another outfit for just such an occasion, but as he prepared to leave, he found himself offended by Larisa's naked body, exposed for all to see. To preserve her decency, he covered her body with pages from *Pravda* and the *Young Communist*, which, being a loyal Party member, he just happened to have with him.

Nine months passed before Chikatilo was seized by his *alter ego* again. This time the victim was a thirteen-year-old girl from a good family. Lyuba Biryuk was waiting at a bus-stop close to her home village of Zaplavskaya on a warm summer's day in 1982 when Chikatilo saw her, chatted to her, then agreed to abandon the wait for the bus and walk towards her home with her. The path took them close to the woods and Lyuba's fate was sealed. Chikatilo's shy, insecure persona was swamped from then on by the monster within him. Over the next six months, he committed as many murders in the many far-flung districts where his job took him. Now he was less choosy over whom he took: these six victims were males and females, aged between nine and sixteen; all they had in common was their powerlessness, which made them easy prey. Chikatilo was essentially a cowardly man, and would never have tried to tackle someone who might fight back or escape. Using the knife he carried with him, he stabbed his victims in a frenzy, his "trademark" being knife-injuries around the eyes. Sometimes he gouged eyes out. Such a thing was rare, inducing the police to speculate that the killer believed the old superstition that a person's eyes are imprinted with the last thing they see before they die, in this case Chikatilo himself. Perhaps the killer was trying to obliterate the accusing, agonized stare of the person dying so cruelly at his hands. Or perhaps he was merely prolonging the suffering, enjoying the screams, causing maximum pain—the pain which gave him such acute pleasure—in the most devastatingly brutal way imaginable. Certainly Chikatilo's other actions with the bodies bore this theory out. Eventually his sensation-seeking necessitated more and more bizarre horrors: he would bite off victims' tongues and breasts and eat them, cut off noses and lips, slice off boys' genitals—or remove the testes, leaving the empty scrotal sac—and excise girls' internal reproductive organs, then devour them on the spot, sometimes cooking them over a rough fire he built at a nearby spot in the forest. So vicious was his butchery that a number of policemen broke down and requested to be removed from the case. Some investigators even theorized that the murders had been committed by Satanists or a gang collecting testicles for transplants.

Most chilling of all, sometimes forensic evidence suggested that the savagery had taken place while the victim still lived, that it was the pain of torture, more than the death, which gave Chikatilo his horrible pleasure. This, too, sets him apart from the majority of sex murderers for, as Dr. J. Paul de River said in his 1950 book, *Crime and the Sexual Psychopath*: "The lust murderer usually, *after killing his victim*, [my italics] tortures, cuts, maims or slashes the victim in the regions on or about the genitalia, rectum, breast in the female, and about the neck, throat and buttocks, as usually these parts contain sexual significance to him and serve as sexual stimulus." In his actions, Chikatilo had more in common with Albert Fish and with a historical monster like Gilles de Rais who, in the fifteenth century, killed, raped and sodomized more than 150 children after inflicting the most barbarous tortures upon them purely for the sadistic pleasure their agonies offered him.

The police in Rostov and its surrounding areas were becoming worried. They were beginning to recognize the killings as the work of one killer, but this fact took time to dawn upon them because the various murders were committed in different districts, with each police force dealing with individual cases. The notion of a serial killer was relatively unknown in the Soviet Union and they were without the sophisticated techniques of the West, such as the Criminal Investigative Analysis Programme, a computer profiling technique developed by the FBI at their Behavioural Sciences Unit in Quantico, Virginia over the previous decade. Here, using information gathered from hundreds of interviews with serious offenders, some on

Death Row, the Unit works to compile psychological profiles of criminals. When a crime is committed, evidence gathered from the scene is translated into behavioural characteristics, enabling an analyst to build up an "offender profile." Although this is used in many varieties of crime, it has proved an invaluable tool for American crime-fighters in apprehending serial killers, for even if a serial killer is crossing State lines, his murders are fed into the same computer and common indicators are then discovered. A sadistic killer's *modus operandi*—the result of his oft-rehearsed fantasies—tells psychologists into which of several categories he might fall. Broadly, the two main ones are the "Organized Nonsocial" killer and the "Disorganized Asocial" killer. The Organized Nonsocial murderer presents a cunning façade of warmth and friendliness to society while secretly committing his carefully-planned and methodical crimes, which he knows will shock that same society; indeed, this is part of his aim. He is also likely to cruise around, looking for a victim and a safe opportunity to commit his crime undetected. The Disorganized Asocial individual, on the other hand, is a loner, a friendless outsider who feels rejected, but who murders in a more uncontrolled and less methodical way and is then likely to abandon the body with no attempt to hide it. In contrast, the Organized Nonsocial type may, in an attempt to control matters further, even go so far as to remove the body and then later put it somewhere else to be found, whereupon he may follow its discovery and the murder inquiry with excitement.

What would the FBI's Behavioural Sciences Unit have made of Andrei Chikatilo? The driven frenzy of the attacks would have slotted him into the "disorganized" mould, as would Chikatilo's alienated personality, yet he was carefully calculating in the extreme. His fifty-three murders bore testimony to that. Without doubt, then, Chikatilo was an organized killer. If he had been a disorganized type, how did he control his violent urges until he had lured his victim to a suitable killing field . . . at least fifty-three times? And his method was to spend hours trying to pick up a suitable victim—indeed, when he was pulled in on one occasion, plain-clothes detectives in Rostov had watched him for *nine hours* while he attempted to persuade one woman after another to go with him. His patient approach to female down-and-outs was friendly and chatty with an invitation to have sex. Children who fell prey to him were usually waiting at bus-stops when he opened a conversation, telling them after he had won their confidence: "I'm going there. We'll never catch a bus from here; I know a short cut." And the child—one little boy was only seven years old—would place his or her small hand in that of this monstrous beast, who led them into the forest . . . in much the same way, Chikatilo would later suggest, that someone had abducted his infant brother Stepan in the 1930s. And their fates were not dissimilar. "He made contact with people very easily," a policeman was to reflect many years later. "He had an amazing talent for it. He could join a bus queue and say to the person in front: 'Hey, where did you buy those beautiful mushrooms?' and before you knew it he would have the whole crowd chatting." At his trial, when Chikatilo himself was asked why children went with him, he had his own suggestion: "I must have had a kind of magnetism," he said.

Meanwhile, Chikatilo carried on what appeared to be a normal public life. His work-mates did not like him, regarding him as robot-like, unable to make independent decisions and controlled by his wife, but Fayina, suspecting nothing of his double life, was contented. He was a "perfect husband," she was to declare later. Chikatilo later revealed to psychologists that Fayina had upset him by having an abortion without his knowledge—as if he had high regard for the sanctity of life—but the couple were not in disharmony. However, it was during 1984 that

Chikatilo's unsatisfactory sex life with his wife ended completely; she even urged him to see a psychiatrist about his loss of libido, but he had found a more rewarding substitute and pursued it with a vengeance. Chikatilo's need for blood was driving him more frequently and to ever more sadistic methods. In two months of summer 1984, he killed ten people—more than one a week. But at the end of 1984 with more than thirty murders on their hands, the police were no nearer catching him. They were, it is true, beset by difficulties. The victims were very different in age, sex and social status, even though a number were drifters, prostitutes, mentally handicapped youngsters and kids from broken homes who ended up on the streets and sleeping in railway stations. Because of this, these people were not reported missing and even that first step in a murder inquiry—the identification of the body—was often a problem. But the police also rejected their most powerful weapon of detection: publicity. A mixture of the customary Soviet secrecy and the desire not to cause panic made the police hush up the news that Rostov had on its streets a sadistic murderer who picked up people at random and slaughtered them in the most unspeakable of ways—and had done this thirty-odd times already. The media, still controlled by the authorities, dutifully obeyed and kept the terrible news quiet.

The vagrant nature of many of the victims was, then, to Chikatilo's advantage, and like Britain's murderer of, mainly, prostitutes, Yorkshire Ripper Peter Sutcliffe, he even tried to pretend to himself that he was performing a street-cleaning service. He was disgusted by the squalor and the promiscuity of the women, the alcoholism, the shabbiness and dirtiness of these fallen people. They were little more than objects to him—"rootless elements," he called them—there solely to provide him with gratification. They deserved what they got. After his arrest Chikatilo openly tried to justify his treatment of these people. "They followed me like dogs," he said. "Vagrants . . . they beg, demand and seize things . . . They crawl into your very soul, demanding money, food, vodka and offering themselves for sex . . . I saw scenes of these vagrants' sex lives and I remembered my humiliation, that I could not prove myself as a real man." But like Jeffrey Dahmer, who despised his own homosexuality but justified his murders on the grounds that his victims were gay, Chikatilo had much in common with the "vermin" he eradicated: like them, he was a misfit, an outsider of a society which he felt had rejected him, rather than the other way round.

But the police were also to be condemned for their sloppiness (as, in fact, the Public Prosecutor's office and the judge at Chikatilo's trial did criticize them.) At the murder-scenes, forensic clues were lost because of the bulldozing clumsiness of the officers; additionally, other items of evidence had simply been mislaid. In their anxiety to clear up the case, the police pinned blame wherever it might stick. Two retarded young men, pulled in for another offence, confessed to ten of the murders, and the police were jubilant. Then, while they were held in custody, more murders occurred, whereupon two more retarded youths were arrested. They also confessed. With each new discovery of a body a succession of mentally handicapped males were arrested and confessed. The police called them "the halfwits" and fought to defend their actions, but while they were content to believe in the guilt of their handicapped youths, they were not putting maximum effort into catching Russia's worst serial killer of all time. Eventually, after the intervention of the Public Prosecutor's Office, the retarded men were freed and the murders acknowledged as the work of one man. Because Chikatilo buried their bodies in woods beside railway tracks, it earned him the nickname "The Forest Strip Killer."

* * *

In September 1984, Chikatilo was arrested by the Rostov police. Officers Zanasovski and Akhmatkhanov were on plain-clothes patrol near the city's central bus station one evening and observed Chikatilo behaving oddly, getting on buses and trying to pick up women—staring at them, smiling and chatting, or pressing up against them—then getting off to catch one bus after another in opposite directions. He was "ill at ease and was always twisting his head from one side to the other . . . I had the impression that he was trying to make sure that he was not being followed," Detective Akhmatkhanov reported. With hindsight, we can assume Chikatilo, carnivorous beast that he was, was clearly out hunting. What Inspector Aleksandr Zanasovski recalled was that this man was the same one he had questioned a couple of weeks earlier, behaving in exactly the same way at the nearby railway station. Chikatilo had let him know he was an educated man, telling the inspector that being a teacher, he liked and was interested in young people. Zanasovski checked with one of the women he had approached and it seemed he had done nothing more than chat in a friendly way. Chikatilo was sent on his way, and now Zanasovski was watching him once more, showing the same persistence.

And what persistence. The officers watched for more than nine hours throughout the night as Chikatilo relentlessly pursued one woman after another. His patience almost paid off when a young girl performed an indecent act with him, but then he returned to his hunt for prey. But the sex act was enough of an excuse for the policemen to arrest Chikatilo for licentious behaviour. When they opened his briefcase and discovered it contained a kitchen knife with an eight-inch blade together with some lengths of rope and a jar of petroleum jelly—and then found out he came from Shakhty, where many murders had been committed—Zanasovski and Akhmatkhanov believed they had caught the serial killer of whom the public, at last, had been told. Chikatilo was questioned for two days during the time he was held for the public conduct offence and confessed, again, to his "sexual weakness" for young girls and his lack of relations with his wife. This, he told officers, was no longer important to him because he was approaching fifty. But the biggest blow to the police was that a blood test showed that Chikatilo's Type A blood did not match the semen type found on and in the victims' bodies, which was AB. Just as nobody thought about bringing in the handful of witnesses who had been the last to see some of the murder victims alive, nobody thought to test Chikatilo's semen type, for it was an accepted scientific fact that blood and semen always matched. Since then, science has proved that in rare instances this is untrue. Chikatilo was an exception to normal humans in so many ways; he was exceptional in this, too, and it was a tremendous stroke of luck for him. The only thing the police had on their captive was the reported theft of a roll of linoleum and a car battery from a company he had worked for in Shakhty—a crime which was to cost him his membership of the Communist Party, causing him enormous shame and increasing his sense of society's injustice. In due course he came up in court over the theft and was sentenced to a year's corrective labour. But because he had already been held in custody for some time, he was freed. He refrained from murdering for many months, but before 1985 was out, two more people had fallen victim to his murderous lust.

The Soviet Union's Department for Crimes of Special Importance became involved in the man-hunt in 1985, when its deputy head, Chief Inspector Issa Kostoyev arrived in Rostov to head up the investigation. More than half a million people had been interviewed by the time Chikatilo was caught. The investigation was so wide that it solved 1,062 unrelated crimes, including ninety-five murders. Every school was contacted, its children urged not to go with strange men and asked if anyone had ever approached them. Psychologists were called upon to take a leaf out of the FBI's book and try to draw up a psychological profile of their serial killer. One was Aleksandr Bukhanovsky, who was also to interview Chikatilo at length when he was finally arrested in December 1990. The profile was remarkably accurate: Bukhanovsky painted a portrait of a middle-aged, self-pitying misfit, heterosexual but impotent. With only the victims' remains and the circumstances of their deaths to work on, Dr. Bukhanovsky suggested that the killer would be apparently normal with a regular job. In addition he believed the subject would be unable to stop killing.

He was right again. 1987: three murders; 1988: three murders; 1989: five murders. As the police began to get more desperate, Chikatilo began using even greater cunning by committing his murders farther afield. Another change of job, into the supplies section of a company in Novocherkassk, gave him even more freedom to travel on business trips and he exploited this, killing in places as far apart as Moscow, the Urals and Leningrad (now St. Petersburg)—evidence of the premeditated nature of his attacks. Predictably, the methods he used changed too: there was less frenzy and more precision in the way he used his knife. The cutting or biting off of male genitals and the excision of a female uterus was followed by his chewing the organs. Uteruses, he said later, "were so beautiful and elastic." Like a surgeon he performed his abominable "operations" upon the helpless, terrified youngsters he had stolen from the streets and from those who loved them. His victims, more often than not, were little boys now, not girls. Like all sadistic killers he began to search for variation. Since his satisfaction came from inflicting pain, rather than from a recognized conventional sexual interest in a person of a particular gender, the identity of the individual became immaterial.

As was also inevitable, the blood-lust began to come upon Chikatilo so frequently that it dominated his life, which revolved around plans for the next sacrifice to his power. 1990 saw him killing a total of eight more people. But as his boldness increased, so too did the alertness of the population. Eye-witness reports began slowly to come in, offering descriptions of a tall, middle-aged man with glasses seen in the vicinity of, or in conversation with, those who were later found murdered. Or he was seen trying to induce small boys to go with him, telling them, "I know your mother, I'll take you to her." Encouraged, the police stepped up their manpower even more. Six hundred police officers in plain clothes rode the trains and buses up and down routes which were judged to be favourites of the killer. Police were to be found staking out the Forest Strip area, hiding in ditches or posing as mushroom-pickers in the woods. And eventually, it paid off.

At four o'clock in the afternoon of 7 November 1990, a sergeant based at the railway station in Donleskhoz watched a tall, middle-aged man with glasses, wearing a grey suit and carrying a shoulder-bag, emerge from the woods and wash his hands and his shoes in a nearby water hydrant. He had a bandaged finger and a red stain on his cheek which looked like blood. Leaves and twigs were stuck to his clothes. The policeman asked for his documents and discovered it was Andrei Chikatilo—a name which meant nothing to him, even though it was soon to cause a chill to run up and down the spines of those who had read or heard of his dreadful acts. Chikatilo, glib and unflustered, was not detained, but when the report of this sighting found its way on to Kostoyev's desk, as it eventually did a full six days later—yet another example of police sloppiness—the name rang a bell with him. He pulled out the file on Andrei Chikatilo from his 1984 arrest, when he was freed because of the difference between his blood and semen type, and was reminded of recent Japanese research which stated that, rarely, this was possible in an individual. The police returned to the woods near the station in Donleskhoz. There, after a long search, they found the body of 22-year-old Sveta Korostik, killed by Chikatilo just before he had so casually chatted to the police officer at the Donleskhoz station. She had suffered many knife wounds, her tongue and nipples had been cut off and were missing and the mutilation was clearly the work of the Forest Strip Murderer. Sveta was to be Chikatilo's last victim.

When investigations were made with Chikatilo's employers, they discovered that his long-distance business trips coincided with places where murders had been committed. But, in an effort to catch Chikatilo red-handed, he was tailed and, as in 1984, detectives watched his determined efforts to pick up youngsters on the trains, particularly those weakling stragglers of the herd, the children who had become separated from the mainstream of passengers. Reluctant to risk Chikatilo murdering again, after a few days they arrested him. For a week, Chikatilo denied the crimes. But this time his blood and semen were both tested and they were discovered to be different. Twenty-one lives would have been saved if only this had been done in 1984. Kostoyev began to subtly suggest to Chikatilo that the crimes could only have been committed by an insane man. Gradually Chikatilo realised that only insanity could save him from the executioner, and, encouraged by the psychiatrist Aleksandr Bukhanovsky, who was brought in to coax words from him, he began to talk. In one statement he described his lifelong depression and humiliation because he had been the butt of people's jokes and because he was impotent. Self-pityingly, he remarked on the unfairness of managements who "took advantage" of his "weak character" to make him leave "without reason" (neglecting to mention his molestation of small girls and the charge of theft which was proven against him). He described his victims as "déclassé elements" and "scum," implying that it was their own fault that they had been killed, and even categorizing them with a private code: EM for easy morals, D for drifter, A for adolescent. He claimed to be unable to control his actions during his perverted sexual acts. "How much of this is my responsibility?" he asked. "What I did was not for sexual pleasure. Rather it brought me some peace of mind . . . What I did, I did after watching videos of perverted sex acts, cruelties, horrors."

Kostoyev charged Chikatilo with thirty-six murders from 1982 to 1990 and also with raping or sodomizing his victims. Chikatilo indignantly denied the latter charges; his impotence would have made that impossible, he said. He was also insulted at any suggestion of theft from his victims. Then he amazed his interrogators by confessing to nineteen more killings, including his first, Lena Zakotnova in Shakhty, whose picture he picked out from a selection of photographs of little girls and for which another man had been found guilty and executed. Understandably, the police were horrified to learn that Chikatilo had been the culprit, but their reluctance to believe this evaporated as he gave details about the killing which only the murderer would have known. His memory for each of his victims and the events surrounding each killing was remarkable, and he took the police to many places where he had buried bodies of people that the police had not even known were missing, or whose murders had been attributed to other, unknown, killers. An important part of any Russian criminal investigation is the "experiment," during which the accused demonstrates in front of a camera exactly how he committed the crime. Using a tailor's dummy, Chikatilo showed how he had murdered each person, including that first time with little Lena. Showing no remorse, he chatted and made jokes as he performed his grisly death-act. The remains of two of the victims Chikatilo remembered killing could not be found, despite his certainty about their location. The police gave these up.

Fayina Chikatilo felt sick. When she was first told her

husband had been arrested, she thought it was because he had been making a nuisance of himself with the authorities, protesting in numerous letters about some garages being built close to his son's house. She could not believe Andrei was really capable of the terrible things they were saying he had done. After all, hadn't he always been a devoted father who loved his own children? How could he perpetrate such abominably evil acts upon other small children? As for these crimes being sexually motivated, she found this hard to understand, because of his lack of interest in sex with her. When she accepted the truth, she also began to fit pieces of the jigsaw puzzle into place: the business trips and the nights away; the blood he sometimes had on his clothes, which he claimed was from cuts he had suffered when unloading goods. Unreasonably, Fayina felt a huge burden of guilt; that she was to blame for trusting him and not inquiring too deeply into his activities. If she had, she said, she would have done something to stop him, but—"I could never imagine him being able to murder one person, let alone fifty-three . . . he could never hurt anyone." Overcoming her repulsion, she visited her husband once, to get his authorization for her to have access to the couple's savings. Hanging his head like a naughty child, Chikatilo could not meet his wife's gaze, but used his pet-name for her. "If only I had listened to you, Fenechka . . . If only I had followed your advice and got treatment," he whined. Fayina was too appalled to have any more to do with Chikatilo, and the two children Ludmilla and Yuri found it equally hard to come to terms with the fact that they had been fathered by such a monster. The family were later forced to change their name and move away after receiving death-threats. "I crossed him out of my life as if he had never existed," Fayina later told writer Peter Conradi.

Chikatilo believed that he could claim that temporary insanity had fired his actions, and suggested that he could be treated. Scientists would be interested in him because he was unique, owing to the number of his victims, which made his case "exceptional," he said. After his confessions, Chikatilo was sent for psychiatric evaluation to the Serbsky Institute in Moscow, where he spent three months being tested by many doctors. In the old Soviet Union, this was the place where the authorities infamously used Soviet psychology as a form of political control rather than to investigate the complexities of the psyche. Here, "enemies of the state" were likely to be certified and interned in asylums, but with the break-up of the Soviet Union, the Serbsky Institute gained a new, healthier profile influenced by Western methods, and under the guidance of psychiatrists like Boris Shostakovich and Andrei Tkachenko, who specialize in the study of the criminally insane, the Serbsky psychiatrists noted that Chikatilo discussed the murders "calmly and coldly," and that he was not deranged enough to fail to realize he was committing wrong. On the contrary, said the reports, he was a sadist who was cautious in the extreme when carrying out his premeditated acts. It was noted that he was even discouraged from murdering when the weather was cold—during the winter months his murder rate dropped away. This "uncontrolled compulsion," it seemed, only took hold when it was convenient and comfortable for Chikatilo. He was declared legally sane.

The trial of Andrei Romanovich Chikatilo began on 14 April 1992 in Rostov-on-Don Regional Court. It was to last six months; perhaps unsurprising, given that the documentary evidence collected by investigators over the previous six months filled 200 volumes, covering, as it did, twelve years of murders committed in an area stretching from southern Russia and Ukraine to the Central Asian republic of Uzbekistan. Although Chikatilo had claimed fifty-five murders, only fifty-three were regarded as conclusive by the police, including Chikatilo's first murder in

Shakhty, that of Lena Zakotnova, for which Alexander Kravchenko had been executed. It took three days for Judge Leonid Akubzhanov to read out the evidence to a court packed with relatives, the media and other spectators magnetized by the ghoulishness of the crimes committed by the world's foremost serial killer; three days of interruptions as people repeatedly erupted into outbursts of anger, tears and abuse. As Chikatilo, dressed in grey trousers and an old shirt decorated with the rings symbol of the 1980 Moscow Olympics, stood or sat staring sullenly from behind the bars of a metal cage designed, not to keep him in, but to keep others out, the prosecutors detailed the grisly crimes he committed against women, boys aged between eight and sixteen, and girls aged between nine and seventeen. Relatives of victims—and even hardened soldiers keeping guard—fainted as they heard how Chikatilo boiled and ate the sawn-off testicles or nipples of his victims, or carved slits in some corpses to use for his own brand of necrophiliac sex, often not bothering to kill his trussed teenage victims before the butchery started. "He was constantly on the look-out for victims," Judge Akubzhanov said. "On holidays, on business trips, visiting relatives. He was always ready to kill."

Chikatilo countered this by remarking coolly at one point: "I did not need to look for them. Every step I took, they were there." He tried to convince the judge that he was a victim of Soviet totalitarianism. He had led a wretched life, having to travel constantly for work, stay in "dirty railway stations and miserable hotels" and put up with the rudeness of his bosses, he said. Then he claimed abnormality. "I am a mistake of nature, a mad beast," he declared—and it was true that Chikatilo appeared far from grandfatherly now. No longer looking like a respectable teacher of literature, his head had been shaved, giving him an evil appearance, and this was compounded when, after spending the early days either silent or making articulate pleas for a new trial on the grounds that everyone, including the judge, had allegedly already found him guilty, he suddenly decided to play crazy.

Portraying the Mr. Hyde figure which the world had expected when the search was on for the "Rostov Ripper," Chikatilo began lolling his head, rolling his eyes, gnashing his teeth and drooling, loudly singing the Communist anthem "Internationale," producing pornographic magazines, rattling the bars of his cage and even, on a couple of occasions, dropping his trousers or tearing off his clothes to wave his penis at the court, screaming: "Look at this useless thing. What do you think I could do with that?" Obviously it was beginning to dawn on Chikatilo that being found insane was his only chance of survival. "I am not a homosexual!" he ranted one day. Another day he yelled: "I have milk in my breasts; I am going to give birth!" Then he suddenly retracted his confession to the murder of Lena Zakotnova. Next, he claimed to remember other murders he had committed, saying at one point that he had killed seventy people. Next, he recanted on six murders to which he had already confessed. Another time-wasting strategy was to declare that he wanted the trial conducted in his native Ukrainian language, and to demand an interpreter. Yet another was to claim hallucinations and offer the belief that the KGB was firing invisible rays at him: standard schizophrenic symptoms suddenly harnessed by a killer playing a madman to Oscar-winning standards. Repeatedly, he was hauled from the court back to his cell and beaten by guards.

Throughout it all, the crowds keened, wailed and shouted. An elderly woman denounced Chikatilo as "a damned soul and an evil sadist." The aunt of one murdered boy shouted at one point: "This trial is rubbing salt into the wounds of the relatives of the victims." Voicing a popular view, she demanded: "Liquidate the criminal. Too much money is being spent on supporting his life." Many others concurred. Chikatilo had confessed, they said. What was the point of having a trial? "What's the use of announcing the verdict? It would have been a better idea to shoot him here at once," said a student from a nearby college.

Several times distraught relatives of victims tried to attack Chikatilo through his bars. Eventually they were penned upstairs in the gallery. One day the brother of a victim hurled a small metal ball at Chikatilo. It flew through the metal bars and missed his head by centimetres. When the guards went to arrest the man, other spectators gathered protectively around him. The guards did not pursue the arrest. The grief of parents who had lost sons and daughters was pitiable. Nina Beletskaya, whose twelve-year-old son Ivan disappeared and was murdered in Zaporozhe, Ukraine in 1987 after going to pick apricots in the forest near their home, broke down while giving evidence. "The day I buried my son, I gave him my word that I would try to live long enough to see his killer with my own eyes," she said. "I wanted to see this man who could rip open my son's stomach and then stuff mud in his mouth so that he would not cry out. I wanted to know what he looked like, to know which mother could bear such an animal. And now I see him." She told reporters: "Look, he's still smiling. He's taken part of my life . . . He's an animal. He doesn't deserve a human trial." Lida Khovata, whose ten-year-old son Alyosha was murdered in August 1989 said: "It's so painful I can't even describe it. I have no wish other than to kill him. I just want this to end."

On 15 October Judge Akubzhanov found Chikatilo guilty on all but one of the murder charges—a confession to the killing of a fifteen-year-old girl offered inadequate evidence—and amid shouts of fury and applause sentenced him to death by shooting—with a single bullet fired in the back of the head. As he spoke, the killer shouted "Swindlers," shrieked and snarled, threw himself around the metal cage and hurled his bench to one side.

Guards tried to grab the spitting and biting man as the angry crowd bayed for his blood. "You gave him nothing! Give him to us, give this murderer to us!" cried one woman. Others screamed: "Give him to us so we can tear him to pieces, as he did to our children!"

Chikatilo's lawyer, Marat Khabibulin, rejected the court's finding that his client was sane and announced that he would appeal to the Supreme Court of the Russian Federation in Moscow against the verdict, claiming the court had not properly evaluated Chikatilo's mental health. If the appeal fails, Chikatilo's death sentence will have to be confirmed by the Russian President's Commission on Pardoning. That may take some time, since in 1992 it was still considering death sentences handed down in 1989. Until that decision, Chikatilo will spend his days in a special cell isolated from ordinary prisoners who would probably kill him if they could. The father of one of his victims works at the Novocherkassk prison, where he is held.

Dr. Alexander Bukhanovsky's scientific fascination with the killer extended to regular visits to Chikatilo during the trial. He would take him his breakfast every day—and the cannibal asked that Bukhanovsky be with him at his execution. The psychiatrist believes that Chikatilo is insane and argues that he should be sent to a mental hospital. Does Chikatilo sit in his cell, reflect on his life and, like Joseph Conrad's evil character Kurtz in *Heart of Darkness*, shrink back in despair to glimpse the stark truth of his own terrible inhumanity, crying out: "The horror, the horror!"? Who can tell? But he certainly enjoys discussing himself with the doctor, Bukhanovsky, who says he is intrigued by both the killer's intelligence and the conflicts within his psyche. "He was a great theatre-goer. He could sit in a performance of something by Chekhov and be moved to tears, but then go out and murder someone," Bukhanovsky said. "His internal world is a thousand times richer than the surface expression of that world."

It was to Alexander Bukhanovsky that Chikatilo gave details of his "dreadful childhood." "When he started telling me about his life it was already the story of his illness," said Dr. Bukhanovsky. Chikatilo told the doctor about his brother Stepan, subject of his mother's fearful tales. "He was told the child was kidnapped, stolen and eaten. He found out about it when he was four. He reacted with such terror to the idea that it was possible to kidnap and eat a child that he remembered it all his life. On the one hand he found it terrible and frightening, on the other he had an unhealthy interest in it and his fantasies were all constantly concerned with it," said the psychiatrist.

Since Chikatilo's dreadful crimes, the stories of how he murdered and devoured his victims have become examples for Russian parents who want to warn their children against going with strangers. Just like the child Andrei Romanovich Chikatilo before them, Russian children are told by their mothers that there are human monsters around, eager to snatch them away, kill them and gobble them up. Andrei Romanovich turned out to be that archetypal bogey-man, that wolf in the forest. But there is one significant difference between the genuine scare-stories told to today's children, and that told to the four-year-old Chikatilo by his mother. For he was told the story; his sister confirmed this. But the authorities checked up on Chikatilo's childhood memories. And they could find no records or documents confirming the birth of a Stepan Chikatilo in Yablochnoye. None of the villagers remembered this boy, still less the terrifying fate which was said to have befallen one of their number.

On the other hand, Chikatilo, in all his impossible monstrosity, really exists outside the imagination.

11

Why?

You maggots make me sick. I am beyond your experience.

Richard Ramirez, the "Night Stalker,"
killer of fifteen in California

"I think you can provide some insight and advance this study."
"And what possible reason could I have to do that?"
"Curiosity."
"About what?"
"About why you're here. About what happened to you."
"Nothing happened to me, Officer Starling. *I* happened. You can't reduce me to a set of influences. You've given up good and evil for behaviourism, Officer Starling. You've got everyone in moral dignity pants—nothing is ever anybody's fault. Look at me, Officer Starling. Can you stand to say I'm evil? Am I evil, Officer Starling? . . . A census taker tried to quantify me once. I ate his liver with some fava beans and a big Amarone."

Thomas Harris: *The Silence of the Lambs*

Jeffrey Dahmer's crimes in Milwaukee came to light in the summer following the release of 1991's Oscar-winning film, *The Silence of the Lambs*. Small wonder, then, that the discovery of a man whose flat was littered with the body parts from eleven corpses, including a human heart in the freezer ("I was saving it to eat later," explained Dahmer) and a set of male genitals in a pot, provoked a rash of "the real Hannibal the Cannibal" headlines. But soon the abhorrence felt towards Dahmer's crimes was to take a new direction: the Russian cannibal killer Andrei Chikatilo, arrested in December 1991, perpetrated such repulsively cruel acts that even Dahmer's paled by comparison. Once again Thomas Harris's most famous creation to be committed to celluloid was called upon to help out the headline-writers: "Russia's Hannibal the Cannibal" shrieked the newspaper stories. Yet Dahmer and Chikatilo could not have been more unlike Anthony Hopkins' sinister psychopath, a man who emitted a tangible, almost magical, aura of sheer power. It was a compelling performance which, rather worryingly, caused Hannibal Lecter to become an anti-hero and cult figure. So worrying, in fact, that Anthony Hopkins—who was knighted in January 1993 and became Sir Anthony—expressed doubts about playing the character in a proposed sequel to the film.

But this fiend was fiction. Real-life monsters are somewhat different. Normally they are not easily identifiable beasts with piercing eyes and an aura of power who instil inexplicable fear in all who encounter them. It is not potency, but inadequacy, which drives them. They more often appear to be quiet, withdrawn people, isolated and lonely, maybe, but regarded as regular guys by many who meet them. They have mothers, fathers, relatives, people who care about them—or at least, they did care at one time. One has to remind oneself that these killers have not just appeared like aliens in our midst, as fully-fledged, evil adults. Once upon a time, they were new-born babies cooed over by their mothers, they were laughing toddlers learning to talk, they were small boys in short pants reciting their five times table and playing boats with bits of sticks in muddy puddles. What on earth happens inside the brains of these children to set them

upon a blood-spattered path of perversity? As a woman
said outside the Rostov court where Chikatilo was tried:
"They kept on explaining how and whom he killed but
nobody explained why. That's the most interesting
thing." So can we answer this question? Can we find
common factors among these killers, something which
makes them prey like carnivorous animals on those
weaker than themselves? Were they born that way? Are
they just genetically evil?

The rash of recent cases of cannibal or vampire killers
might also pose the question: is this sort of horrific murder actually becoming more common in the twentieth
century—and if so, why? Or have such crimes always
happened? As was noted in the introductory chapter,
there have certainly been instances in past centuries' history to indicate that sadistic killers existed then, as now. [1]
Claiming that such bloody acts were the work of werewolves, for instance, would seem to support this hypothesis, but documentation is muddied by the persecution,
superstition and hysteria which accompanied medieval
law enforcement. Even setting these prejudices aside, the
incidence of such crimes cannot be comprehensively as-
sessed, owing to the limitations of communication in past
ages. Of course, even the most bloody of those crimes
would not necessarily involve cannibalism or blood-
drinking, although this is just one optional aspect of a
crime which is the work of those we call sadistic killers.
Sadistic sex murders make up eighteen per cent of all
mass killings—and cannibals fall among their ranks. Fear,
mutilation and the infliction of suffering are essential

---

[1] That sado-necrophilia and necrophilia is not a new phenomenon can
be seen in the sixteenth-century writings of the jurist Damhoudere who
recommended the death penalty for lower-class people and exile if the
culprit was an "honourable"—or upper-class—person, on the grounds
that such a person does not "respect the goal and the measure of
natural love, but uses the dead body sexually, behaving as if he copu-
lated with a piece of wood or stone."

ingredients for sexual gratification in the sadistic killer—
or lust-murderer, as he is sometimes called. The sight or
feel of blood stimulates them, often they move on to
tasting blood, then biting . . . swallowing. In these killers, the advance to cannibalism might seem almost im-
perceptible; this aspect of deviant sexual behaviour is
contained within essentially the same framework. And by
virtue of the compulsive nature of their drive, sadistic
killers develop into serial killers if not caught. [2] Similarly,
in striving to "perfect" their crime and reap its sensual
rewards—satisfactions which are destined never to live
up to the fantasies they have entertained for years—they
enter an "improvement continuum" and become more
and more experimental in their brutality.

Over and over again in the preceding chapters, we can
see this pattern repeating itself: Andrei Chikatilo's mutilations became ever more frenzied and bloody, his infliction of torture on his victims gathered momentum and
for the Russian killer to achieve satisfaction necessitated
greater suffering and pain on the part of his victims, together with cannibalizing their bodies. Jeffrey Dahmer's
modus operandi became similarly more channelled. In his
childhood his necrophiliac satisfaction came from dead
animals. When he moved on to killing humans, at first he
did not keep any "mementos" of his victims and if one
had not known of Dahmer's childhood history the dismemberment might almost seem to have been born of
expedience. Later in his killing career he began preserving their heads, genitals, bones or other organs. While
Dahmer's perverted desires appeared at first to be adequately met by his actions of drugging, strangling, having

[2] Serial killers are distinct from mass murderers in that serial killers kill
one or two people at a time, repeating this until they are caught,
whereas mass murderers wipe out crowds of people at one time, for
instance, by shooting—and may frequently turn the gun upon themselves after such an act of slaughter.

sex with male corpses, mutilation and dismemberment, as
his killing methods became more streamlined, he demanded greater and greater stimulation—and achieved it
in a number of ways, including cannibalism. It has been
suggested that Dahmer was different from many serial
killers in that his power and domination thrill did not
come from observing his victims scream, suffer and beg
for their lives; his pleasure began post-mortem. He could
even be seen as merciful, because he drugged them. But
one has to consider the way that over time Dahmer graduated to wilder and more bizarre behaviours, eventually
drilling the heads of his drugged victims in the belief he
could make them into "zombies." If he had not been
caught, would he have ultimately needed to see the suffering of his victims to achieve that same elusive satisfaction which his fantasies promised? Eventually, if his
victim-count had reached the staggering heights of
Chikatilo's, would he have begun behaving like the Russian ripper?

Others who rape and mutilate follow the same ghastly
pattern. Just as Dahmer and Chikatilo turned to cannibalism to provide their "buzz," who knows how many
other sadistic killers—certainly those whose perversions
include necrophilia—would have got around to cannibalizing their victims as that supreme act of power when
primitive bestiality ruled their actions? I am thinking
here of killers like Neville Heath and William Heirens.
Heath was apprehended after two sadistic murders of
women in Britain in 1946 during which he inflicted terrible mutilations, including the biting-off and mangling of
breasts; Heirens, a fetishist who stole women's underwear from washing-lines and was sexually stimulated by
breaking and entering houses to burgle them, also managed only two mutilation murders—including one of a
six-year-old girl whom he kidnapped from her bedroom
as she lay asleep and whose body he dismembered—before his arrest in 1946. It is interesting, although chilling,

to speculate on the depths to which these two murderers would have sunk if they had killed more people. It was noted that the sadistic fantasies which Heirens had enjoyed for many years "far exceeded" those he had carried out.

It is undoubtedly true that serial killers are on the increase, especially in the States. At the beginning of the century there was about one murder a year for every 100,000 people, a figure which climbed to a peak in the 1930s, dropped dramatically post-war, but then rose inexorably during the 1960s to make it ten in 100,000 by 1980 —a tenfold rise since 1900. Thirty years ago, in almost all homicides, the killer had some relationship with his victim. But twenty years on, in the 1980s, 25 per cent of murders were "stranger murders"—accounted for, say sociologists, by increased mobility and a society which is impersonal and filled with sexual and violent images. Now, in the 1990s, there is a murder epidemic: the USA homicide rate has trebled since the 1960s, and according to FBI estimates there are between thirty and fifty serial killers on the loose in America. While Great Britain is unable to match the USA proportionately—mainly because of its more restrictive firearms laws—murder and violent crime are on the increase there also.

What is most alarming is the nature of the offender. More and more often, we are hearing more about sadistic "killing for kicks"—"recreational murder" or "wilding" as it is sometimes known. Most horrifyingly of all, such sexual sadism is increasingly inflicted by people in groups. That such sadistic individuals are able to seek out and find others of a similarly perverted persuasion, instead of being alienated by virtue of their inclinations, must make us question the nature of our society. The "wilding" case that shocked New York was that of a young woman jogger who was set upon by a gang of youths who held her for some time and repeatedly raped and tortured her, finally leaving her for dead, and the case of the sixteen-year-old girl in Manchester, England, who was abducted and tortured—including having her teeth pulled out and her flesh scrubbed off with a wire brush—then doused with petrol and set on fire. Before she died, she told police that her persecutors were a group of several men . . . and one woman.

It is exceptionally rare for women to indulge in sadistic behaviour; perhaps because the sense of inadequacy, low self-esteem, powerlessness and frustration which manifests as aggression to others in male sadistic killers is often turned inwards in women, resulting in such things as self-mutilation and suicide. But again, increasingly, cruel murderers are not exclusively male . . . or adult. The crime which really stopped Britain in its tracks, in February 1993, was the sadistic "killing for kicks" of a two-year-old child who had been abducted from a shopping centre in Liverpool. When his body was later discovered the little boy had suffered such appalling injuries that it made policemen weep in shock—but the security cameras in the shopping centre had captured his abductors on video-film, and the suspects were later arrested. They were two ten-year-old boys who, according to allegation, had previously limited their tortures to neighbourhood animals.

So who is to blame for this shocking state of affairs? What makes people commit crimes like mutilation, cannibalism or vampirism? Have we created a climate in which the sadistic murderer can flourish? It has become common, over the past few decades, to blame a criminal's antisocial deeds upon everyone and everything except the criminal himself. Parents are blamed, peer-pressure is blamed. Racism, poverty and unemployment, substandard housing and tower blocks are blamed. Schools are blamed for imposing too much discipline. Schools are blamed for not imposing enough discipline. Churches are seen as having failed in their duty. The media, together with the film industry and comic books, are blamed for glamorizing crime and violence. Even advertising is blamed, for offering a criminal desirable images of goods and a lifestyle which he cannot attain. When the poor commit crimes they are seen as victims of a society which has deprived them of hope; seeing privilege and wealth all around them robs them of self-esteem. But when middle-class youths similarly break the law, we suggest that they too are casualties of society, rebelling against middle-class values of materialism and the pressures to succeed which have been placed upon them by their parents.

As Stanton E. Samenow points out in his book *Inside the Criminal Mind*, economic hard times have been associated with an increase in crime . . . but then, so have good times:

> Sociological explanations for crime, plausible as they may seem, are simplistic. If they were correct, we'd have far more criminals than we do. Criminals come from all kinds of families and neighbourhoods. Most poor people are law-abiding, and most kids from broken homes are not delinquents. Children may bear the scars of neglect and deprivation for life, but most do not become criminals. The environment does have an effect, but people perceive and react to similar conditions of life very differently.

Psychological studies of adopted children who are psychopaths or who have become criminals suggest that heredity may play a large part in each of these types. Some of the studies have found a higher-than-average proportion of both in adopted children whose biological relatives were criminals or antisocial personalities. Samenow puts his own view bluntly: focusing on forces outside the criminal is futile, he says, because it is criminals who cause crime, not family or social factors. Sure, he says, remedy intolerable social conditions, because this is a worthwhile task, but do not expect criminals to change because of such efforts. Samenow's is an unfashionable view, in its way just as extreme as those psychologists and sociologists who cast around for social causes of crime while ignoring the criminal, but it is borne out in part by much social planning of the 1960s which was based on the assumption that improving conditions in inner-city high-crime areas would reduce the crime and murder rate in these places—after all, the stress caused to laboratory rats by poor conditions and overcrowding makes them, too, behave in unaccustomed antisocial, violent, cannibalistic and murderous ways. However, despite some cities operating urban renewal schemes—better houses, better schools, better health-care—the crime rate has increased, not decreased.

As for such conditions being more likely to predispose people to becoming serial or sadistic killers, although these killers are always more than eager to lay the blame anywhere but upon themselves, it is interesting to note that among those whom we may consider to be the most oppressed in our urban midst—ethnic minorities—it is extremely rare to find a serial killer. Although in America the murder rate among black males is ten times higher than among white males, serial killing is not generally their province. The profile of an archetypal serial killer, according to VICAP (the Violent Criminal Apprehension Programme) at the FBI's National Centre for the Analysis of Violent Crime in Quantico, begins "single white male, aged 20s or 30s . . ."

But in this book I am concentrating on the sadistic murderers among serial killers. It is true that they are not a novel phenomenon, [3] but whereas during the last cen-

---

[3] In Richard von Krafft-Ebing's *Psychopathia Sexualis*, published in 1886, the psychiatrist classes the "lust-murderer" as "cruelty, murderous lust extending to anthropophagy." Krafft-Ebing tells of Leger, a 19-year-old who "wanders about eight days in a forest, there catches a

tury the appearance of such men was so unusual as to cause the sort of panic which Jack the Ripper evoked, now they are far from unique. Accordingly psychiatrists, while not always understanding the motivation for sadistic murders, can assess those murderers who have been apprehended and endeavour to point to predisposing and diagnostic factors which, it is hoped, could help us to pinpoint the individuals who are likely to develop in this deviant way. A classic study of the sadistic murderer was written by Robert P. Brittain in 1970 where he lists many characteristics which are commonly found among these men. A glance at the individuals contained in this book will amply bear out Dr. Brittain's theories. Among them are:

- Usually introspective and withdrawn, he has few associates and no close friends and enjoys solitary pursuits like reading or going to the cinema alone, often to see horror films.
- He feels inadequate and inferior, except in regard to his crimes, which make him feel god-like, and is likely to offend when he has suffered a loss of self-esteem, such as loss of job, or being ridiculed by someone, especially in a sexual context.
- He can be a hypochondriac and display squeamishness.
- He has an elaborate fantasy life, imagining sadistic scenes which he acts out in his killings. He is fascinated by atrocities and excited by cruelty, such as that committed by the Nazis, and collects books or pictures of such images.
- He has an inordinate interest in weapons, often having a large collection which he may lovingly handle, and even endow some with pet names.

girl twelve years old, violates her . . . tears out her heart, eats of it, drinks the blood, and buries the remains."

- He is usually under thirty-five, unmarried and of high intelligence.
- He is usually sexually dysfunctional, has usually had little or no experience of normal sexual intercourse, and may hate all females.
- Many take jobs which satisfy their sadistic inclinations, such as butchery or slaughter-house work—in much the same way that necrophiles often obtain jobs as mortuary attendants and grave-diggers.
- He has a strong, ambivalent relationship with his mother, both loving and hating her. He is often seen as a "mother's boy" when adult. Sometimes he commits matricide.
- Sometimes the father is excessively punitive and authoritarian.
- There is a great interest in pornography, particularly sadistic pornography.
- A history of cruelty to animals is particularly significant when it relates to cats, dogs, birds and farm animals. Stabbing or hanging is common, although worse cruelties can be inflicted.
- The method of killing his human victims is almost always strangling, which gives him a greater sense of power over his victims, playing with them "like a cat with a mouse."
- Although these are sexually motivated crimes, sexual intercourse or orgasm does not always occur. Sometimes the murderer masturbates and sometimes a penis-substitute—such as a piece of wood or a knife—is used to violate the victim.
- When captured and institutionalized in hospitals or prisons, he is very well behaved, which can result in his being released or sent to a less secure unit.

Trying to assess the motivation of such men is no new thing. There are certainly common childhood factors which could be seen as influential and, indeed, there are common behaviour patterns displayed in childhood by sadists which many investigators regard as predictive. The three most common of these are a preoccupation with fire-setting, sometimes seen in children as young as five or six; cruelty to animals such as dogs, birds and cats (animals which scream, bleed and show fear), rather than the common, if horrid, practice of pulling the wings off flies; finally—and most surprisingly, since it is not obviously hostile or destructive, but more usually connected with stress—is *enuresis*, that is, regular bed-wetting which continues beyond the age of twelve. Other factors are often indicative of violence in adult life, such as observing that the child indulges in prolonged day-dreaming (in fact, he may be engaged in sadistic fantasies), and persistent lying and aggression.

Of the three main behaviours, many psychologists believe that if a child displays two-thirds of this triad, eventual aggression towards people is indicated. And of the three, deliberate, repetitive infliction of severe injuries upon animals is arguably the most specific sign. Studies have shown that children who are cruel to animals also show other aggressive behaviours such as temper tantrums, bullying and fighting. It is easy to perceive that a child who is not only unable to feel any empathy with the suffering of an intelligent animal not far below a human being on the phylogenetic scale, but is also eager to witness or inflict that suffering is not displaying normal behaviour (and neither, one might suggest, are grown men who display the same traits by revelling in cock-fighting, dog-fighting or badger-baiting). However, there are also other influences at work here. Many studies have also shown that severe parental punishments can foster aggression in children, predisposing them to animal cruelty. Some parents actively encourage their children to violate cultural norms and behave in aggressive ways, both with animals and other children, and since children model themselves upon their parents, in such instances it would be more surprising if a child developed into a sensitive human being than if he became a bully and a thug. The absence of a "stable and emotionally available father figure" will also increase the likelihood of a boy showing cruelty to dogs or cats, researcher Dr. Alan R. Felthous claims, and points out that in a study of thirty-one "motiveless" murderers, eighteen had a history of parental deprivation together with "remorseless physical brutality" by a parent. Convincing statistics, until one pauses to consider that the remaining thirteen murderers presumably had not.

However, what does seem to be clear is that serial killers in general almost invariably suffer childhoods of emotional deprivation, are often from broken homes, with a weak or absent father-figure and a dominant mother. Discipline and demonstration of affection is inconsistent. Sometimes, crime is a way of life in families. Emotional abuse is very common, but there is also a relationship between killers who mutilate their victims and sexual abuse in childhood. Sexually abused murderers are more likely to mutilate their victims (and to have begun their sadistic career by torturing animals) than those not sexually abused, according to one 1986 study. [4] Because the sadistic killer does not come from an environment of love and understanding, he grows up feeling rejected, alienated, worthless, frustrated by social failure, impotent and powerless. The relationship with the mother is usually dysfunctional—perhaps unsurprising since the child usually relies on its mother to fulfil its love and nurturing needs. According to Robert Ressler, the FBI detective whose excellent book *Whoever Fights Monsters* delves into the lives of many serial killers, all these children grew up without any limits set upon their

[4] "Murderers who Rape and Mutilate": Ressler, Burgess, Hartman, Douglas and McCormack, *Journal of Interpersonal Violence*, Vol. 1, No. 3, September 1986.

behaviour, without being taught right from wrong and without any comprehension that they must interact with and accommodate other people in the world around them. Consequently they are stunted at an egocentric stage of infantile development—that stage when babies believe they are the centre of the universe and that others are there merely to fulfil their selfish demands. Normal development involves learning that this is not the case, and educating children in these things—socializing them —is the task of the loving mother during the first half-dozen years of an infant's life, says Ressler. But the mothers of these killers, in addition to falling down on this duty, also deprived their offspring of attention and affection. They never properly, actively, *loved* their children but instead ignored them, pushed them out of the way. Relationships with other members of the family, such as siblings, were also absent. A perfect example here would be Ed Kemper, who told Ressler of returning home from school one day at the age of ten to find that he was being banished to the basement because he was so abnormally hulking that he was making his sisters uncomfortable.

But is blaming sadistic murder on unhappy childhoods actually mistaking correlations for causes? There have always been bad homes, and in many of them other siblings of the offender have been equally badly treated, yet they have not become serial killers. Stanton E. Samenow, with his customary cynicism regarding the extent to which environment can shape an individual, remarks that criminals often claim that they were rejected by everyone of importance in their lives, but rarely say why. Suggesting that these embryo criminals are sneaky, defiant, untruthful, argumentative and manipulative of their parents, he suggests that it is the criminal who rejects his parents rather than vice versa. Criminals may tell horrific tales of their deprived childhoods to portray themselves as victims, gain sympathy and avoid blame. But Samenow urges a deeper look into family relationships: "We ought not to limit our inquiries to what parents have done to children but strive to determine what children have done to their parents," he advises. And perhaps, in this context, it might be worth reminding ourselves that Kemper was freely fantasizing by the time he was incarcerated in that basement, that long before puberty he had decapitated and cut the hands from his sister's doll and that as a child of seven he had said about a teacher he had a crush on: "If I kiss her, I would have to kill her first."

When people ask whether such men as Kemper, Gein, Fish and the rest are born or made, perhaps the truth lies somewhere between the two: that something in their neurological make-up has given them a predisposition towards such deviant behaviour and that real or imagined emotional deprivations in childhood enable this predisposition to surface, just as someone whose genetic make-up means they are likely to suffer heart trouble will be more likely to bring this on if they eat fatty foods or take up parachuting. The question that this invites, though, is: does that mean killers like those in this book would have been diverted from their blood-drenched lusts if they had been loved and valued as children? Robert Ressler believes that the millions of people from deprived backgrounds as bad as, or worse, than those suffered by the killers catalogued here, but who do not grow up to kill, are "saved" by forming other attachments—"rescued by strong hands," as he says—in pre-adolescence. In his book *Hunting Humans*, Elliott Leyton asserts something similar, suggesting that the vast majority of people who may have the same tainted origins can be averted from their murderous destiny by being "touched" by some individual or institution that makes their lives bearable and offers them fulfilment. Leyton acknowledges, however, that this theory is impossible to prove in any scientific fashion, for we only have the end results to guide us. Florida psychologist Ann McMillan is doubtful and offers as an example Gerald Stano, murderer of thirty-five women, who was fostered at only six months old and later adopted by a loving couple. He still turned out to be a monster. "Sometimes it's not going to matter who raises them," says McMillan. "If the parents were Mary and Joseph, it would still turn out the same."

We have no clear evidence that, to cite a couple of examples, Richard Chase was the abused victim of an unhappy childhood or that Jeffrey Dahmer's childhood was emotionally barren—we know, for instance, that he had a doting grandmother. His time in the army offered another opportunity for fulfilment and integration, but he achieved neither. Much the same applies to Andrei Chikatilo. His childhood might have been economically harsh, but as far as is possible to ascertain his mother was caring and although he was ribbed at school, this seems to have been no more severe than it is for thousands of youngsters. In addition, he had an attentive wife and a family who loved him. In fact, Chikatilo's psychiatrist Aleksandr Bukhanovsky appears to suggest that the principle reason that Chikatilo became the cannibal killer of fifty-odd people was because he had been told a frightening story about cannibalism in his childhood—which is exactly what Albert Fish gave as the "reason" behind his deviant crimes.

Leyton also suggests that the serial killer is a product of his age and can be judged according to social theory principles. His ideas can be compared to Colin Wilson's somewhat startling assertion in his book *The Serial Killers* that there were no sex-killers before the late nineteenth century, mainly because life was hard for the working classes, and when they committed murder the motive was robbery, not sex. Economic deprivation makes sex a secondary issue, Wilson states. Leyton suggests that murder is a form of class assertion, since serial killers are primarily from the working classes or the lower middle classes, but feel alienated from and rejected by that class or the class they wish to join. To illustrate his point, he suggests that Gilles de Rais, who raped, tortured and killed 150 children in fifteenth-century France, was expressing an aristocratic fear of the power of the peasants who were advancing themselves at this time and threatening his autocracy. Therefore, by murdering the children of peasants, de Rais was imposing the tyranny of his class. From here, Leyton goes on to say that murders like those committed by Kemper, whom he offers as an example, are not primarily sexual but social, citing Kemper's claims that he targeted young upper-class women—"I was swashbuckling, I was destroying only society's finest young girls"—together with his evidently weak sex drive (normal sex drive, that is) as supportive of his suggestion.

Apart from the notion that self-esteem and self-aggrandisement play a part, these suggestions are questionable. "Death, not sex was the ecstasy," says Leyton interpreting the sexual aspect as merely a secondary benefit because it came after death. Other researchers have also suggested that the relief a killer feels is only coincidentally sexual. But this is applying healthy sexual norms to extreme deviance where the powerful sexual drive is operating at a much more primitive level than in normal people. It ignores the sadistic fantasies which preoccupy such men and are used as a masturbatory aid. Death and blood are irrevocably tied up with sex because sexual stimulation is achieved *only* by incorporating them into the fantasy or the reality. These things *replace* normal sexual stimulation . . . but that does not make the murder non-sexual. The fact that lust-killers invariably kill within the sphere of their own sexual preferences would seem to indicate this. The stalking of a victim parallels foreplay and the killing is the orgasm, offering either physical or mental release. The American sex-killer David Berkowitz once explained that after his first murder "I felt happy . . . That built-up tension dissipated temporarily. While I didn't have a physical, sexual orgasm, I certainly had a mental one." Dr. Martin Orne, a psychiatrist from the University of Pennsylvania, believes sexual gratification is the primary motive and suggests that this might be why the victims of serial killers are usually superficially alike. "The killers may simply pick victims that fit their sexual fantasies."

Sex and aggression become inextricably linked early in life for these men and they are unable to differentiate between them by the time they are adults—but how this happens is not precisely known. Can it really be as simple a matter as classical conditioning, as some suggest? It has been speculated that the physiological arousal from inflicting and experiencing pain is not unlike sexual excitement; therefore in the early stages of sexualization, it might be harder for some individuals to discriminate between them, especially if the pain-inducing act also includes sexual elements. Kroll and Gein both blamed their perverted behaviour on seeing some pigs being butchered when in their teens—and this awakened their sex-drives. Albert Fish spoke of the cruelty he suffered and witnessed in his childhood; the infant Peter Kurten saw his brutal father rape his wife and thirteen-year-old daughter and then, at nine, would enjoy watching the local rat-catcher torture and sexually violate animals, reinforcing sex and cruelty in the child's mind. Jeffrey Dahmer found himself powerfully sexually attracted to viscera about the time he began dissecting animals at school and would masturbate while thinking about this, sexualizing something which for almost everyone else, is non-sexual. Some psychiatrists [5] argue that the nature of the first sexual experience followed by orgasm at a critical stage of a person's development may be crucial for any establishment of sexual deviation, which is then maintained by fantasies of that behaviour.

[5] McGuire, R.J., Carlisle, J.M. and Young, B.G. (1965) "Sexual deviations as conditioned behaviour: a hypothesis." *Behaviour Research and Therapy.* 3.

But can we really say this sort of childhood incident actually conditions such extreme deviation—or is it just an aggravating factor? For Fish, it must be remembered, recalled his childhood beatings with a pleasure which we assume his companions did not experience. Most people would find the sight of pigs being butchered anything but sexually stimulating—but not Kroll or Gein. Dahmer's class-mates also dissected animals in the biology lab—yet they did not find animal entrails sexy and were not, as Dahmer told police that he was, sexually aroused by the heat which came from a body which he was disembowelling. So do people really *learn* to enjoy such things, or are humans born with cruelty as a component of their nature? And if so, does that apply to *some* humans or *all* humans?

It is a fact that killing becomes easier after the first time; research among the armed forces confirms that. Psychologist Paul Cameron, who conducted such research in 1976, also found that people who had killed before—as soldiers, for example—were more likely than those who have never killed at all to say they would murder for money, suggesting that inhibitions about murder are overcome relatively easily. But are some people more likely to kill than others? If we imagine a scale of psychopathy (or sociopathy)—that is, a continuum along which each of us may be placed according to the degree of sociopathic traits we display, like narcissism, lack of reliability and responsibility, poverty of deep emotions, lack of shame and untruthfulness—might we hypothesize that, depending how far along this scale an individual is, life-events may elicit certain aggressive behaviours more readily from some people than from others?

Professor Anthony Storr, who has made a study of aggression and destructiveness, points out that some aggression is necessary in humans for advancement and survival. Total passivity (as demonstrated by the fictional Eloi in Wells' story of *The Time Machine*) would ultimately result in our annihilation. But Professor Storr points out that compared to other animals, humans show a "marked hereditary predisposition toward aggressive behaviour" and are exceptionally destructive. Between 1820 and 1945 a total of 59 million people died as a result of "war, murder or other lethal activities" according to one researcher. [6] History has, indeed, shown us that the brutally aggressive instincts of man—and it does seem that it is primarily adult male aggression which can be aroused with relative ease—are not far beneath the veneer of civilization, fuelled by the complexity of other primitive emotional mechanisms. In some countries, although adulterous women are no longer eaten, they are still stoned to death. To appreciate the human capacity for deliberately causing suffering and agony, with an excuse that one is just following orders, we need to look no further back than half a century, when the Nazi atrocities against the Jews were little different from the witch-trials of the Middle Ages. Even more recently, the inhuman cruelties of American soldiers towards unarmed Vietnamese villagers whom they massacred at My Lai in 1969 were repeated in 1990s Bosnia. Allowing for the propaganda machine, it seems clear that atrocities were perpetrated on all sides, but the Serbs and the Croats were the aggressors who committed acts of genocide upon the Muslims who had been, quite literally, their neighbours. Meanwhile they could cite as "justification" the instruction from President Franjo Tudjman of Croatia that

> Genocide is a natural phenomenon, in harmony with the societal and mythologically divine nature. Genocide is not only permitted, it is recommended, even commanded by the word of the Almighty, whenever it is useful for the survival or the restoration of the kingdom

[6] Lewis F. Richardson, *Statistics of Deadly Quarrels*, London: Stevens and Sons, 1960, p. 153.

of the chosen nation, or for the preservation and spreading of its one and only correct faith. [7]

When these are ideals which are embraced publicly and urged upon people whose compliance with authority—especially religious authority—is total, it seems obvious that human primitive impulses have not changed much over the millennia and that the "civilized" world is no more civilized than it was centuries—tens of centuries—ago. But the perpetrators of unspeakable cruelties were not, and are not, all what we would perceive as psychopaths, psychotic, deranged, mentally ill—call them what you will. The Nazi concentration camp guards could not all have been sexual sadists. The Croat soldiers who, in April 1993 set fire to Muslim women and children, who allegedly made weeping mothers hold their babies while they shot the infants dead—these were apparently "normal" men.

Enormous numbers of "normal" people can evidently be induced to see others as not human, as disposable objects with no worth, as being there to fulfil their own selfish desires—or in this case, the desire of the State. They may have done this by abdicating personal responsibility and citing their obedience to authority, but, all the same, they have eschewed any constraints of conscience and have detached themselves from the suffering of the helpless human being they are torturing without mercy—exactly like our monsters under observation in these pages. "We cannot assume that the forces which account for aggression between nation-states are the same as those which drive individuals," says Anthony Storr. Maybe the motives are different, but aren't the same distancing devices at work? Can't we relate the ability of psychotic killers to reduce humans to the status of dispos-

[7] *The Balkan Conflict and International Reaction: American and Serbian Options* by G.C. Raju (Thomas, 1992).

able objects to what supposedly un-psychotic "normal" people do in a war setting when they kill or degrade?

This transformation in the sadistic killer's imagination of living human being into inanimate doll is an oft-repeated pattern, enabling him to feel powerful. Krafft-Ebing (1886) suggested that "mastering and possessing an absolutely defenceless human object . . . is part of sadism"—as it is, indeed, a primary ingredient of rape. Denigrating, dominating, hurting and humiliating a victim offers a sadist ultimate control and it is the control which is the overwhelming motivating force. The more extreme the controlling devices are, the more powerful the controller is in his own mind, and the more helpless the victim, the more like an object he or she becomes. Chikatilo blindfolded his victims and cut out their tongues to prevent them seeing and speaking; Dahmer became obsessed with turning his homosexual conquests into zombies by drilling into their heads; Kroll turned to killing children when he tired of his rubber sex-doll—but his view that they were equally disposable prevailed; Kürten regarded all his victims simply as throwaway objects for his enjoyment and never expressed remorse about their fates; Chase admitted killing baby David Ferreira and decapitating him to "get at the blood," but said that at the time he thought the baby was "something else"; Kemper described "making a doll out of a human being . . . and carrying out my fantasies with . . . a living human doll." And the ultimate control is devouring a victim.

Relating the actions and thinking of lone sadists to "normal" human beings who are able to inflict terrible cruelties on their perceived enemies during war, we can see in operation one of the primary faculties which humans, alone among the animal kingdom, possess: imagination. We may assume that imagination is a worthy quality, responsible for all technological and scientific achievement, not to mention great art and literature. But it is also imagination which is exploited by leaders to incite a group's hatred against an opposing faction—or country, religion or race—and unleash aggression upon them. A group's obedience to authority is also known to rob them of conscience because they abdicate their own personal responsibility and assign it to their leaders.

This entire process can be related to the psychopathic sadistic lust-killer. Imagination inspires him and, devoid of conscience or the societal inhibitory devices which constrain normal men, he simply lives out his fantasies, amply demonstrating, in microcosm, man's potential for cruelty and destructiveness which history has demonstrated in macrocosm. In the male, unlike the female, aggression is linked with sexuality to a greater degree because it is the male hormone testosterone which drives both—interestingly, it has been suggested that boys who grow up to be sex killers are often regarded in childhood as being very highly sexed—so we should not, perhaps, be too surprised to learn that one study has shown that some normal men engage in fantasies which are controlling and sadistic. [8] Yet only a fraction of these few, it seems, fail to contain such fantasies within their imaginations and allow them to spill out into the horrific reality contained in this book and elsewhere. Why this happens, and why only some men entertain such controlling fantasies in the first place while others do not, has not been answered satisfactorily, although causes such as childhood sexual assaults, feelings of inadequacy and poor social relationships are suggested as possible factors. What does seem likely is that the reality of a normal man's life is rewarding enough for him to keep his fantasies locked up in his head, whereas the sadistic killer's real life is so unsatisfactory to him that the fantasies assume a dispro-

[8] Crepault, C. and Couture, M. (1980) "Men's erotic fantasies." *Archives of Sexual Behaviour*, 9, 565-81.

portionate importance and come to take the place of reality.

For fantasy is a key to identifying the sadistic killer. In childhood and adolescence he retreats into his violent imagination instead of forming relationships with others, until one day the fantasies spill out and he ritually acts out his blood-drenched dream. Points out Colin Wilson in his book about serial killers: "For the sexual criminal, the most important step is the one that bridges the gap between fantasy and actuality." The fantasy can sometimes be so rich that it alone can induce orgasm. During one of his terms of imprisonment, Peter Kurten had no need to masturbate or indulge in homosexual acts with his fellow-prisoners, but perfected a technique whereby he imagined sadistic acts or scenes of death and disaster and this would cause him to ejaculate.

The "imaginative revolution"—an advance in our imaginative powers over the past couple of centuries—can, suggests Colin Wilson, account for the rise in fetishism (sexual stimulation derived from a non-erotic, inanimate object) and other sexual perversions. Hundreds of years ago, he claims in his book *The Misfits*, imaginative powers regarding sexuality were more limited (although perhaps the wealth of ancient mythology from all cultures which contains numerous aspects of both erotica and deviation could challenge this assumption). Quoting Tolstoy's view that there is so much leisure in the modern world that people spend all their time dreaming about sex, distorting and exaggerating the sexual image, Wilson looks at various forms of sexual abnormality and concludes that sexuality has evolved to a "higher" level, beyond that of mere reproduction, to a "symbolic" level in which people can be stimulated by ideas. One might hope that increased imagination might result in increased empathy for those who suffer, but Wilson draws attention to the reverse side of the coin: the imagined cruelties advanced by the Marquis de Sade as sexually stimulating ideas. Pornography increasingly became available during the Victorian era and its sometimes bizarre nature taught people how to use their imaginations, he suggests. The down-side of this galvanizing effect of discovering an imaginative world of satisfaction was sex-crime which, according to Wilson, only began occurring significantly in the nineteenth century.

The debate about the correlation between sex-crime and pornography continues today. If we were to look for a logical link between pornographic images and the thought-processes of rapists and sex killers, the most obvious would be the depersonalization and degradation of the victim. Without doubt, pornography turns women into objects to be manipulated sexually for male gratification in the same way that rapists, sadists and murderers perceive them. And like a pornographic picture, a corpse is non-threatening. It is not going to remark on the smallness of the killer's penis—yet another inferiority complex from which many lust-murderers suffer. Yet, despite studies like that in 1983 by American sociologists Straus and Baron which showed that rates of forcible rape were higher in states where *Playboy* sold better, most researchers have, for years, dismissed any suggestion that the increasing availability of pornography incites men to sexually attack women. [9] However, they have perhaps been asking the wrong question. Psychologists Edward Donnerstein and Neil Malamuth asked the right one: could *aggressive* pornography increase observers' atti-

[9] In 1970, when aggressive pornography was much rarer than it is now, the Commission on Obscenity and Pornography concluded that pornographic materials did not have a "harmful" effect; in 1973, Howard, Liptzin and Riefler concluded that pornography was "an innocuous stimulus which leads quickly to satiation" and decided that public concern was misplaced; also in 1973 Mann, Sidmann and Starr concluded that viewing erotic films did not produce "harmful social consequences."

tudes about sexual aggression towards women? And their answer was a resounding "yes." Incorporating others' findings into their own research, they conclude that exposure to such material leads to an increase in aggressive sexual fantasies and influences perceptions of women, making aggressive acts such as rape seem more acceptable. They also reiterated the concerns of 1976 pornography research conducted by Gager and Schurr, which focused on sexual sadism being presented as a source of sexual pleasure for women, who, after their initial resistance is overcome, thereafter "wallow in physical abuse and degradation." Say Gager and Schurr: "It is the pattern of horror which we have seen in our examination of sex cases translated again and again into actual assaults."

As has been quoted elsewhere, it was the Marquis de Sade who said there is no better way to know death than to link it with a licentious image. The man who gave his name to sadism as a sexual perversion died in 1814, proving that such deviance is nothing new. However, a hundred years ago those few who practised it did so in shame and secrecy. Awareness of it was limited, in the main, to the medical profession. Now, with hard-core pornography more freely obtainable, there is little sexual behaviour which remains a mystery and what is particularly worrying is that violent pornography of the bondage-and-sadism type is increasingly prevalent and widely available in the Western world, inexorably attracting sexual sadists and feeding their fantasies with a fusion of sexuality and aggression. It is perhaps only to be expected that "snuff" movies, in which a victim (usually a woman or child) is allegedly killed after being subjected to prolonged sexual violation, are obviously aimed at an audience of people who entertain sadistic fantasies—and are, presumably, made by such people, too.

Movie-makers might deny it, but perhaps it is the same audience to whom they are appealing in their ever-increasing output of "slasher" films which are a tribute to those special-effects wizards who have ceased creating screen magic in favour of screen mutilation. Could the increase in violence and sexual aggression, the rise in the number of sadistic killers this century to an all-time-high, have any link with·the violent images which are constantly offered as entertainment to young people, and are particularly cherished by young men? Do the celebrated "freedoms" which Western society promotes offer, in reality, a reinforcement of individuals' bad behaviour and deviant desires by suggesting that nothing is abnormal? For example, whereas once societal restraints demanded that sado-masochistic desire be concealed as being perverted and damaging, nowadays it is being trotted out as just another option for the sexually adventurous.

Indictments of screen violence and its influence on children have been made by psychologists for many years —Albert Bandura and Alberta Siegel conclusively demonstrated that it increases aggressive behaviour in children exposed to it—but this has been disregarded as we note the increasingly imaginative, graphic and gratuitous violence and sexual aggression on general release in the cinema. Has no one stopped to consider the brutalizing effect of such a bloody diet on those whose emotions have already been flattened by their experience of life? Doesn't violence on the screen feed the imagination in entirely the wrong way? Aren't fantasies even given a direction by such images? Among those whose genes make them so inclined, are these factors possibly enabling the arousal and liberation of that immersed instinct for blood, violence and sexual aggression which we have seen so often (in war settings in particular)—yes, and even the instinct for cannibalism? At liberty among us, sometimes sanctioned by society, are people who enjoy inflicting unspeakable cruelty on living creatures for no other reason than fun—hunters, badger-baiters, the dog-fighting fraternity—all people deriving pleasure from causing pain and making blood spurt. How far removed is this primitive urge from the same power-driven compulsion which controls the sexual sadist?

Many murderers in this book found enjoyment in sadistic pornography in preference to classical "normal" pornography. Gein's dark crypt was stacked with it—and so was Dahmer's bedroom. Chikatilo even claimed that sadistic pornography had incited his acts. A 1980s FBI survey of sex murderers showed that seventy per cent of them felt "sexually incompetent" and relied heavily on visual stimuli such as pornography. But while saying that such images may reinforce the acceptability of sexual aggression in someone's mind, it takes an unlikely leap of the imagination to declare that it is violent pornography which actually *causes* a man to become a sadistic cannibal killer. Ed Kemper pored over detective magazines for pictures of corpses, read pornographic magazines and watched "snuff" movies, but said, with some honesty: "That didn't make me mean. It just fuelled the fire."

But what starts this particular fire in the first place? We might be able to attribute most crime—including murder—to social conditions, psychodynamics, personality disorders, resentments and lusts, but even the most amoral of criminals would balk at the idea of being sexually stimulated by disembowelment, blood-drinking and flesh-eating . . . wouldn't they? But then, how many of these would find rape arousing? How many would still find it stimulating if the rape was accompanied by injury which draws blood—because the sight of blood sparks some excitement in their instinctive response? The number of men who do respond to such images may be fewer as the images increase in violence and bloodiness, finally degenerating into cannibalism—but maybe it's simply a matter of degree. There is certainly no shortage of cases within psychiatric and psychoanalytical literature which confirm the sensual fascination which blood and pain exert upon some people.

If we acknowledge that vampirism and cannibalism

played a part in human evolution, then we may accept that at the deeper levels of the psyche common to all modern humans must be some vestiges of these activities and supernatural beliefs, in the same way that the human body contains vestiges of our evolutionary stages. Psychologist Carl Gustav Jung called this concept the "collective unconscious," identifying various archetypal images that make contact with some primitive aspect of man—and one of these archaic vestiges is likely to be an appetite for blood. "An archetype is like an old watercourse along which the water of life has flowed for centuries, digging a deep channel for itself. The longer it has flowed in this channel the more likely it is that sooner or later the water will return to its old bed," said Jung. [10] The combined spiritual and sexual power attached to blood runs like a secret underground stream in the primitive depths of the human subconscious, dating back to man's early religions and superstitions, harnessed to his desire to eat human meat and drink human blood. Are cannibal killers functioning at this same primitive level?

In normal sexual relations, biting is not considered to be a perversion and neither is the love-bite—but when is a love-bite considered deviant? Vampirism is classed as a perversion by researchers such as Krafft-Ebing—although it is usually found in association with other psychiatric disorders such as schizophrenia and mental retardation—but blood-drinking which does not necessarily result in death is suspected to be more common than most of us may imagine. However, few patients or offenders are likely to confide such activities on their own initiative, says Herschel Prins, a professor of clinical criminology who is one of Britain's foremost researchers into vampiristic activity as part of bizarre sexual behaviour. He speaks of the "dual but highly related worlds of

[10] "Wotan" in *Collected Works* vol. 10: *Civilisation in Transition.* (1964/70).

mythical and clinical vampirism," and explains sadistic, biting fantasies as an extension of the vampire's "kiss." He also links the subconscious urges which feed such fantasies and behaviour with the notion of being able to perpetuate life, which the vampire, in its "undead" state, has achieved, being able to balance life and death. In his book *Bizarre Behaviours* Professor Prins gives several examples of people with no apparent associated mental condition whose desire to drink blood has brought them to the attention of the police or psychiatrists, one nineteen-year-old man saying he believed fresh human blood had a "supernatural quality" which would grant him immortality. As sexologist Havelock Ellis said in 1903:

> The result of the love-bite in its extreme form is to shed blood . . . the mingled feelings of close contact, of passionate gripping, of symbolic devouring . . . with some persons . . . the love-bite is really associated with a conscious desire, even if more or less restrained, to draw blood, a real delight in this process, a love of blood. Probably this only occurs in persons who are not absolutely normal . . . [11]

A pair of researchers [12] in 1971 reported a ritual practised by a married couple:

> As a prelude to sexual intercourse, the young man would draw blood by cutting a small incision on the palm of his wife's right hand. She would then stimulate his penis, using the blood of her right palm as a lubricant. Normal intercourse would then ensue, and the moment the wife felt her husband ejaculating, she was required to dig her nails deep into the small of his back or buttocks.

[11] Havelock Ellis, quoted in *Vampires, Werewolves and Demons*, Richard Noll, 1992 (Brunner/Mazel, New York).
[12] Lazarus and Davison, 1971, in *Abnormal Psychology*, Davison and Neale.

Among other reported cases are those of a twenty-year-old man in prison for larceny, who submitted to homosexual acts in return for being allowed to suck his partner's blood, because the sight of blood had excited him sexually since he was eight years old and had been stimulated by the sight of dogs which had been run over by cars; cases of both men and women who reported violent sexual excitement when sucking blood from an incision in a partner's flesh; of a man who enjoyed drinking his own blood so much that he perfected a technique of directing blood from an artery directly into his mouth; more unusual still, of a disturbed woman whose fantasy was to capture a docile young girl, "to kiss her breasts, then tear or bite them off and eat them . . . I would at last find my way to the heart and then drink the heart's blood, then pluck out the heart and perhaps eat it." [13]

Many researchers besides Professor Prins [14] are of the opinion that erotic vampiristic and cannibalistic impulses are by no means rarities. Professor Prins poses the question: is vampirism merely a pathological extension of the "love-bite" which is practised in normal sexual relations, possibly serving to satisfy very basic oral/sadistic needs which are present, to a greater or lesser extent, in all of us?

What is "normal"? What is the point at which vampiristic behaviour begins and ends on the "normal" continuum? Could *all* sexual behaviour be placed on such a continuum, with loving, reciprocal, non-injurious sex placed at the top, and with the imaginary graph-line plunging downwards through behaviour such as so-called date-rape . . . what might be termed "ordinary" rape

[13] Quoted in *Vampires, Werewolves and Demons*, Richard Noll, 1992 (Brunner/Mazel, New York).
[14] For example, R.L. Vanden Bergh and J.F. Kelly in "Vampirism," *Archives of General Psychiatry*, 11.

. . . rape with excessive violence, infliction of injury, mutilation? On such a continuum, which is irrevocably tied up with the assertion of power, primitive deviant behaviour like vampirism, sadism, and cannibalism would be down at the lowest point, as urges which are only enacted by the few . . . down into the depths of man's unconscious, towards the primitive, the ungodly, the unspeakable: the depraved cannibal killers at the bottom of the slope.

Writers of fiction have exploited our subconscious primeval urges towards blood-letting and blood-drinking and, when the vampire took centre-stage, the sexual aspect was powerfully reinforced. The myth of the male vampire was a pervasive form of inspiration for the romantic poets and gothic writers of the late eighteenth and early nineteenth centuries, producing a romantic male archetype, a "Fatal Man" who, according to Mario Praz, can be identified in works ranging from Milton's Satan to Byron's heroes. By the time that Stoker wrote *Dracula* in 1897 there were also other nineteenth-century concerns to exploit. Charles Darwin's evolutionary theories published between 1859 and 1871 served to heighten fears that "higher" and "lower" urges struggled for primacy within a single individual and that the more savage, degenerate side of human nature constantly bubbled beneath the surface façade of civilization. Such ideas inspired other books such as Oscar Wilde's *The Picture of Dorian Gray* in 1891 and Robert Louis Stevenson's *The Strange Case of Dr. Jekyll and Mr. Hyde* in 1886.

The evolution of the vampire from historical legend into nineteenth-century fiction created a fiend quite unlike all other fearsome supernatural monsters because of the mesmeric seduction and blatant forbidden pleasure of sexuality involved in the blood-letting process, inspired, one can speculate, by the Romanian vampire Nosferat, which raped women at the same time as sucking their blood. As with the cannibal killers contained in this book, the three main components of sexuality, blood and death became fused in Stoker's vampire. For instance, when the half-asleep Jonathan Harker is surrounded by three beautiful vampire women at Dracula's castle, his feelings are ambiguous:

> There was something about them that made me uneasy, some longing and at the same time some deadly fear. I felt in my heart a wicked, burning desire that they would kiss me with those red lips . . . I lay quiet . . . in an agony of delightful anticipation . . . The fair girl went on her knees and bent over me, fairly gloating. There was a deliberate voluptuousness which was both thrilling and repulsive.

> *Dracula*, pp.37-8

The blatant sexual symbolism in the above passage leaves nothing to the imagination of the sophisticated twentieth-century reader, any more than does the scene where, in a curious reversal of the usual relationship between vampire and victim, Dracula forces Mina Harker to drink blood from his chest—symbolically an act of enforced fellatio with blood being a substitute for semen: [15]

> With his left hand he held both Mrs. Harker's hands . . . his right hand gripped her by the back of the neck, forcing her face down on his bosom. Her white nightdress was smeared with blood, and a thin stream trickled down the man's bare breast . . . The attitude of the two had a terrible resemblance to a child forcing a kitten's nose into a saucer of milk to compel it to drink.

> *Dracula*, p.282

[15] According to C.F. Bentley, in his article "The Monster in The Bedroom: Sexual Symbolism in Bram Stoker's *Dracula*," *Literature and Psychology*, 22 (1972)

Historically, this suggestion of sexual symbolism has much to commend it. If we glance backwards through the sort of belief-systems catalogued in an earlier chapter, including modern-day cultist activity, one learns that blood, semen, urine and other body substances play a part, each thought to be endowed with special mystical or medicinal powers which could be absorbed by others to their benefit; seminal fluid from animals was thought to ensure virility and, according to folklore, vampires and succubi craved human semen as well as blood. And as has been shown, the most significant spiritual life-essence, assigned a special importance, was blood. [16]   Fictionally, vampirism is also used as a metaphor for interpreting interpersonal dynamics, in which one person absorbs the energy, exploits or destroys another—something else which finds its roots in primitive human practises such as eating one's enemies or the corpses of venerated tribal elders. As in myth, the victim of a vampire's bite also becomes a vampire—there is a merging of the feeder and the victim. Could this be partly what drives the cannibal or vampire killer? Certainly, the reasons they have variously offered might point in such a direction. Just as Britain's infamous necrophile serial killer Dennis Nilson declared that he killed, sexually violated and dismembered fifteen young men because he wanted company and his actions ensured they would always be with him, something similar was said by Jeffrey Dahmer. He, too, tried to control and keep his victims around because they wanted to leave. Dr. Judith Becker, hired by Dahmer's attorney Gerald Boyle, said at the trial that Dahmer admitted that cannibalism gave him a sexual thrill. "He felt that the man was a part of him and he internalized him.

---

[16] In some cultures one of the measures designed to prevent a corpse becoming a vampire was to drink some of the corpse's blood and eat its flesh, sometimes boiling the heart in oil. This was practised until as late as the nineteenth century.

He reported having an erection while eating it," she revealed. Ed Kemper said he cut flesh from his victims' legs and ate it because "I wanted them to be a part of me— and now they are" and in court he explained that he had killed the hitch-hikers because "that was the only way they could be mine. I had their spirits. I still have them." Would it not be logic of a sort to relate Issei Sagawa's sexual and cannibalistic preference for large, healthy women to his smallness, a desire to absorb the robustness of a victim to counter his own weakness? As the anthropologist M. Sahlins observed: "Cannibalism is always 'symbolic', even when it is real." [17]   In trying to ascribe motives to cannibal killers, there might also be something to be considered in yet another theme explored by Bram Stoker in *Dracula*, using the psychiatric patient, Renfield. On one occasion Renfield cuts a doctor's wrist, then falls to the floor to lick up the spilt blood, repeating over and over: "The blood is the life! The blood is the life!" As well as offering a nudge to the Christian reader with reminders of spiritual teachings with this line, the theory that drinking blood is necessary to maintain one's own life has been seen in twentieth-century clinical cases, including that of Richard Chase, who bears an uncanny resemblance to Renfield—it might be recalled that he even earned the nickname "Dracula" from fellow-patients at a psychiatric hospital because he used to kill birds and drink their blood. In another incident in *Dracula*, Renfield traps flies in his room until one day the flies are seen to be diminishing and Renfield is seen to have some spiders, which he feeds on his flies. Some time later, the spiders have disappeared and Renfield is keeping sparrows. A request for a pet cat is refused and soon

[17] Sahlins, M., "Raw women, cooked men and other 'great things' of the Fiji Islands." In P. Brown and D. Tuzin (eds.), *The Ethnography of Cannibalism*. Washington: The Society for Psychological Anthropology (1983).

afterwards, the birds go missing. Renfield later vomits them up. In the story, the doctor wonders what would have happened if Renfield had been permitted to have a cat—and the reader is well able to guess.

> "My homicidal maniac is of a peculiar kind. I shall have to invent a new classification for him, and call him a zoophagous (life-eating) maniac; what he desires is to absorb as many lives as he can, and he has laid himself out to achieve it in a cumulative way . . . I wonder at how many lives he values a man?"
>
> *Dracula*, pp.70-71

12

Madness . . . But Method in It?

. . . for to define true madness,
What is't but to be nothing else but mad?

Hamlet, Act II, Sc.ii

It is always tempting to declare as mad the actions of
terrorists, tyrants and sexually sadistic murderers—of
anyone, in fact, who commits acts so unthinkably heinous, so challenging to our concept of humanity that our
gut reaction is to declare that these people must be deranged. But are the truly crazy capable of systematic,
carefully-planned and chillingly-executed murder? Are
they really sick or just sickening? Do not all these types
of killers share certain traits which make them dangerous, such as single-minded certainty of purpose and the
unashamed ruthlessness to carry out that purpose and
reap its reward—that reward being, in the case of sexual
sadists and cannibal killers, erotic gratification? It is common for criminals to claim insanity, but is this just to
"beat the rap"? Then again, in what way can a man be
judged sane who talks, as Kemper did, of the sexual thrill
obtained from decapitating somebody—"You hear that
little pop and pull their heads off and hold their heads up
by the hair. Whipping their heads off, their body sitting

there. That'd get me off." To murder for a motive, such as greed or jealousy or revenge—that can be understood, if not condoned—but in their horror, most people would declare that such a man as Kemper *must* be crazy to do what he did. But in a court of law, while trying to decide whether or not someone is insane, you cannot just say "he is nuts" without defining what you mean by "nuts." At Jeffrey Dahmer's trial, his defending attorney Gerald Boyle contended that Dahmer's lethal perversions showed he was a mentally diseased human being—"not an evil man but a sick man whose acts grew to a level of a mental illness, an illness that has been growing and growing to the point where he was not able to conform his conduct to the law . . . he was isolated in his own mind." District Attorney Michael McCann countered by reminding the jury that the case was about Dahmer's state of mind when he killed, not about the gore surrounding the deaths, for unnatural acts do not necessarily point to insanity in the legal sense. "You may feel sex with a dead body is an unnatural act," McCann told the jury, but added: "This is a lawsuit about responsibility for killing fifteen men. Not responsibility for dismemberment. Not responsibility for having sex with a dead body." And he pointed out that Dahmer acted rationally and in his own self-interest—for instance, he always wore a condom. "Mr. Dahmer knew at all times that what he was doing was wrong . . . The issue here is going to be responsibility," McCann said.

The issue of responsibility also arose after Andrei Chikatilo was found guilty and sentenced to death in 1992. His defence lawyer Marad Khabibulin chose a more novel way to claim insanity and overturn the conviction by denying that Chikatilo had ever committed the murders. The guilty verdict was mainly based on Chikatilo's confessions, which were dubious, he said, "because . . . he is not sane, therefore his evidence is inadmissible, so the verdict should be overturned." It was true that much of the evidence in the investigation did indeed come from Chikatilo's own highly detailed confessions of the killings—this was how some of the victims' bodies were found by the police. Despite Chikatilo's bizarre courtroom behaviour, which included ranting incoherently and drooling, Judge Akubzhanov said Chikatilo's remarkable self-control during and after the crimes indicated otherwise: he had fastidiously prepared for his attacks by carrying spare clothes in case his became covered in blood. "Literally, several minutes after committing a bestial murder and mutilating his victims, he walked calmly out of the forest and began a conversation about mushrooms with people at the bus stop," said the judge. "At every stage of his crimes, he was in total command of his actions. His conscience didn't bother him at all. He has an iron psyche and nerves of steel."

The main problem for courts in deciding whether someone is sane or insane is that the legal criteria differ significantly from the medical criteria. This is not a new argument; it has been the source of dispute for hundreds of years. In the olden days, on those occasions when dangerous behaviour was not being attributed to demonic possession, witchcraft or werewolfery, the courts of thirteenth-century England operated a "wild beast test," for people judged to be either "idiots" or "lunatics." An idiot was born mentally retarded and judged not to be responsible for criminal acts; idiocy was tested by asking him to count twenty pennies, name his mother or father and give his age. For someone to be judged a lunatic (madness manifesting later in life), it had to be proved that his mental abilities were no greater than those of a wild beast. A few centuries later it became accepted that "lunatics" could be suffering from temporary insanity—not having understanding at the time of the crime—and then the test of understanding became "whether or not the accused hath yet ordinarily as great understanding as ordinarily a child of fourteen years hath."

In 1839 the distinction between the insane and the sane murderer was drawn up by American psychiatrist Dr. Isaac Ray. The difference, he claimed, was in method and motive and in the subsequent behaviour of the killer. The insane murderer, he said, does not plan methodically, but falls prey to his homicidal impulses "and then voluntarily surrenders himself to the constituted authorities." As has been evidenced by the cunning and skill of all of the murderers considered in this book, some of whom readers may consider to have deserved the tag of insanity, such a definition is open to question. The present system dates back a century, to the trial of Daniel McNaghten in Britain. McNaghten fired a gun at police chief Sir Robert Peel, but was found not guilty by reason of insanity and spent twenty-one years in an institution. From then on, the "McNaghten Rules" came into force, designed to exclude from criminal responsibility those who "at the time of the committing of the act" are suffering "a defect of reason" or "disease of the mind, as to not know the nature and quality of the act . . . or, if he did know it, that he did not know he was doing what was wrong." Such a lack of blameworthiness, meaning the ability not to be able to distinguish between moral and immoral behaviour, right and wrong, is still applied to young children and "idiots"—people who require hospitalization rather than imprisonment. Thus the insanity plea in court is black and white: you are either sane or you are not; either controlled and organized or irrational, impulsive and out of control. The danger is that offences which are bizarre and disgusting sometimes mean the criminal can be judged on the repulsiveness of his act rather than the mental state he was in when he committed it. And the problem for juries is that killers do not exhibit the accepted signs of insanity: look at Dahmer, look at Sagawa—yes, look even at Chikatilo who only began behaving like a madman in court when he perceived that in this way he might escape execution.

The burden of proving insanity lies with the defence. Bearing in mind the conflict between legal and medical criteria, Dr. Donald Lunde, who studied Ed Kemper in depth, claims that mass murderers and serial killers are "almost always insane." Lunde believes they fall broadly into two groups: the sexual sadists and the paranoid schizophrenics. Previous chapters have detailed the identifying factors of sexual sadism; the latter condition is one of psychoses frequently characterised by an aggressive, suspicious attitude, by delusions of grandeur and/or persecution and by hallucinations, such as auditory hallucinations in which the killer "hears voices" ordering him to kill—claimed, for instance, in the cases of Britain's Yorkshire Ripper, Peter Sutcliffe, who reported hearing God tell him to kill prostitutes (and, presumably, to mutilate them sexually, too), Herbert Mullin of Santa Cruz who believed that killing people would avert an earthquake, and New York's "Son of Sam," David Berkowitz, who told psychiatrists that he killed because he had been ordered to do so by his neighbour's dog which was speaking with the voice of a demon.

But many psychiatrists would agree that most serial murderers are neither psychotic in the accepted sense, nor, notes Richard Rappaport, a North-western University psychiatrist in the USA, do they go through the sort of emotional breakdown experienced after the event by many "spree" murderers. Sadistic and serial killers invariably fall into the category of having an antisocial personality disorder—but is this due to an intrinsic neural impairment which prevents them from assessing the needs of others and can it therefore be deemed insanity? Criminal psychologist Dr. Silvano Arieti said, after examining Boston Strangler Albert DeSalvo, who killed thirteen women in a frenzied eighteen months up to January 1964, that he was not "insane in the legal sense, nor psychotic in the medical sense. He is a sociopath, and only that. The law does not recognize a sociopath as having a mental illness which will excuse criminal responsibility. I thoroughly disagree with the law on this point."

Sociopath is another word for psychopath and "antisocial personality" is yet another interchangeable term for this personality disorder, one aspect of which is "narcissistic personality disorder," in which the totally self-centred person has a grandiose view of his own uniqueness and abilities. Some sadistic killers display this aspect by their enormous vanity, relishing the fame which their crimes ultimately win them—offering their thoughts as "experts," for example. Sociopathy has its diagnostic roots in the early nineteenth century, when French doctor Philippe Pinel studied an aristocrat who had whipped a horse, kicked a dog to death and tossed a peasant woman into a well. He declared the man to be suffering from *"manie sans delire"*—insanity without apparent derangement. This was translated as "moral insanity" in 1835 by English psychiatrist James Prichard, because it fell outside the usual ethical and legal codes.

A sociopath is not necessarily a criminal. Hervey Cleckley, a recognized expert on sociopathy, provided the classic description in 1976, including such diagnostic criteria as gross egocentricity and callousness which demands self-gratification regardless of the cost to others, no sense of responsibility, no capacity to experience or feel guilt or empathy with others, untruthfulness, absence of delusions, poorly-integrated sex-life, low frustration tolerance, easy arousability and sometimes explosiveness, considerable superficial charm, above-average intelligence and a failure to learn from experience or punishment (although it is arguable that serial killers *do* learn from experience: they learn what they wish to learn; as can be seen from the cannibal killers in this book, they note their mistakes and learn how to be more successful killers without getting caught). There is no remorse with psychopaths. They are so emotionally flattened that they are chillingly indifferent to any suffering they have caused. Note the words of David Bullock, aged twenty-one, who murdered six people at random in Manhattan and told the judge he did it because it "makes me happy . . . It was in the Christmas spirit . . . something to amuse myself."

Killers like the ones under discussion display a mixture of tremendous vanity, a desire for fame and extraordinarily illogical thought-processes. The vanity is obviously part of their obsession with themselves. Chikatilo, for instance, believed that because of his conflicting blood and semen type, he was unique and possessed two souls; when Albert Fish was caught he remarked regretfully: "I'm past my best." John George Haigh was a monstrously narcissistic man, vain about his forgery skills and his disposal of the bodies of those he murdered. His vanity extended to his desire to be commemorated in wax at Madame Tussaud's Chamber of Horrors—and he even bequeathed the waxworks company a suit of his clothes, to make sure the model of him looked elegant enough. Often it is this very vanity which ensures murderers are caught for their crimes, for in their narcissism, they believe they are far more clever than those who try to catch them. Sometimes they are so keen to reassure themselves of this superiority that they take risks by associating with the police who are conducting the murder hunt. Ed Kemper spent a lot of time hanging around a Santa Cruz bar with off-duty policemen, asking them questions about the murders he had committed, and he even applied to join the police force. Peter Kurten went to a bar near the scene of one crime to listen to people talking with horror about the murder and to read the publicity about the case.

Arrest frequently offers these men an opportunity for recognition and notoriety for the first time in their lives. Police interviews enable them to talk in minute (and sexually stimulating) detail about their crimes, as the centre of attention. Sometimes killers—like Issei Sagawa—enjoy writing autobiographies containing detailed accounts of their sex crimes. Other killers confess to more crimes than they have committed in order to be "the best" murderer. For example Chikatilo told the police chief who had arrested him of another prisoner boasting about having killed five people. "How would he have felt if I'd said I was in for fifty-five?" said Chikatilo, laughing heartily.

The lack of logic which killers sometimes display also sets them apart from normal people. Ridiculous indignation is often expressed about comparatively trivial details of their appalling crimes, as if some injustice is being done to them. Albert Fish was hurt and angry when a New York newspaper called him "a sixty-five-year-old ogre." He was also shocked when he learned that he was being charged with kidnapping Grace Budd. But Mr. and Mrs. Budd had given him their permission to take Grace away with him, he protested to his psychiatrist, so how could he have kidnapped her? David "Son of Sam" Berkowitz displayed the same illogical thought processes when one of his victims displayed fear. "I wasn't going to rob her, or touch her or rape her. I just wanted to kill her," he said. Andrei Chikatilo was insulted at any suggestion that he stole from his victims and Ed Gein was similarly outraged at the police accusation that he stole the cash register at the hardware shop where he had killed an elderly woman, whom he had afterwards dismembered and eaten. Just as Issei Sagawa spoke of his terrible crime as though it was a piece of mischief, Jeffrey Dahmer never seemed to grasp the full horror of his acts. Milwaukee police detective Dennis Murphy, who conducted sixty hours of interviews with Dahmer, said Dahmer reminded him of a guy who had been caught doing "something wrong and was a little embarrassed about it."

Psychopaths are probably the largest group of recidivists, and attempts to cure them are always unsuccessful, says Cleckley. After thirty years' work with psychopaths, using a variety of therapeutic approaches, he reached the depressing conclusion (depressing, because psychiatrists do not like to confess the failure of their methods): "There is no evidence to demonstrate or to indicate that psychiatry has yet found a therapy that cures or pro-foundly changes the psychopath." But we come back to the legal core of the matter: does this make them insane, according to the McNaghten Rules? It is, after all, not that psychopaths are in such mental disarray that they are unable to distinguish between right and wrong; just that they don't care. Their mental impairment robs them of the ability to care. Does that mental impairment then make them insane? Or are they, as Jack Levin says in his book *Mass Murder*, "evil, not crazy"?

Despite their primitive behaviour, serial killers are by no means Neanderthal in their intelligence levels. A psy-chotic murderer would often be far too disorganized and irrational to execute his crimes successfully. Often "an impulse to kill" is more correctly interpreted as a desire which becomes a habit. Abnormal, maybe, but a habit is not necessarily uncontrollable. Psychiatrists agree that a person must have high intelligence or a large amount of low cunning to get away with murder over and over again. FBI consultant Professor Park Elliott Dietz puts it succinctly: "In order to be serially successful with murder —that is, simply, not to get caught, a person has to have both the intelligence and the means to evade detection. He has to be reasonably well-integrated socially. He is not likely to be an alcoholic or a drug user. And he usu-ally owns a car." He adds: "One of the reasons serial killers have been so hard to catch is our old assumption that they must be frothing at the mouth . . . If that were true, they would be easy to spot. What is really disquiet-ing is that people who act normal can commit these un-speakable crimes."

In England more murderers are judged to be insane than in America, where there seems to be a greater fear that if found insane the killer will somehow escape punishment and spend only a short time incarcerated. Where the punishment for murder is execution, the public's understandable desire for revenge also comes into play, particularly in the most sadistic cases. Prosecutor Stephen Kay encapsulated this desire during the murder trial of Lawrence Bittaker and Roy Norris who horribly tortured and killed five teenage girls in California in the 1980s: he apologized to the jury that the maximum penalty was "only" the death penalty—a sentiment which would have been approved of by any relative of Dahmer's or Chikatilo's victims. Yet there are some who would say that the death penalty is preferable to a lifetime in prison. As Douglas Clark, the sadistic murderer of six women, said—and he was fearfully well-qualified to say it —"There are a hell of a lot worse things that can happen than to die in the gas chamber." Interestingly, when Albert Fish was found sane and guilty and sent to the electric chair in the 1930s, it was later revealed that the jury did not really believe him to be sane, but there were few people in New York who wished to see Fish escape with his life, as he would have done if an insanity verdict had been brought in.

In fact it is not true in principle or practice that people sent to prison are deprived of their liberty for longer periods than if they are judged insane and sent to a secure psychiatric unit for treatment: statistics demonstrate that generally the reverse applies. The median time served by people convicted of first-degree murder in the USA is ten and a half years, and for second degree murder, five years. "Life imprisonment" in both Britain and the United States is frequently an oxymoron—that is, a contradiction in terms. But statistics are made up of exceptions. Public fear is justified when they learn of frightening instances on both sides of the Atlantic where psychiatrists and psychologists ignore the advice of experts like Cleckley. Individuals who have committed the most abominable crimes are allowed out of high-security hospitals on unaccompanied shopping trips. Others are released on parole after mental health tribunals take the word of optimistic psychiatrists that the patient is "safe" —that is, cured of his deviant impulses.

Over and over, we hear of people committing the most grotesque murders almost as soon as they have been released. In this book alone we have several glaring examples of psychiatric complacency. Police records show that at one hospital—from which he escaped—vampire killer Richard Chase was described as a "violent mental patient." Nevertheless, he was allowed to re-enter society. Peter Kurten was repeatedly set free or sentenced to only a few years for attacks on women, despite having a history of such attacks, and the story is similar regarding Fritz Haarmann. Ed Kemper was released as cured from a mental hospital where he had been "treated" after he had murdered his grandparents. At Albert Fish's trial, his defence attorney James Dempsey indicated the shrunken, grey-haired old man peeping through the open fingers of his hands spread across his face and declared that Fish "was insane in 1928 and is insane today." Bellevue Hospital, which had discharged Fish as safe in 1930 had a lot to account for, he said. Issei Sagawa was released as cured from the Japanese hospital to which he had been transferred; he is a free man today.

Dr. Donald Lunde suggests that assessing someone on grounds of "treatability" and "dangerousness" would be more worthwhile than trying to label them sane or insane, for if someone was found to be dangerous but suffering from a treatable mental disease, he could then be treated in a hospital. However, sadly this "treatment" sometimes has the killers laughing up their sleeves at the psychologists and psychiatrists who attend them. Fooling the psychologists seems a remarkably easy task for a glib psychopath, whether it is before or after they have been tried and sentenced. The smart, educated criminal can fake schizophrenia, epilepsy, amnesia and even Multiple Personality Disorder in pursuit of an insanity verdict and, he hopes, incarceration in a hospital with the prospect of earlier release.

The aforementioned sadistic killer David "Son of Sam" Berkowitz convinced two court-appointed psychiatrists that he was deluded into believing that his neighbour's dog, possessed by a 3,000-year-old demon, had barked instructions at him ordering him to kill, because the demonic forces wished to drink the victim's blood. Another psychiatrist, David Abrahamsen, remained unconvinced and it was he who persuaded the court that Berkowitz was sane, saying he had failed to display any other indicators of insanity, especially demonstrating "clear-headed cunning" in avoiding detection for a whole year. Berkowitz was found sane and given a twenty-five-year sentence. Three years later, in 1979, Berkowitz admitted he had invented the talking dog story to try and fool the authorities into believing he was insane. Far from being seized by an uncontrollable compulsion to kill, Berkowitz—like Andrei Chikatilo, Joachim Kroll, Ed Kemper and others in this book—would roam around for hours searching for suitable victims and stalking them. Every night Berkowitz was out hunting, but only attacked someone when he thought it was safe to do so.

Such careful premeditation defies the legal definition of insanity. But just as cunning killers are able to fake insanity and fool psychologists, they are equally well able to feign normality and rehabilitation, as has been amply illustrated by the cannibal killers under consideration. Jeffrey Dahmer, on bail awaiting a court hearing on an enticement and assault charge, so convinced the psychologist who had monitored him for months that he was recovering from his social problems that his jail sentence was kept to a minimum. But during the time that the psychologist had been seeing Dahmer, he had killed several people, the last one only a matter of weeks before he was due to be sentenced. As he appeared in court to hear experts declare him a changed and repentant man, at home in his Milwaukee flat was his latest souvenir: Anthony Sears' boiled head.

Similarly, some years after Ed Kemper had been released from Atascadero, his mother fought to have his juvenile record of the murder of his grandparents set aside, or "sealed," so he could begin life afresh without a blot on his character. In September, 1972, he was seen by two psychiatrists, who remarked on the excellent progress he had made, what a well-adjusted young man he was, and how he presented no danger to society, recommending the sealing of his records—which was performed two months later. One of the psychiatrists remarked that he was pleased that Ed had given up riding a motor-cycle "since this seemed more a threat to his life and health than any threat he is presently to anyone else." At the time of the interviews, Kemper had already killed, mutilated and fed upon the corpses of several women. Indeed, his latest murder had been four days before his visit to the psychiatrists. He had dismembered the body and flushed the body fluids down the drain before burying the hands in one county and the torso in another. He did not get rid of the head, but kept it in the boot of his car, where it remained during his interview with one of the psychiatrists, who was to declare him "a very well-adjusted young man who had initiative, intelligence and who was free of any psychiatric illness."

It is of grave concern that psychiatrists can be "conned" by such dangerous individuals, especially since they, of all people, should be aware of the psychopath's legendary charm, intelligence, cunning and ability to lie convincingly. Then comes the second part of the game: if someone can fool a psychiatrist into thinking he is insane, he may later fool them into thinking he has regained his sanity—and be freed. And as has been proved, at the cost of victims' lives, psychiatrists sometimes seem danger-ously inclined to interpret a killer's exhibited compliance as a real change of inner personality. As Cleckley says, the psychopath "is much more likely than others who have committed serious crimes to convince his psychotherapist that treatment has been effective, that it has brought true insight and profound changes that now make him no longer a danger to society." He is also often clever and convincing enough to "make the therapist feel also that the cure was specifically effected through cherished items of the therapist's creed of psychiatric theory." But, adds Cleckley: "The daily papers report many cases of armed robbery, rape and murder resulting from such confidently optimistic estimates of therapeutic success." Going even further, Cleckley adds that there has been "a gross overestimation" of the influence which the psychiatric treatment of criminals has had, "whether or not they are psychopaths," and suggests that this miscalculation has played "a major role in these tragic events."

A clever killer who has had any dealings with psychologists or psychology is more than capable of putting his acquired knowledge to use, either for self-entertainment to reassure him of his own superiority, or for more practical, devious purposes. Just as Kemper, for example, enjoyed playing with interviewers and reporters (ghoulishly amusing himself on one occasion by telling one shocked woman that when he saw a pretty girl ". . . one side of me says, 'Wow, what an attractive chick, I'd like to talk to her . . .' The other side of me says, 'I wonder how her head would look on a stick?' "), he also tried to confuse psychologists by seriously offering varying and conflicting explanations for his acts on different occasions. He would begin interviews by giving psychologists the Minnesota Multiphasic Personality Inventory, a personality assessment device which he had learned inside out during his teenage years in the mental hospital where he had been placed after murdering his grandparents . . . and from where he was later released to indulge in many more barbaric murders.

Keeping society safe from a potentially dangerous person appears to be well-nigh impossible if that person has not yet committed a crime. Even when the crime is a serious one which falls short of murder, sentencing practices shy away from ensuring that life means life. Rehabilitation experiments are being conducted all the time as murderers sentenced to "life" are declared, after only a few years, to have paid their debt to society or to have been "cured" and are then sent out into the community to test that theory. But who, one might ask, are the guinea pigs?

Prevention being better than cure, it should be a source of optimism that psychiatrists are able to cite predisposing factors which should help us to pinpoint the individuals who are likely to develop in this deviant way. But in reality, this knowledge does us little good for, as they say, all cows eat grass but not everything that eats grass is a cow. For example, all sexual sadists may have practised first on animals, but not every child sadist will grow up to be a sadistic killer (although, as an adult he may well sublimate his enjoyment of inflicting suffering on others using alternative power-driven methods). Torturing animals in childhood is more common than sadistic murder, therefore it cannot always be seen as a forecast of future hell. Using childhood behaviour to predict adult criminality is thus strewn with pitfalls. Even if we know that little Johnny wets the bed, starts fires, skins dogs, pores over Nazi literature and has a passion for weapons, what on earth can we do about it if such a "murder-prone" child has not committed a "serious" crime? It might be recalled that Fritz Haarmann's father had tried to have his son committed when he sensed the potential dangerousness of the boy, but doctors refused the request, declaring the child to be safe.

Clearly we cannot lock someone away for life because

of what he *might* do in the future, but to offer treatment to such a youngster when his sadistic impulses first become evident could possibly deflect him from worse crime. Two psychiatrists, Daniel S. Hellman and Nathan Blackman, suggested in 1966 that "the detection and early management" of such children "might well forestall a career of violent crime" in the adult, [1] yet it is difficult to see how this could be achieved without infringing an individual's rights and liberties and also risking stigmatizing the child—perhaps thereby inclining him even more towards dangerousness. Hervey Cleckley is an advocate of early identification and positive action, pointing out that if a youngster shows signs of schizophrenic illness or any other psychiatric disorder apart from psychopathy, he can usually be dealt with before he has committed a crime. Something similar should be available for psychopaths, he says, for "perhaps all or nearly all of these patients will . . . eventually commit antisocial acts." Solving such a sensitive problem must be a major challenge to modern psychologists, but it is clearly one which needs attention.

[1] Hellman and Blackman, "Enuresis, Firesetting, and Cruelty to Animals," *American Journal of Psychiatry 122* (1966) 1431-1435.

13

Future Tense?

Sade lived in an atmosphere of unreality, a world of dreams inside his own head. He was one of the privileged few who could afford that indulgence. Two centuries later, an affluent society has created conditions that could spawn potential de Sades by the thousand.

Colin Wilson: *The Serial Killers*

In a sense it should be irrelevant whether the court decides if sociopathy can be labelled "insanity" or not. What is important—and where the system has frequently failed society in its anxiety not to victimize the criminal—is that such a person is incarcerated for the rest of his life with no prospect of release, ever—in which case, the "insanity" defence might as well be abolished completely. The evidence clearly shows that there is no hope of rehabilitating or otherwise reforming sexual sadists whose fantasies have escaped into reality. Psychiatric opinion is primarily behind Hervey Cleckley, the classic authority on psychopathy, who says: "There is no evidence to demonstrate or to indicate that psychiatry has yet found a therapy that cures or profoundly changes the psychopath." The sadistic killer is beyond redemption. He is driven by his terrible fantasies, and those fantasies are unlikely to abate just because a man is imprisoned for carrying out the murderous delights of his twisted imagination. He may, of course, say that he fantasizes no longer, but fantasies are not thrown aside so easily. The Marquis de Sade is sometimes defended by people who point out that the aristocratic sadist never actually killed anyone, but merely indulged in a rich fantasy life. However, it might be worth remembering that the Marquis de Sade was kept locked up and not unleashed upon society. If he had been, who knows whether he would have acted out the fantasies which so excited him? As Ed Kemper said in an interview with FBI man Robert Ressler: "What I needed to have was a particular experience with a person, and to possess them in the way I wanted to; I had to evict them from their human bodies." In other words, remarks Ressler "in order to have his sexual fantasies fulfilled, he had to kill his partner." Dr. Bernard Defer, one of Issei Sagawa's psychiatrists in France, made the same point in 1992, when he expressed concern about Sagawa's release from a Japanese mental hospital: "Sexual desire, especially perverse desire, is something lasting, something permanent. It forms part of the personality."

The execution of men like Fish and Chikatilo serves no useful purpose. It may fulfil the public's desire for revenge and quell our outrage somewhat, but it is of no use for future detection and expanding our database of knowledge. Such individuals may not deserve any more merciful treatment than they showed their victims, but the death penalty is no deterrent to these perverts—as the activities of Andrei Chikatilo show. At least if they are behind bars they can, as guinea-pigs, be studied and evaluated in the hope of finding some way of identifying and preventing others following the same sinister path.

Tracking that path should be of prime importance. For instance, when any arrest is made there may be signs of worse to come for those who take the trouble to seek them out. [1] As Brittain said of those who commit lesser sexual crimes: "It does not follow that all who commit such acts are potentially sexual murderers and many may only be social nuisances; it does follow, however, that such offenders should be examined most carefully because a proportion, however small, are potentially very dangerous." Carrying out background research on offenders—from sources other than the criminal himself—might reveal information which could influence the way the authorities deal with him. For instance, the American sadistic killer Duane Samples had his application for parole supported by psychologists until FBI man Robert Ressler discovered Samples had fed them lies and had a long history of disembowelment fantasies. But all too often, the most information about a killer comes after his arrest, from journalists or writers researching the case, and this can reveal the shocking laxness of the authorities. Psychiatrists may counter that, unlike journalists and FBI officers, they do not have the experience, time or inclination to leave their offices and investigate the past, to put in "leg-work" before making decisions on the future freedom or imprisonment of potentially dangerous criminals. However, if they are not prepared to do this to satisfy themselves that a person is not a threat to society, then they owe that society the protection of keeping a potential murderer out of circulation for good.

If lifetime imprisonment is an answer for the convicted sadistic killer, what about the question of prevention? We might be able to identify the behaviour of cannibal and vampire killers by declaring it to be necrophilia combined

---

[1] For example, some burglaries are sexually motivated. William Heirens, who murdered and mutilated two females, one of whom was a small child, had shown early and unusual signs of severe disturbance: he had begun stealing women's underwear from clothes lines at age nine and progressed to burglary three years later. He would experience erection and sometimes orgasm as he broke into a house through the window.

with infantile oralism and sadism; that, to paraphrase one researcher, it occurs where myth, fantasy and reality converge—but that is just putting a condition in a pigeon-hole, not dealing with it. The essential question "What makes such monsters?" has no succinct answer. Genetic predispositions and childhood influences; twentieth-century expectations conflicting with social deprivation; the increasing presence of violent and sexual imagery. All these may combine to form a perverse continuity with the shadow of man's innate primitive aggression, with the mythical blood-beliefs tied to sexual impulses which overcome civilized reason. Perhaps these are more easily aroused in particular individuals: those whose dark side —"the invisible saurian tail that man still drags behind him" as Jung described it—casts a darker shadow than it does in most other people.

But if the wretched and loveless home-lives of such individuals are the spur to sadism and cannibalism, then how many others in the world were also born with similar predispositions to sadistic crime, including the sex-related desire to feast on the bodies of their fellow-humans, but whose upbringings have, for whatever reason, screened this subconscious appetite from view . . . so far? Even more worrying: can the substantial increase in the number of serial killers, in violent sex-crime, in sadistic acts and in "killing for kicks" really be due to all those social factors like poor mothering and the breakdown of the family? To unemployment and poverty? To the lack of constraints like discipline in homes, schools and countries? To the similar ebbing of religious influence? To the gratuitous violence to which the film industry is so devoted—especially sexual violence—and the increase in sadistic pornography?

If we really believe that such social inadequacies provide a fertile soil in which the aberrant individual can blossom, then the Western lifestyle is fertilizing that soil liberally. As Elliot Leyton says in his book *Hunting Humans*:

> If we were charged with the responsibility for designing
> a society in which all structural and cultural mechanisms
> leaned towards the creation of the killers of strangers,
> we could do no better than to present the purchaser with
> the shape of modern America.

Modern civilization—and I use the phrase loosely—is already trying to cope with one twentieth-century plague: AIDS. Let us hope we pay attention to another, the latest fatal infection of violence which is gradually corrupting our society.

Bibliography

Books

Barber, Paul, *Vampires, Burial, and Death: Folklore and Reality* (Yale University Press, New Haven, CT, 1988)

Berg, Karl, *The Sadist* (Heinemann, 1933)

Biondi, Ray and Hecox, Walt, *The Dracula Killer* (Titan Books, 1992)

Boar, Roger and Blundell, Nigel, *The World's Most Infamous Murders* (Hamlyn Publishing, 1990)

Cleckley, Hervey Milton, *The Mask of Sanity* (C.V. Mosby, St. Louis, MO, 1982)

Conradi, Peter, *The Red Ripper* (True Crime Books, 1992)

Davison, Gerald C. and Neale, John M., *Abnormal Psychology: An Experimental Clinical Approach* (Wiley, 1982)

Dunning, John, *Strange Deaths* (Arrow Books, 1987)

Gollmar, Robert, *Edward Gein: America's Most Bizarre Murderer* (Hallberg, Delavan, WI, 1981)

Heimer, Mel, *The Cannibal: The Case of Albert Fish* (Xanadu Publications, 1971)

Holmes, Ronald, *The Legend of Sawney Bean* (Frederick Muller Ltd, 1975)

Krafft-Ebing, R., *Psychopathia Sexualis* (F.A. Davis, Philadelphia, PA, 1892)

Levin, Jack and Fox, James Alan, *Mass Murder: America's Growing Menace* (Plenum Press, New York, 1985)

Leyton, Elliot, *Hunting Humans: The Rise of the Modern Multiple Murderer* (Penguin Books, 1986)

Lloyd, Georgina, *One Was Not Enough: True Stories of Multiple Murderers* (Bantam Books, 1989)

Lourie, Richard, *Hunting the Devil: The Search for the Russian Ripper* (Grafton Books, 1993)

Lunde, Donald T., *Murder and Madness* (W.W. Norton, New York, 1979)

Marriner, Brian, *Cannibalism, The Last Taboo* (Arrow Books, 1992)

Nash, Jay Robert, *Encyclopedia of World Crime* (Crimebooks Inc, Wilmette, IL, 1990)

Nash, Jay Robert, *Compendium of World Crime* (Harrap, 1983)

Nash, Jay Robert, *Bloodletters and Badmen* (M. Evans, New York, 1972)

Noll, Richard (Ed.), *Vampires, Werewolves and Demons: Twentieth Century Reports in the Psychiatric Literature* (Brunner/Mazel, Inc., New York, 1992)

Playfair, Giles, *Crime in our Century* (Sidgwick and Jackson, 1977)

Praz, Mario, *The Romantic Agony* (OUP, 1970)

Prins, Herschel, *Bizarre Behaviours: Boundaries of Psychiatric Disorder* (Tavistock/Routledge, 1990)

Ressler, Robert K. and Shachtman, Tom, *Whoever Fights Monsters* (Simon and Schuster, 1992)

Robbins, Rossell Hope, *Encyclopedia of Witchcraft and Demonology* (Peter Nevill Ltd, 1959)

Samenow, Stanton E., *Inside the Criminal Mind* (Times Books, New York, 1984)

Schlesinger, L.B., and Revitch, E. (Eds.) *Sexual Dynamics of Antisocial Behaviour* (Charles C. Thomas, Springfield, IL, 1983)

Schwartz, Anne E., *The Man Who Could Not Kill Enough* (Mondo Books, 1992)

Storr, Anthony, *Human Destructiveness: The Roots of Genocide and Human Cruelty* (Routledge, 1991)

Wilson, Colin, and Seaman, Donald, *The Serial Killers: A Study in the Psychology of Violence* (W.H. Allen, 1990)

Wilson, Colin, and Seaman, Donald, *Encyclopaedia of Modern Murder* (Pan Books, 1986)

Wilson, Colin *The Misfits: A Study of Sexual Outsiders* (Grafton Books, 1988)

Woodward, Ian, *The Werewolf Delusion* (Paddington Press, 1979)

Articles

Bentley, C.F., "The Monster in The Bedroom: Sexual Symbolism in Bram Stoker's *Dracula*," *Literature and Psychology*, 22 (1972)

Boukhabza, D. and Yesavage, J., "Cannibalism and Vampirism in Paranoid Schizophrenia," *Journal of Clinical Psychiatry*, 42 (1981)

Brittain, R.P., "The Sadistic Murderer," *Medicine, Science and the Law*, 10 (1970)

Burton-Bradley, B.G., "Cannibalism for Cargo," *Journal of Nervous and Mental Disease*, 163 (1976)

Felthous, Alan R., "Childhood Cruelty to Cats, Dogs and Other Animals," *Bulletin of the American Academy of Psychology and the Law*, 9 (1981)

Garelik, Glenn and Maranto, Gina, "Multiple Murderers" *Discover* (July 1984)

Hellman, Daniel S. and Blackman, Nathan, "Enuresis, Firesetting and Cruelty to Animals: a Triad, Predictive of Adult Crime," *American Journal of Psychiatry*, 122 (June 1966)

Hemphill, R.E. and Zabow, T. "Clinical Vampirism: A presentation of three cases and a re-evaluation of Haigh, the 'Acid-Bath Murderer,'" *South African Medical Journal*, 63 (1983)

McCarthy, Terry, "Japan's Dr. Lecter: no straitjacket required," *The Independent* (February 9, 1992)

MacCulloch, M.J. et al., "Sadistic Fantasy, Sadistic Behaviour and Offending," *British Journal of Psychiatry* 143 (1983)

McGill, Peter, "Portrait of a Cannibal" (Issei Sagawa), *Observer Magazine* (May 24, 1992)

McGill, Peter, "And tonight, folks, meet the man who ate his girlfriend . . . ," *The Observer* (March 8, 1992)

Pitman, Joanna, "How I tasted tea and whisky with a cannibal" (Issei Sagawa), *The Times* (January 25, 1992)

Prins, Herschel, "Vampirism—a Clinical Condition," *British Journal of Psychiatry* 146 (1985)

Prins, Herschel, "Vampirism—Legendary or Clinical Phenomenon?," *Medicine, Science and the Law*, 24 (1984)

Ressler, Robert K. et al., "Murderers Who Rape and Mutilate," *Journal of Interpersonal Violence* (September 1986)

Starr, Mark et al., "The Random Killers," *Newsweek* (November 26, 1984)

Index